WHAT THE CRITICS A...
www.askthedream...

D1539732

"Take two pillows and e-mai... ... ... the morning."
—*Yahoo.com (Daily Pick for June 4, 1998)*

"Unravel the meaning at www.askthedreamdoctor.com."
—*Los Angeles Times*

"Ask the Dream Doctor. Someone who truly understands the psyche developed this page."
—*Access Guide to the Web, Volume 2*

"Where to get help? www.askthedreamdoctor.com."
—*Arizona Republic*

PRAISE FOR
Ask the Dream Doctor

"McPhee's book provides an excellent addition to the new dream symbol approach which carefully avoids assigning a single meaning to a dream image while skillfully showing the dreamer how a dream image can function as a metaphor in guiding one's life and giving examples. All the classic dreams are in the book. . . . I enjoyed the inclusion of real dreams, the tips for interpretation, and the thoughtful associations to common dream images."
—*Richard Wilkerson, editor, Electric Dreams,*
www.dreamgate.com/electric-dreams

Ask the Dream Doctor

Charles Lambert McPhee

Delta Trade Paperbacks

A DELTA BOOK

Published by
Dell Publishing
a division of
Random House, Inc.
1540 Broadway
New York, New York 10036

Book design by Virginia Norey

Dell books may be purchased for
business or promotional use or for special sales.
For information please write to: Special Markets Department,
Random House, Inc., 1540 Broadway, New York, NY 10036.

Library of Congress Cataloging-in-Publication Data
McPhee, Charles Lambert.
    Ask the dream doctor / Charles Lambert McPhee.
       p.   cm.
    ISBN 0-440-50926-2
    1. Dream interpretation.   I. Title.
BF1078.M375   2002
154.6'3—dc21   2001058254

Printed in the United States of America
Published simultaneously in Canada
July 2002

RRH   10 9 8 7 6 5 4 3 2 1

For Petra

AUTHOR'S NOTE

Thanks to Oxygen Media, LLC, for providing a selection of dreams included in this book. You can find Oxygen at www. oxygen.com.

Thanks to supanet, Ltd. for providing a selection of dreams included in this book. You can find supanet at www.supanet.com.

✳ ✳ ✳

C O N T E N T S

x ✳ **Contents**

xii * **Contents**

Ask the
Dream Doctor

Introduction

Dream interpretation is enjoying a fabulous liberation from so much of the superstition—and simple bad information—that historically has drained the field of its natural potential. Recent advances in sleep disorders medicine have enabled us to peer for the first time beneath the surface events of sleep, to understand the physical causes of some of our most powerful dreams. The Internet has allowed us to gather very large quantities of data about dreams that demonstrate, very convincingly, the relationship between their metaphoric language and the everyday thoughts and concerns of dreamers. Houses in dreams are consistent metaphors for the self. Cats are feminine symbols associated with pregnancy and childbearing. Dreams about being unprepared for an exam in high school reflect feelings of being tested in our waking lives. Tornadoes represent fears of families being separated due to violent emotional storms. It's all there in the data, and today we can prove it.

The "Ask the Dream Doctor" web site first appeared on-line on March 15, 1998. Since its inception, over three hundred thousand dreams (and growing) have been gathered from Internet visitors from over eighty-five countries around the world. The resulting database is the largest collection of dreams in the world. The database is searchable by keywords, by age, sex, gender, and relationship status, and by geographical location: city, state, and country. Today, to learn what single female teens in Australia are dreaming about, we need merely to enter search parameters and let a computer quickly sort the dreams. We may not be surprised to learn that the girls are dreaming about boys, but perhaps our eyebrows will raise when we read consistently about symbols such as water and vampires, throwing punches that can't connect, about flying high above the Earth, and about friends and loved ones dying. These are the same themes we see in teens from the United States, the United Kingdom, Canada, Malaysia, Japan, and India. In fact, these common dream themes appear in every culture. The evidence is overwhelming. Beneath the surface of our geographic and cultural diversity, we are all speaking a common language.

As a person who spends his entire life communicating about dreams— on the Internet, through books, and on the radio—for me, the most fascinating aspect of the current state of the art is how little most people know about using dreams in their practical, everyday lives. Despite the pioneering work of Drs. Sigmund Freud and Carl Jung, and in part because of the recent work of Drs. Francis Crick and Alan Hobson, who have proposed that dreams are meaningless, the value of dreamwork today is suspended in limbo. Many people believe that dreams are random events whose contents possess no correlation with their daily lives. If you are suddenly afflicted with nightmares since your divorce, the reasoning goes, perhaps this is only a coincidence. The information contained in this book, however, powerfully demonstrates that "random" theories are last century's news. *Ask the Dream Doctor* instructs us that dreams are honest and intelligent portraits of our inner emotional lives. Dreams are practical tools to improve self-understanding, to enhance communication in our romantic relationships and with our children, to identify dangerous and unhealthy relationships in our lives, to broaden our spiritual perspective, and to empower ourselves to become the people we truly wish to be. Understanding the images of our dreams is the key to understanding better the artist who is their creator: our self.

The first step on the road to empowerment is to learn how to recall dreams better. To this end, "How to Remember Dreams" follows this introduction. Read it through and put it into practice as you enjoy this book. In two short weeks, you will have recalled more dreams than you ever imagined possible.

The second step is to learn to understand the meaning of your dreams on a daily basis. Most of us miss the connection between our dreams and our everyday lives because we focus on the literal, surface appearances of dreams. Dreams, however, express their meaning in the great economic language of metaphor, a basic language that allows human beings in a dizzying array of cultures to grapple with the same universal life issues: birth, death, pain, separation, identity, family, status, self-esteem, love, and romance, to name but a few. As you read this book, the outlines of this universal language will gradually become visible to you. Indeed, by sharing our dreams, we learn that we all have much more in common with each other than we do differences.

I have been moved to tears many times as I have sat at my computer, reading the powerful and heroic tales of everyday people faced with burning life decisions—all revealed in their dreams. Souls are in progress, decisions are being forged, and attempts at sense and understanding are being made. You, too, will share in these honest and courageous dreamers' lives, and in their accounts will witness your own reflection. Their willingness to share their stories is a selfless and generous gift to us all. All the names and identifying information in the dreams have been changed to protect the privacy of the dreamers.

How to Remember Dreams

The key to remembering dreams is to learn how to wake up slowly—so that you prolong contact with your subconscious mind. Waking up S L O W L Y means that you lie still in bed, keeping your eyes closed, not talking or worrying about the schedule of the day, and working diligently to try to remember what it was you were just dreaming about—because you always dream just before you wake up in the morning.

If you don't immediately recall a specific image or sequence from a dream, it is important nevertheless to remain still, and allow yourself time to evaluate your feelings. Dreams always leave us with an emotional hangover. Did you wake up feeling tense, frustrated, happy, sad, or worried?

Once you've tuned in to your feelings, you want to answer four questions about your dream in a dream journal that you keep faithfully at your bedside.

- What was the key image in the dream?
- What was the key feeling?
- Where was the dream located?
- What situation in my waking life does the dream remind me of?

These four questions and answers will help identify the dream's meaning, and will help you recall the dream later, when you have more time to reflect on it in a clearheaded state.

The next step to having a rich dream life is the simplest of all. Before you go to bed at night, confirm your intention to remember your dreams and to wake up slowly the following morning.

It sounds simple—and it is! I have taught thousands of people to successfully remember their dreams using this same method. If you follow these easy steps for two weeks, I guarantee that you will soon be starring in your dreams. This daily practice is the foundation of an active, exciting, and deeply rewarding relationship with your subconscious mind.

Dream
Symbols

Airplane

Airplanes: Because of their associations with big trips, airplanes frequently symbolize significant transitions and attempts to reach new destinations in our lives. Common destinations include career goals—a new job position with "elevated" responsibility, recognition, or financial reward—or a change in social status, such as marriage or a committed relationship.

Plane crashes, losses of power, and trouble in flight are common dreams that reflect anxiety about our ability to reach a destination. If a dreamer has a fear of flying, the dreams may reflect literal anxieties prior to a trip, or may occur when a child is traveling. Plane crash dreams should not be interpreted as precognitive.

♦ **Interpretation tip:** If you dream about flying in a plane (or of watching them fall from the sky), ask yourself what goal—career or social—is weighing on your mind.

* * *

The dreams that follow illustrate different aspects of airplane dreams. In the first, a dreamer's life is turned "Upside Down" by an illness in the family. In "Falling Plane," a hopeful young woman wonders if a romantic reunion will lead to a committed relationship. "Plane Crash" instructs us that flying dreams can also represent the routine stresses of everyday living; major issues are not always indicated. In yet another romance dream, "Boyfriend Dies" reveals a deeper fear camouflaged as concern about air travel. Finally, "Crash Landing" shows us a woman in transition, nervous about her ability to achieve the "lofty" career goals she has set for herself. Will she survive her big debut?

Airplane Dreams

"Upside Down"

Last night I had a dream that was quite disturbing. I boarded an airplane, but it was a small, older plane with approximately ten seats and no roof. I was nervous getting on because of the plane's appearance, but I went anyway even though I knew it was odd.

As soon as the plane took off I was dangling upside down and hanging on by wrapping my knees around a bar above me. I had to hold on to another bar below my head with my hands. There were other people doing the same thing but I have no idea who these people were. The pilot's back was turned to me because he was flying this plane and he never turned around or uttered a word—but he did have a scarf flying in the wind like an old-time pilot in an army movie.

We landed and I remember thinking, "Wow, we made it." But I knew I had to go back the same way I had come, and I was planning to do that even though the ride was horrible.

The next thing I knew I was standing in what was supposed to be my bathroom (but the colors were different and the dimensions too) but the toilet was smashed in four pieces and it appeared my ex had done this.

Let me tell you what has been going on in my life recently; this may help. I am trying to leave a five-year failed relationship that has been mostly unhappy. My mother passed away five years ago of a stroke and my father had a severe stroke this year. I am currently moving into my father's home to help care for him because he cannot be left alone. I am also a single parent of a fifteen-year-old and I work full-time. Perhaps this dream signifies the turbulence in my life. But I do not quite understand the toilet part.

–Lauren, Age 35, Single, USA

Given the background Lauren provides, this dream is not difficult to understand. Lauren's life has been turned "upside down" by a stroke in her family. Because Lauren is the primary caregiver for her father, her life will be impacted the most.

Lauren's airplane dream functions as a metaphor for the change in her life caused by her father's illness. The pilot of the plane—now determining the course of her "life path"—is almost certainly her father. In the dream, Lauren notes his age, lack of movement, and absence of speech—all characteristics associated with stroke.

Even though the ride is "horrible," Lauren plans to return the same way. This segment of the dream reflects Lauren's resolve to complete the trip (take care of her father), despite the fact that the "journey," right now, is rough. Her father is fortunate to have such a loving daughter.

The toilet in Lauren's dream appears incongruous, until we recognize toilets as common symbols for the "release" and "elimination" of private and "pent-up" emotions. Lauren reflects that the toilet, which no longer operates, appears to have been smashed by her ex. Is it a coincidence that Lauren also tells us she is trying to leave a five-year failed relationship? The toilet (that no longer functions) reflects Lauren's difficulty "eliminating" this relationship from her life.

Lauren's dream reflects her concerns about two primary relationships in her life: her father, and her ex. The dream confirms Lauren's commitment to her father, whose life has been thrown into chaos by illness, and it identifies an area of lingering emotional irresolution with her ex. What is the message of her dream? The journey that lies ahead will not be easy. If Lauren wishes to arrive safely, and turn her life "right-side up," she needs emotional strength and clarity. Lauren will lighten her load considerably if she can resolve her relationship with her ex.

"Falling Plane"

I had a boyfriend my freshman year of high school who I went out with for several months before he had to move to Georgia. We didn't talk for five years, but in May of my freshman year in college, I found his E-mail address and we've been talking via E-mail for eight months now. We are going to be seeing each other for the first time in years over my winter break (he goes to school in Florida, and I go to the University of California). Although we are three thousand miles apart and haven't seen each other in years, I have always thought he was "the one," and my feelings have never changed.

I had two of the same dreams—one was a few weeks ago, the other occurred last night. I was dancing with him and having an incredible time. But then suddenly the dream flipped around, and I was in an airplane flying to meet him. However, the airplane started having trouble, and the engines went out. The plane began drifting aimlessly through the air, but it never crashed. All I could think about was him as I was sitting in the falling plane, but I wasn't scared or anything.

In the first dream I had, the airplane made an emergency landing and I was all right. But in the second one, the plane never landed, but also never crashed.

I woke up before I could finish the dream, but when I awoke, I wasn't in a panic or anything. Is there anything significant to this?

–Kayla, Age 19, Single, USA

Kayla's airplane dream, like Lauren's "upside-down" dream, functions as a metaphor for a big change in her life. Kayla is excited, and nervous, about reuniting with an old boyfriend—a boyfriend whom she secretly has considered "the one" for many years. Will Kayla arrive at her hoped-for destination—a committed relationship?

Kayla's dream begins by reflecting her excitement and anticipation of great times ahead. She and her crush dance together and have "an incredible time." Soon, however, a shadow of uncertainty enters her dream. Will this romance really "get off the ground"?

The dream shifts suddenly. Kayla is now flying on a plane, alone, en route to meet her old boyfriend. At this point in the dream, the airplane functions both as a literal allusion to her upcoming plane flight (she will fly home to see him over winter break) and it symbolizes her fears for the relationship. The engines soon quit, and the plane enters a free fall. Falling in dreams symbolizes insecurity (lack of support) and uncertainty about the future. (We don't know where we are "going to land.") Significantly, though, Kayla does not panic, and her plane never crashes. Indeed, Kayla's response appears to be one of levelheaded coolness in the face of an honestly recognized unknown. Kayla has no reason to panic, and she has every reason to be hopeful.

"Plane Crash"

I have had this dream about planes crashing for about four years or so. I am on a plane and it crashes, but we always manage to land either in a small neighborhood, in the middle of a forest, in water, etc.

Sometimes I am not on the plane, I just see a plane crash or many planes crashing around me. There is so much panic as we are going down—I am always so scared. But after we crash or emergency land it turns into kind of funny stuff, like there's a tivoli there (a park), I am in the water making phone calls, I sign up for a neighborhood meeting. . . .

These dreams have made me scared of flying. Help!

–Emma, Age 31, Married, USA

Emma, as anyone might be, is puzzled by the meaning of her plane crash dreams. Are the dreams precognitive? Should Emma be careful flying in the future? Are the dreams warnings?

While plane crash dreams occasionally represent literal fears of flying (in Emma's case, her dreams are *causing* fears of flying), the dreams more likely reflect everyday anxieties in Emma's life.

To understand her dreams, Emma needs to think back to identify what major events were occurring in her life at the time the dreams began—that set the dreams in motion, so to speak. Her dreams may reflect anxiety about achieving any of life's uncertain milestones: getting married, buying a house, moving into a certain neighborhood, becoming a mother, or achieving a desired position or status in her career.

Because Emma consistently emerges from her plane crash dreams unhurt, her dreams suggest occasional doubts about her ability to reach a destination more than they suggest real problems. As Emma herself observes, after the crash she often winds up in rather amusing or mundane everyday scenarios. She begins making phone calls, or she signs up for a neighborhood meeting while standing or floating in water. In this way, the dream informs us that *big* issues are not indicated here. The dreams also show us that Emma, despite her occasional nerves, actually handles these concerns with proficiency and skill. (Business as usual . . .)

Four years ago (when her dreams began), Emma almost certainly assumed a greater degree of responsibility in her life. (Parenting is a likely candidate. . . . Don't we all wonder if we will survive it?) If Emma can identify, four years later, what set her recurring dreams in motion, she will have solved their enigma. In the meantime, Emma should also recognize that—so far—she has always reached her destinations "safe and sound." This is a travel record anyone can be proud of!

"Boyfriend Dies"

I live in Mexico and have a boyfriend who lives in Texas. I had the worst nightmare and have no idea why. I dreamt that he was on a plane, and I saw the plane when it started to fall and hit the ground—tail first. Strangely, I saw that he was sitting in the back section of the plane, so I instantly knew that he was dead. I was crying forever.

Then, I saw that he was alive and okay. That's all that I remember.

I am really worried about this dream because he is going to visit his parents over Thanksgiving, and his parents live on the East Coast, so obviously he is taking a plane.

Please tell me what this dream means, it has me really worried.

–Destiny, Age 23, Single, Mexico

Destiny's airplane dream, like Kayla's ("Falling Plane"), reflects both literal and symbolic concerns. Destiny knows that her boyfriend soon will be traveling to the East Coast by airplane, to visit his parents. As she worries about being separated from her lover, an airplane crash may be one of several fears that occupy her mind. In her dream Destiny witnesses a grisly accident, and knows instantly that her boyfriend was killed. Curiously, though, after a good cry, Destiny's boyfriend miraculously reappears. He is "alive and okay."

What is the meaning of this curious dream resurrection? Is the dream yielding to Destiny's wishes, and providing her with a happy ending, as her grief grows too much to be borne? Or is the dream telling us that a literal death, really, never was the issue? Indeed, that the death Destiny fears is symbolic?

Death in dreams is a consistent metaphor for change and separation, and should almost never be interpreted literally. Accordingly, the death Destiny fears is most likely a change in her relationship. Her boyfriend is returning home for a family holiday. For whatever reason, Destiny is not included in this reunion. Is Destiny worried about the influence her boyfriend's family will have on their relationship? Will they accept Destiny and approve of her, or will her boyfriend return from his trip with a change of heart? Destiny is left at home waiting, her dreams filled with hope, fear, and suspense.

"Crash Landing"

I just woke up from a nap and had the most memorable dream. It stands out in my mind because I don't often remember my dreams.

I was at my mother's house, where I grew up. My older brother (who is sick with AIDS and lives with my mother) was there and it was storming, very dark and gloomy. I was there, kind of hiding out or procrastinating. This part of the dream is a bit unclear for me, but I know I had the lead in a play the next day and I was trying to avoid preparing for it. I was supposed to contact someone about the play but I didn't do it, and I was trying to avoid it altogether.

Then we heard a pilot communicating over a radio. He was describing this awful storm. I ran out on the front porch and looked up in the sky to see a big jet struggling. Then it crashed across the street, right in front of me. We both took off running toward it, when I realized it might explode because of the fuel. There was this sickening smell of fuel or oil.

So my brother and I ran behind my mother's house, where a smaller plane had just crashed. It had people we knew on it and someone on the plane had something to do with that play I was in. I started to talk to them, but then I woke up.

I should note that I'm an attorney who just switched from a larger firm to a smaller firm, in the same town. Two partners at the old firm just decided to start their own firm and asked me to join them. Two days ago we had an open house/party to announce our opening and it was well attended. Everyone is positive about the new firm and they were describing the firm as "the premiere" law firm and "up and coming." I personally am excited but nervous about the whole thing.

–Sierra, Age 31, Married, USA

Sierra's career is heading in a new direction. She has set her goals high, and exposed herself to risk by leaving an older, larger law firm. As Sierra faces the prospect of building a new business from the ground up, does she occasionally wonder if her new venture will "take flight"? Will she successfully arrive at her new, hoped-for, career destination?

Given the background Sierra provides, it's not difficult to understand that she feels she has just stepped off a big plane (the large law firm she has left) onto the wings of a smaller one (her new firm). Both planes, however, in a stormy environment that represents emotional turbulence, are forced to make crash landings. What is the meaning? Sierra has "burned her bridges" with her old firm, and now, she confesses, she is nervous about her future with her new firm.

A subplot of Sierra's dream is her desire to avoid preparing for a lead role in a play that she knows she is scheduled to perform tomorrow. Just at this moment, she rushes outside to witness the plane crashes. When Sierra reaches the wreckage of the smaller plane (her new law firm), she is aware that the person she needed to speak to about "her performance" is riding on this plane.

The message of Sierra's dream is clear: Sierra has the entrepreneur's jitters! She has stepped away from a more secure position with a larger firm (that apparently felt like a sinking ship) to test the winds of working with a smaller team. Like an actress on opening night, Sierra is nervous about her performance—procrastinating and wondering if she will survive. Now that Sierra has entered the big leagues, though, and decided to shoot for new "professional heights," there really is no option but to suit up and play. The pressure's on, and we're sure Sierra will "rise" to the occasion.

Attacked

Attacked: Dreams about attack rarely reflect literal fears of physical violence in our waking lives. Instead, they almost always reflect feelings of emotional attack. In heated arguments with friends, lovers, and coworkers, it helps to remember that words, also, can "sting like a bullet," and "cut like a knife."

Is the attacker someone we know? If so, we are alerted to the fact that we feel emotionally threatened, or injured, by this person. Is the attacker an animal? We may be wrestling with a primitive instinct or emotional drive, such as the desire to defend our family or, in women, the drive to bear children. If an attacker is disguised, we are alerted to the possible operation of repression inside us; we are struggling with an issue we "refuse to recognize" honestly. If we are preparing for battle or war, rest assured we are anticipating a challenging period at work, or in our personal life. If we resist our attackers, it is a positive sign of self-esteem and confidence. If we are unable to defend ourselves (we can not find a weapon, or our gun misfires), the dream is reflecting feelings of powerlessness against whomever, or whatever, the attacker represents. Dreams about being a victim of attack reflect feelings of powerlessness in waking life. Dreams about attack are common in children, and often reflect feelings of hostility or aggression encountered at school, or in the child's social life.

Attackers may also represent internal struggles—"battles" with drug, alcohol, and food addictions—and struggles against social pressures to conform. Common attack themes—being chased by a group of men who wish to capture and assault the dreamer—may reflect literal fears of violence in waking life.

Please also see: "Chase" and "Violence."

◆ **Interpretation tip:** If you dream about being shot at or chased, try to identify where you feel emotionally attacked in your waking life. If you experience recurring themes of attack in your dreams, try to confront your attackers in your dreams, and ask them to identify themselves.

✳ ✳ ✳

The dreams that follow illustrate different aspects of attack in dreams. "Shot in the Stomach" reflects the feelings of a young woman who has just received an emotional blow—delivered with an air of authority. "Attacked by Men in Suits" reminds us that our work environments, occasionally, can become war zones. Our final entry, "Kill My Student," reveals that the battles we wage are often against ourselves.

Attack Dreams

"Shot in the Stomach"

My boyfriend and I recently broke up. We'd been together for about ten months when he said that he wanted some "fun and freedom." Before we broke up we were somewhat engaged. I've had two dreams after the breakup.

The first one was the day after. We were in a car in front of a military compound and someone shot and hit me in the stomach. The bullet was meant for me and was a direct hit. When I found out I was shot, I was bleeding a lot, but my boyfriend (or ex) did not seem to notice or did not seem to care. When he finally did notice, he said he had to go do some kind of mission.

After he left, I drove off in a car going in the opposite direction of the way he went, and my wound was still painful, but the bleeding had slowly begun to stop. When I woke up, I felt a pain in my stomach where I supposedly got shot.

My second dream was last night. There was some kind of crisis going on, and a lot of people were called on to perform a job, and he was one of those people. After he went to prepare, I heard stories of how people were getting killed, so I ran to stop him from going. When I got there, nobody was left except him. I begged him not to go, and he told me he wasn't. Afterward he gave me a ring and put it on my ring finger, and we walked away in each other's arms.

What do these dreams mean? I wake up feeling scared and frightened, not knowing what to do!

–Brooke, Age 19, Single, USA

Brooke's dreams almost certainly reflect distress in light of her boyfriend's recent announcement—that he wants to be single, so that he can enjoy his "fun and freedom." His decision apparently was delivered with an air of authority and finality, which reminds Brooke of a military environment. The bullet that strikes her in the stomach represents the emotional pain she feels. Brooke's fear of death symbolizes her desire to avoid change and separation. Brooke is afraid that if her boyfriend goes ahead with his secret mission, she may "lose him forever."

Are we able to recognize the familiar symbols that so freely populate this dream? After Brooke is shot (absorbs the impact of her boyfriend's painful news), she drives off alone in a car (symbol of the self—of the "direction we are headed" in our lives), "going the opposite direction of the way he went." Her wound is bleeding, which shows that Brooke is emotionally injured and in pain. In her second dream, after Brooke convinces her boyfriend not go on his "mission," he gives her a ring—a symbol of commitment—and in Brooke's case, a sign that her "engagement" still is on.

Will Brooke's dream come true? Will her boyfriend, after a few sniffs around the neighborhood, decide to return home and resume the engagement? Will his symbolic death be avoided? Brooke's dream hints at the future, but offers no guarantees.

"Attacked by Men in Suits"

I have been dreaming about people attacking me lately, for about three weeks, almost every night. Sometimes there are men in suits and ties, sometimes men in black. Not like robbers, but soldiers on a night mission, or just soldiers—all with guns.

The part that bothers me is that I always have a gun but it doesn't work. I either fire and hit the person, but they don't seem to have been hit, or the gun doesn't work. Sometimes I am a soldier and am trying to protect the people around me. Most of the time I don't know the people I'm with.

I have been a little stressed out at work since I started my new job almost two years ago. My coworker is very moody and the slightest thing will set her off. She is very two-faced. She can be nice to me one minute and a total witch the next. Everyone in the office knows how she is but the ones in charge won't do anything. They feel that if we ignore her moods, they will go away. Ignoring the moods is just not working. I like my job and the other people I work with and can not afford to leave it, or I probably would have by now.

–Jenna, Age 28, Married, USA

Jenna is burdened at her office with an unstable and verbally violent coworker. She has requested assistance from "the ones in charge" (the men in suits), but her requests, so far, have been met with a conspiracy of silence. The soldiers in uniform (Jenna also appears as a soldier) are common dream symbols for authority, and reflect the hierarchy of the organization for which she works.

Curiously, the abusive coworker who is the source of Jenna's immediate problems is not directly represented. Instead, Jenna is pursued by organized groups—sometimes men in suits, sometimes soldiers on a night mission. This aspect of the dream reveals that Jenna's consistent inability to receive support from her coworkers and upper management has caused her to feel attacked by her entire organization. Will anyone acknowledge her request for assistance?

The gun that does not fire symbolizes Jenna's sense of powerlessness. The darkness in her dreams is a metaphor for conspiracy, and for Jenna's inability to see the future. To restore power to her gun, Jenna needs to consult, immediately, with a human resources advisor. Jenna is entitled to a consistent and emotionally hospitable workplace. If Jenna can make "the suits" in her company obey their own policies and procedures, she will shine needed light into her workplace, and she will restore power to her gun.

"Kill My Student"

I am an instructor and I dreamed that I killed one of my students (I don't know the reason). I hit her head with a shovel. My anguish and desperation was so great that I was beside myself. I went to the director of the school and told her. She said to me not to worry and we proceeded to throw the body into a well.

Later I found her dentures (she was a young woman) and it looked just like the plastic plate that I use to whiten my teeth. My terror began again as I didn't know how to dispose of that evidence. I went back to the director and she was very busy and she couldn't find a time for me in her appointment book, but once again she said not to worry.

So I thought either burn the dentures or cut them in pieces. Once I arrived at that decision I began to walk home (my car was in the shop). I walked but I couldn't find my way. I walked and walked very anxiously and aimlessly and began to think, "What will I tell my grandchildren and children when the police catch me in the years ahead?" (My kids are not even married yet.)

The desperation and anguish grew stronger and I was so scared. At that moment I thought I would do anything if this whole thing weren't true. Finally I woke up and I was quite shaken by all these feelings. But a few minutes later I felt this powerful sense of relief and gratitude for my good fortune in life. I thought how much I should appreciate all my experiences and how much I shouldn't take my life for granted.

I am fifty-two years old, and recently moved after living almost twenty-five years in another state. I am going through a big transition in my life, where I know that a change is coming, but I do not know how it will affect me. I am content, and almost feel guilty for not having any preoccupations. I love where I live and I do not need to be terribly concerned about my finances. Yet I often wonder why I was put on this planet and how can I direct my life to make a greater difference in this world. I feel numb at times, and though this dream was scary and painful, when I woke up I felt a sense of renewal through the experience of all these bad feelings.

Something else that I think is important is the fact that I finally decided to look for professional help (medically) to control my emotional eating, which leads me to binge uncontrollably. As a result of this condition I gained a lot of weight even though I am not obese. I have always been a strong advocate against the use of medications. I am a professional teacher and counselor on natural healing methods, yet here I am, using drugs to help suppress my appetite. I already know what to eat, how to exercise, and the emotions that trigger my binges, yet I still can't control my eating habits. I feel like such a hypocrite to even talk to my students about a healthy lifestyle.

I guess there is a sense of doing something wrong and feeling ashamed of it (taking drugs?). The possibility of being in jail and being totally deprived of my freedom is sort of what I am feeling right now. It feels at times like I am trapped in my own jail—that's how desperate I feel.

—Sara, Age 52, Divorced, USA

After all of Sara's hard work—all her training, learning, and striving to practice what she preaches—does she ever feel like her eating disorder sometimes just gets loose and whacks her over the head—with a giant shovel (spoon)? Anyone who has battled a self-destructive habit knows what it's like to be a victim of a compulsive behavior.

Because Sara is an instructor of natural healing methods, her recent decision to accept medical care has caused her distress. Not only is her decision an admission that nonmedical treatments do not work in all cases, it makes her feel like a hypocrite in front of her students, who look to her for guidance and support.

Sara plays both roles in the internal struggle represented by her dream. Her eating disorder (role one) hits the student (role two) on the head with a shovel. The clue that identifies Sara as the student who is killed is her discovery of the victim's "dental record." The dentures remind Sara specifically of the plate she uses for whitening her teeth at night. Positive identification?

Sara feels tremendous guilt for her actions, and asks an authority figure (the school director) for assistance. The director then helps Sara to bury the evidence—a reflection of Sara's desire to conceal her behavior from her students. Still fearful that she will be discovered, Sara next spends a significant portion of her dream worrying about what she will tell her "children and grandchildren," a continuing reference to her students, who look to her for guidance and leadership. As the dream ends, Sara's car is in the shop—a symbol of powerlessness—and she is unable to find her way. Clearly, Sara has lost her direction.

Sara's dream is a potent invitation for her to consider being honest with her students. When she awoke, she felt a cathartic sense of release from experiencing "all those bad feelings." If she wishes to role-model this gift of authenticity, Sara needs to tell her students her decision, and she should not be afraid to share with them her true identity: a sympathetic student, who is also on the road to empowerment.

Baby

Baby: Babies in dreams often reflect literal concerns about the birth cycle and the responsibilities of parenthood. Babies also can symbolize new projects, business developments, and relationships that a dreamer is "nurturing" in waking life. In romantic relationships, babies can represent the "product" of the relationship. Is the baby healthy, happy, and strong? Or is it weak, and in danger of dying? Giving birth can symbolize a new stage of growth and personal development. Neglected babies are common metaphors for a dreamer's untended "inner child." Crying babies and big babies may represent adults we know in waking life, who act like babies, and are unable to care for themselves.

Common Baby Dreams:

Abandoned baby: Common dream among women who are unprepared for the responsibilities of motherhood. A baby is present, but the dreamer shows a willful disregard for the child. The dreamer is resisting social pressures to have children, or may fear an accidental pregnancy for which she is unprepared due to career, financial, or emotional reasons.

Disappearing baby: Common dream in the wake of an abortion, miscarriage, or actual death of a child. The baby is present, but then suddenly disappears. The dreamer may feel misgivings that she has done something to harm the baby.

Happy baby: Powerful dream frequently experienced by women who are happily anticipating motherhood. The mother can see and hold her newborn child, and is elated.

Neglected/forgotten babies: Common dream among first-time mothers reflecting literal anxieties about the continuous responsibilities of motherhood. In more experienced mothers, a dream about a neglected baby (the product of a romantic relationship) may symbolize neglect of the relationship with one's partner. Also can symbolize neglect of oneself. The dreamer is not caring for his or her "inner child."

Talking baby: Frequent dream among new and expectant mothers. The mother and newborn are able to converse fluently. The dreams reflect a new mother's anticipation of her relationship with her child. The conversations often are not profound, and may express routine thoughts and concerns occupying the mother's mind.

Tiny baby: Familiar dream mechanism for representing a child whose arrival is distant in the future. Common among women who have chosen to delay parenting for career, relationship, or financial reasons.

Unprepared-for baby: Common among couples who are trying to conceive, or who are experiencing difficulty becoming pregnant due to medical complications. The dream is similar to dreams about being unprepared to take an exam in school or college. Will the dreamer pass the test, and make the transition to motherhood?

◆ Interpretation tip: If you dream about babies or about giving birth, first decide if your dream reflects literal or symbolic concerns. Are you curious about childbirth, anxious to begin the process, or nervous that you already may be pregnant? If literal concerns do not apply, ask what new project, business development, or romantic relationship in your waking life is being represented.

✳ ✳ ✳

Depending on the context of our waking lives, dreams about babies alternate freely between literal and symbolic meanings. In "Broken Baby," a dreamer's newborn is delivered in pieces, a chilling commentary on the status of her foundering marriage. Another symbolic dream, "Wounded Baby," illustrates the use of babies as metaphors for new projects and business developments that we nurture from the ground up. Our third dream, "New Baby," signifies a period of personal growth and development for our dreamer. Our final entry, "Giving Birth," reflects a woman in transition, who is ready to leave her past behind, for an uncertain but promising future. This chapter concludes with a series of literal baby dreams, all of which are common when babies are on our minds.

Symbolic Baby Dreams

"Broken Baby"

I recently got married and moved across the country. I've been very depressed, unhappy with my marriage and experiencing great feelings of disappointment and being trapped. I love my husband very much—he's the kindest, most honest and gentle man I've ever met in my entire life—but I'm not attracted to him anymore.

Recently, I've been having a lot of dreams about babies and giving birth. My most vivid dream was that I had given birth to a sickly, underweight child. I was attempting to breast-feed and squeezed my right breast and all that came out was blood and pus. My child could not breast-feed and didn't eat for his first two days. When I could finally nurse, it was very difficult and he only ate once.

Other dreams I've had about babies included giving birth to plastic doll children that fell apart on delivery, and lots of dreams about breast-feeding children that didn't exist at all. I did have an abortion eight months ago (before my husband and I were married) but I don't know why these dreams would be tied to it since I don't feel any guilt about the abortion. I didn't want a baby and neither did my husband at that time. We do plan on having children in the future, but no time immediately.

–Christina, Age 27, Married, USA

If we know that babies in dreams are often literal representations of hopes and fears concerning childbirth, and that they also represent the "product of a romantic relationship," then Christina's recurring dreams quickly make sense. Christina recently decided to terminate a pregnancy, and she is involved in a troubled marriage.

The images contained in Christina's dreams are disturbing. The sickly, underweight child that she delivers and attempts to nurture represents the status of her foundering marriage. Christina informs us that she is depressed and unhappy, and feels trapped in her new life. The blood and pus that flow from her breast show us that Christina no longer feels she can give her marriage the emotional food it requires.

Christina's dreams about doll children falling apart on delivery, and of breast-feeding nonexistent babies, are both common in the aftermath of abortion. The first dream graphically represents the abortion procedure she underwent. The second reflects the physical and emotional preparation of her body for being a mother (breast-feeding), coupled with her awareness that the child "no longer exists."

Christina tells us that her dreams surprise her, because her decision to terminate her pregnancy was made prior to her marriage, and because she feels no guilt about it. Is the true meaning of her dreams, accordingly, that she does not wish to make a second error in judgment?

Christina's dreams reflect difficult events from her past and present, but they also carry a potent message for her future. Christina needs to take her marriage to an emergency room (relationship counselor) to see if she can bring it back to life—before she brings other parties (babies) into the equation. The image of the sickly child is foreboding: Christina should not bring new children into her home, unless they have the healthy family they need to nurture their growth.

"Wounded Baby"

In my dream I was looking after someone else's baby like it was my own. I was in a largish house and for no reason a strange man stabbed the baby in the neck. I was horrified. I think I called a doctor or ambulance and the baby was patched up and fine.

I discovered a garden to the house. It was full of blossoming trees and green grass. I thought I'd like to go out there. At this point I was semiconscious of the baby's mother, as I had been wondering what to do with the baby.

Then, the strange man appeared again and stabbed the baby. I hadn't been concentrating on looking after the baby, but was more interested in the garden. This time the wound was huge and I could see in graphic detail a hole from the neck down to the shoulder. I knew the baby wouldn't survive.

I called an ambulance, but no one came quickly enough. I thought the mother would be so angry with me. I saw the baby go blue. I knew it was dying. I tried to resuscitate it, but it shriveled up in front of me. I accepted it, but thought I ought to have grieved more, felt more. I didn't seem to have any emotions at all. It was dead and that was that.

At the moment I am in a state of flux regarding my career. I have been working in the same place for nine months, hoping it would continue, but it seems that it may all be finished by the end of the year. I haven't given up entirely, but my hopes are waning. I have been thinking of starting up my own business, and perhaps that is symbolized by the garden. Can you help me solve this mystery?

–Mary, Age 30, Single, England

Mary has identified the symbolic significance of the garden in her dream precisely. With her hopes waning for continued employment with her current company, Mary naturally has begun to look elsewhere—for areas of "new growth."

Mary's dream reveals how babies often symbolize new projects in our lives, that we are nurturing and helping to grow from the ground up. Given that Mary's current employer is experiencing trouble "surviving," it is clear that the baby in her dream symbolizes her current job. The attacks the baby receives represent the "setbacks" and "financial losses" that have occurred in the company. In the dream Mary is committed to caring for this baby, yet she also fears that perhaps the end is near. When the baby dies, Mary is puzzled that she does not feel a greater sense of grief or loss. This is another clue that the baby she holds really symbolizes the "death of her job," and does not reflect concerns about a real child.

As the dream concludes, Mary accepts the baby's death, but remains intrigued by new opportunities that appear to exist in a garden. Mary's desire to start her own business is strong. In dreams to come, the new baby Mary will be carrying will be her own. It will be another "baby business" that a concerned parent is helping to grow.

"New Baby"

Background information: I am twenty-four years old and just moved back in with my mother so I can finish college. I recently received a new position at work, somewhat of a promotion. Basically I am starting a new everything. A relationship also just recently ended with no explanation. He just stopped calling and returning calls. I work a lot of hours with not much personal time.

In my dream I was standing in the middle of nowhere (white and foggy) and was handed a baby, by a person that I could not see. It was almost like the baby just appeared.

I knew the baby looked familiar but I couldn't place the face. Then my mother appeared and said that the baby was me, and that I was granted the greatest gift—to be able to see myself. I just remember feeling every emotion possible at that time, and then woke up feeling the same way . . . (every emotion still going through me).

This dream happened a while ago, but it is always on my mind.

–Faith, Age 24, Single, USA

Faith tells us that she is "starting a new everything" in her life. She recently received a new position at work (a promotion), and she decided to move back home with her mother, so she can finish her college education. Faith is even starting a new phase in her romantic life. A man she was seeing recently stopped calling, leaving the door open to new romance in her future. Is it such a surprise that Faith's dream represents this period of new beginnings by showing her as a newborn?

Faith's dream reflects her multiple new statuses in waking life, but it also references a new phase in Faith's personal and spiritual growth. The color white, and clouds, are both associated with spirituality in dreams. Because Faith is in a "white and foggy" location when the baby appears, a spiritual insight into herself is indicated. Faith's mother next explains that the ability to "see herself" is a great gift. Indeed, from a spiritual perspective, the ability to "see oneself" is equivalent to the universal spiritual admonition to "know thyself." The better we are able to see ourselves, the better "parents"—to our developing souls—we can be.

In a powerful moment of enlightenment and atonement (at-one-ment), Faith experiences "every emotion possible" in her dream and awakens deeply moved. Her memory of the dream, she writes, "is always on my mind." The dream has encouraged Faith that, even in the midst of great change, she knows what is required for her to develop into a strong and healthy personality. With love and attention, Faith's "baby" will grow into everything Faith desires her to be.

"Giving Birth"

I have a strong urge to bear down and realize that I am pregnant and ready to give birth. At first I cannot figure out how this could be and then I do bear down and this whole baby comes out of me. I am telling my sister and my husband and a third person that I gave birth without any pains or contractions. Then I notice that I am torn and bleeding and will have to drive myself to the hospital. While I am trying to get to the hospital I am desperately trying to clean and nurse the new baby, who has fallen into some water.

This dream about giving birth was followed by a two-week period of one or two dreams every night about death—my own and others. In one dream I was building a straw-bale house with my husband, and I was trying to explain to him about weight distribution of the second floor onto the main floor. I suddenly realized that I would die before finishing the house, and then I did die. My body lay heavily on the ground and I floated up through the opening of the unfinished house. I felt this overwhelming sensation of lightness. Then I looked back unemotionally at my dead body.

In real life I am married to a nice man, and we have been building a life together, which is fine, and far from finished. But the level of love is quite low, and we are not connected on any spiritual level. At the same time these dreams started, I was overwhelmed with the idea that I needed to go to Australia and follow some intuitive desire. This need to go there has been extremely strong, and very unexplained; not at all the way things usually are for me. In an awake state, as well as in a dream state, everything has been telling me that I must go.

Based upon these dreams, I have decided to go. I will be leaving in three weeks.

–Jada, Age 42, Married, USA

Jada is "giving birth" to a new aspect of herself. Because Jada drives herself to the hospital, her dream suggests she feels alone in this "new birth" project—without much support from family or friends. The dream also suggests that Jada fears for the life of this new development. As she drives, her baby falls into some water, and Jada works "desperately" trying to clean and nurse it. Jada is still uncertain if this new aspect of her personality will survive.

Jada's dream about building a new house with her husband is explained by Jada's comment upon her marriage: "We have been building a life together, which is fine, and far from finished." Two details included in her dream, however, foreshadow impermanence in the relationship. The house is constructed with hay bales, which are not the sturdiest or most enduring of building materials. Jada also observes an imbalance in the weight distribution between the upper and lower floors of the house, an allusion to the spiritual imbalance that Jada perceives in her relationship. (Upper floors in houses represent consciousness and spiritual aspects of the self, while lower levels represent the body and everyday living.) Jada would like to see more attention paid to spiritual issues in her life. While contemplating the house, Jada suddenly realizes she will "die" (will move on) before it is completed. When she dies, she releases her heavy body in exchange for an overwhelming sensation of lightness.

Jada's unemotional response to her death indicates that she is not afraid of the symbolic change that it represents. On the contrary, Jada is anticipating her rebirth, and suspects that when it does occur, it will feel like the release of a heavy weight. Based upon these dreams, Jada has courageously booked a trip to Australia—the first step on the journey of her "new life."

Literal Baby Dreams

"Abandoned Babies"

Hello. I am eighteen and I am not sexually active. I don't have plans to marry, nor do I have a strong desire to have kids. But I keep dreaming about *babies*!

In one dream I was in the hospital where they place all the newborns, and I was looking at all of them saying how cute they are. I would pick up one or two and kiss them. Then I said, "I wish I had a baby," and all of a sudden I was pregnant, and with one gentle, painless push—I gave birth.

The child, my "daughter," was absolutely beautiful. But I did not feel like carrying or kissing her. I had no maternal instincts whatsoever. A doctor came in and got after me. "How can it be that you are nice to all the babies but yours?" I looked at the doctor but had no answer. The other babies were simply more appealing. I got up and picked up another child and rocked it in my arms, and ignored my own child, who was then crying!!!

–*Mia, Age 18, Single, Mexico*

In typical dream fashion, as soon as Mia begins wishing for a baby, she miraculously delivers! Immediately, however, her mixed emotions begin to show. While Mia finds her baby girl "beautiful," she also observes that she experiences "no maternal instincts whatsoever." Mia begins to ignore her, and even the doctor is perplexed by Mia's callousness!

Mia's dream is common among women who are unprepared for the responsibilities of motherhood. The meaning of her dream is clear: Babies look cute from a distance, but Mia is not ready yet to assume the responsibilities of motherhood.

"Disappearing Baby"

I keep dreaming about playing with a baby and suddenly the baby disappears and I can't find it anywhere. Why is this happening to me? I lost a child before it was born last year. I also sometimes dream that I am pregnant and that I will be delivering the baby in a week or so, but I am not pregnant.

–*Sabrina, Age 29, Married, USA*

In the aftermath of her miscarriage, the meaning of Sabrina's dream is clear: Sabrina was expecting to be playing with her new baby by now. In the dream Sabrina is confused by the baby's absence, just as she still must, today, be confused by her recent experience of miscarriage. Sabrina's second dream reflects a literal desire to be pregnant again.

"Happy Baby"

I am now nine months pregnant and due in two and a half weeks. During the past three months I kept having dreams that the baby was born. I have always gotten to hold the baby and see the face and it felt so real that I woke up and was so disappointed that the ordeal was not over with. In all the dreams I was very happy and content. What could this possibly mean?

–*Leah, Age 24, Married, USA*

Leah's dream is entirely transparent. Leah is anxiously anticipating the birth of her new baby, and for three months has been imagining the event occurring in her dreams. Is a fear of delivery (we assume this is her first child) also in evidence? Leah is disappointed when she awakens from her dream—that "the ordeal" is not over.

Leah's contentment when she holds her child is a positive sign. Leah is prepared for her child, and does not anticipate difficulties or complications—physical or emotional—with becoming a mother.

"Talking Baby"

I had a dream that my husband gave birth to our baby; however, the baby was an infant or at least he came into the world with a full head of hair and was speaking fluently like a young child. As I entered the room this child asked if I was his mummy and I replied yes, and the child held on to me so tight.

It was a nice kind of dream but I am at a loss to understand it. I didn't give birth to it as has happened before; I am sure my husband did. And I felt very happy. I have been married to a great guy for two years and we are planning to start our family this year. However, my husband has a lot of changes to go through first (an operation, a workers' compensation claim, and change of job), just to name a few things.

–*Vanessa, Age 29, Married, Australia*

Vanessa has a talking baby dream with a twist: In the dream, the baby asks if Vanessa is his mother. The reason the baby does not know? He was delivered by his dad!

Vanessa's dream reflects her happy anticipation of becoming a mother, and includes her awareness of current obstacles to reaching her goal. She is waiting on her husband to complete several events (operation, workers' comp claim, new job) before they can start their family. Vanessa is prepared for her child to arrive, but she is waiting on her husband to "deliver" the child!

"Tiny Baby"

I had a dream that I had a baby. But the baby was very small. First of all I was disappointed, but then I thought that a small baby is actually very convenient. I can bring it anywhere, and it will fit into a matchbox.

Then I got hungry, and I put the baby on my plate as I started eating my lunch. All of a sudden I realized that I had accidentally swallowed the baby. I got very upset. I started spitting out the food I had in my mouth. All I could get out was the skeleton, and it looked like an embryo skeleton. I was horrified, but then I thought, "Oh well! It was small anyway," and I felt relieved.

Background: I am getting married in a couple of months. My future husband and I would love to have children but we want to wait a couple of years. I don't know if it matters, but I am currently taking the pill. Any thoughts?

–Melissa, Age 31, Engaged, USA

Melissa's baby is so small—it fits neatly into a matchbox! In dream-speak, this is a familiar metaphor that informs us that Melissa's baby most likely is an event that is distant in the future—perhaps even only at the conceptual stage?

Melissa and her husband would love to have children, but have decided to wait a few years. Is Melissa's dream a reminder that, each day she swallows a birth control pill, she is also "swallowing" (suppressing) her desire for children? If so, the day will soon come when Melissa can forego the birth control pills, and allow her baby to grow.

"Unprepared for Baby"

I've had this dream, twice now, that I was pregnant and about to have a baby and I am on my way to the hospital. When I get there I am in a bed about to give birth, and I can see myself a huffin' and puffin'. Then I'm at my house getting ready to go show the baby off when I realize I don't have a car seat. I'm looking and looking but no seat! Then I wake up.

My husband and I are trying to get pregnant, but we're having trouble. This dream happened before I even started to find out there would be trouble getting pregnant. We do not have any other children.

–Madison, Age 27, Married, USA

Madison's inability to locate a car seat—as she prepares to show off her new baby—reveals her awareness that an obstacle lies in her path to childbirth. Madison and her husband are making a strong effort to conceive (a huffin' and puffin'), but the absence of the baby, and the social context of the dream, inform us that time is passing by. Madison feels the expectant eyes of family and friends upon her. Where is her baby?

Madison insists the dreams began before she was aware of any difficulties. If this is so, Madison is hardly alone among women who have dreams that foreshadow either pregnancy or difficulty in conception.

Bathroom

Bathroom: Common setting in dreams for feelings relating to shame and "release of private emotions." If a dreamer searches for a toilet but can not find a private location (all the stalls are exposed, or strangers are present, causing the dreamer to be uncomfortable), a lack of privacy is indicated, or the dream may indicate fear of expressing one's "private emotions"—about which one feels ashamed or embarrassed—in public. If the toilet area is filthy or flooded, with the toilet bowl backed up or otherwise not functioning, difficulty "eliminating" emotions—a blockage—is indicated. Defecation dreams also are common in the aftermath of lover's quarrels and other intense arguments. Is someone burdening you with a "load of crap"?

Dreams about searching for a bathroom in which to urinate may also reflect literal pressure upon your bladder during sleep. Do you have to go when you awaken?

♦ **Interpretation tip:** Are you "holding back" some private emotions that you "need to release"? It's time to invite a good friend over, and "get it out of your system"!

* * *

Bathroom dreams are amusing to read, but they also reflect dreamers wrestling with difficult feelings and awarenesses. Our first dream shows a man in transition, concerned about public perceptions of his lifestyle choices. Does his sex life really belong "In the Toilet"? Our next dream, "Urgent Need," details a descent into some primitive behaviors: A woman's lover behaves like an animal. In "Private Business," a young woman's need for privacy is explored. Does everyone really need to know the details of her medical condition? Our final dream, "Bowel Movement," is a humorous example of how dreams sometimes represent all that "bathroom talk"—a bit more literally than we might expect!

Bathroom Dreams

"In the Toilet"

I'm in the process of adopting a baby. Also, my company may transfer to another city. I am also preparing my home to be sold. I've had this recurring dream. A handsome man, with brown hair and blue eyes, and I are trying to meet but we can't seem to connect. There are obstacles that keep us from getting together. The next thing I know we are in a bathroom becoming very intimate with one another. I look over my shoulder and see a child on a toilet seat. I tell the man we should not do this now, in front of the child. He says it's okay, as long as we do not let her see.

While this is going on, the first child leaves and a second child enters and proceeds to sit on the toilet. Then the dream ends.

This is such a strange dream that I can't make heads or tails out of it. Can you help me?

–Ryan, Age 34, Single, USA

As a gay man, Ryan has endured a lifetime's worth of social stigma. Straight society says he is queer, and mainstream religions tell him he is going to hell. As if things weren't difficult enough, Ryan now wishes to adopt a child. While gay adoption is legal in most states in the USA, the debate about the suitability of gays as parents continues socially.

Bathrooms in dreams are common settings for feelings related to guilt and shame. Most of us, in our potty training days, learned from our parents that defecating was a dirty process. When we are taught as children that going to the bathroom is dirty, it is easy for us to continue to experience shame and guilt about performing the act as adults.

The difficulty Ryan experiences connecting with his dream partner suggests a real-life struggle to achieve a relationship with a mate. Even when he does connect, however, Ryan's sexual activity, rather than being performed freely and in private, is attempted warily before an audience of observing eyes. And yes, it is in a bathroom (the closet?).

The issue addressed by Ryan's dream is not whether he and a future mate ever would perform sex directly in front of a child—an act any responsible parent would regret. On the contrary, the setting of the bathroom directs us to consider feelings of shame learned many years ago. Is Ryan's sexual orientation dirty? Does it belong hidden in the closet? Is he fit to be a parent? And finally, how will his future children perceive his lifestyle?

"Urgent Need"

After having been divorced for fourteen years, I am newly engaged to a very nice man. During that time I have only dated two or three times. My fiancé is quite a bit overweight, at around three hundred seventy-five pounds. I am of normal build with a few extra pounds. His eating habits are atrocious. Other than that, we are very much alike and are the same age. He recently bought a house for us, but my name isn't on it, and he plans to leave it to his daughters when he dies.

I dreamed we were walking outside. He was wearing nothing but his underwear, and I was wearing a T-shirt. We were both barefooted. We came to the zoo and decided that it would be fun to go in and see the animals. We were only there for a short time when his need to go to the bathroom overcame him. He actually climbed into the "white gorilla's" environment and defecated right where anyone walking by could see him. I was aghast and mortified. I ran screaming from the zoo, and didn't see him again until we were at home.

–Nicole, Age 51, Engaged, USA

The setting of the zoo in this dream lets us know some primitive issues are being addressed. And, given the background Nicole has provided, it's not hard to figure them out. Her fiancé's eating habits "are atrocious." Does she sometimes think he acts like an animal (a "white gorilla," to be specific)?

Dreams about defecation typically concern issues of self-control and shame. If we dream about searching for a bathroom but are never able to find one, we are encouraged to ask ourselves what emotional issue we are "holding on to" (control), that we need to release. If a dream bathroom is in a public space, which causes us to be self-conscious, the dream suggests that we feel ashamed of an emotional issue, or feel unable to release it, because we are concerned about what others may think.

Judging by Nicole's dream, neither of these scenarios applies to her fiancé. On the contrary, his public defecation at the zoo represents his inability to control his eating disorder—no matter who is present. It is also significant that Nicole and her partner are both dressed only in their underwear as they walk around the zoo. Their partial attire suggests they are exposed and seeing each other plainly. In her dream, her fiancé's behavior sends Nicole running for the door. Will Nicole run for the door in her waking life as well?

"Private Business"

I was going into a public bathroom and the stall I walked into had three girls standing there, letting me get by. They just stayed in while I started to go number two. It seemed normal. I kept going number two and a different set of people came in and waited there. People kept coming through—like it was a waiting area for other stalls that really were private. I kept going number two like it was never-ending.

I just found out that I may have had a bacterial infection since I was age eleven. I am always sick and I have gotten worse over the last two years. The doctor has been giving me medicine because I have had diarrhea for the last year. I just got over it. She said food used to just rot in my stomach.

I am glad I am getting better but I do not know for sure when or if I will get completely well. I am on my second round of treatment; the first round did not work. I have been sick, flulike, and had to miss one day of work this week. The doctor has cut sugar and starch from my diet. I hate that when I go out to eat with my coworkers my food choices are noticeable and have to be explained. It is embarrassing to me. Please advise. Thanks.

—Samantha, Age 32, Single, USA

Samantha is a woman who could use a little more privacy in her life! Just when she thinks she is getting over one problem (diarrhea), her restricted diet is making her feel embarrassed all over again. Will she ever be free of this nagging medical condition, and not have to air her laundry in public? (Or at least get her own stall?)

Samantha's dream is a good illustration of the associations that bathrooms hold in our minds. Bathrooms in real life are locations where private behaviors are performed. The bathroom in Samantha's dream, though, is anything but private. As the dream begins, Samantha has three girls standing around while she performs her business. They leave soon enough, but then another group of people come in and take their place. All the while Samantha is going number two—for what seems like an eternity.

The long time Samantha spends in the bathroom is a reference to her recent medical problem, which kept her in the bathroom (literally) with chronic diarrhea, for almost a year. The symbolic message represented by the parade of onlookers, however, is one of embarrassment; everyone knows too much about her private issues.

Has Samantha asked her doctor what answers she can give if people ask about her food choices? Samantha needs an answer that will satisfy people quickly, that will restore her privacy.

"Bowel Movement"

My dream was very strange, and I need help interpreting it. My boyfriend of five years was intentionally having a bowel movement on my face. I kept screaming for him to stop, but he didn't. He left the room and I put it in a place where he was sure to step on it when he came back in the room.

We are very much in love and have been dating for five years. I am ready for marriage but unfortunately he is not. So I have been feeling very rejected by him. The day before his roommate was talking to him about buying another house together like a business deal. I told my boyfriend in a fit of anger and frustration that if they bought another house together I would break up with him. His feelings were very hurt and he assured me that he was not going to do that. Anyway the next night he said something that really hurt my feelings. And I let him know that I thought it was cruel. He said that my threat to break up with him was cruel. So anyway he was basically trying to get back at me. Needless to say, our relationship has been off lately because of my need for a commitment and his bad attitude about it.

–Cynthia, Age 25, Single, USA

When the "s— gets thick" in a relationship, it often spills over into our dreams. "Take that," says Cynthia, as she piles a stool in her lover's path. Cynthia knows he will step in it (step in his own s—) and it will serve him right for all the "crap" she has had to put up with lately.

The play on words reflected in this dream may strike us as offensive, but the dream is an excellent illustration of how dreams often literally embody slang metaphors. The day before Cynthia had this dream, she felt that her lover was "dumping his emotions" unfairly on her. (She felt that he was treating her "poorly," also known as "like s—.") Her subsequent dream reflects these emotions, and her motivation to show her boyfriend what it feels like in return.

Betrayal

Betrayal: Dreams about being betrayed in a romantic relationship typically represent emotional feelings of insecurity, or literal fears of infidelity. If the betrayal occurs in a business context, one may be concerned about being lied to or defrauded by a partner. Betrayal dreams often occur for years in the wake of actual betrayals by real-life partners.

Infidelity: Dreams about infidelity on behalf of the dreamer may indicate romantic attractions outside the primary relationship, and can be indicators of sexual dissatisfaction with one's partner.

◆ **Interpretation tip:** Betrayal dreams often reflect our insecurities, rather than being literal indicators of betrayal. Before you accuse a partner of wandering, perform an inventory of your own self-esteem.

* * *

Ah, betrayal. Nothing awakens us quicker than a dream about a partner casting aside vows of fidelity. Is the lover faceless? Is he or she someone we know—a "good friend," somebody from the office, or from the neighborhood? We wake up feeling suspicious, but uncertain whether our dream is grounds for accusation. Is our dream communicating with us, trying desperately to send a message—to recognize clues that surely must be laid before our eyes? Or is our dream simply a cruel mirror—reflecting fears and feelings of inadequacy—as we perpetually perceive ourselves as unworthy of love and commitment?

Each of the dreams that follow illustrates a different aspect of the betrayal spectrum. "My Husband Is Cheating" reflects doubts that commonly attend a young woman's transition to motherhood. "Faceless Woman" instructs us that affairs and separations do injure relationships—deeply—and that damaged trust often requires years to heal. "Laughing at Me" yields powerful insight into the dynamics of low self-esteem, the true culprit in many dreams about betrayal and infidelity. Our final entry, "Ocean of Betrayal," demonstrates that, given the right circumstances, even betrayers can feel betrayed.

Betrayal Dreams

"My Husband Is Cheating"

I am a twenty-six-year-old stay-at-home mother of a ten-month-old. Lately I have been having dreams that my husband is cheating on me. It has been mostly strangers and once a prostitute, and I catch him in the act almost every time.

The most recent dream, however, was quite troubling as it was my eighteen-year-old sister who was the "other woman." I have no issues with her and am actually quite close to her. My husband and I are still having sex regularly (once a week) though not as often as before our son was born. I didn't suspect my husband of anything until I continued to have these dreams, and now I am suspicious of him and feel that I can't trust him.

–Gina, Age 26, Married, USA

Gina describes herself as a twenty-six-year-old stay-at-home mother. Though she has no reason to suspect her partner, a recent series of infidelity dreams has driven her to suspicion. What does he do, she wonders, each day at work? And with whom?

Gina's dreams may be caused by her new responsibilities as a stay-at-home mother—which keep her home while her husband still is free to roam the world—but a deeper concern almost certainly also is present. Like many new mothers, Gina may be questioning her desirability and attractiveness after the delivery of her child, and after making her transition in role from lover to mother.

The fact that Gina's dreams show her husband with various, nondescript partners (including a prostitute) indicates there is not a specific woman with whom she suspects he is having an affair. Similarly, the inclusion of her sister in a recent dream is doubly significant. Gina reports that she is "quite close" with her sister. In light of this closeness, her sister is an unlikely candidate for suspicions of infidelity. What is the significance, then, of her sister's appearance in these dreams? Most likely it is her age. Her sister is eighteen years old—a young age—at a time when our dreamer, suddenly, is feeling much older.

Because Gina has no reason to distrust her husband, and because these dreams most likely reflect, to some extent, her own insecurities as she transitions to her new role as a mother, Gina is advised to voice her fears to her husband as an expression of insecurity, and not as an accusation of infidelity. As they begin this exciting period of their lives together, both partners must respect each other's needs and concerns. Just as the dreamer is concerned with staying attractive on the home front, her husband, with a new family, is occupied with staying active in the business world. These dreams demonstrate a need for increased love, support, and reassurance, during a normal period of transition in a relationship.

"Faceless Woman"

Every night for the past two years I have had the same dream. It always starts with me sitting in my car in the driveway, getting ready to go into the house. I get to the door and try to open it but drop everything in my hands. Then I try to open the door again but the handle won't turn. Finally I get the door open and go in to find my husband sitting on the couch with another woman. I slowly walk around the couch to see her face and I can't. She doesn't have a face. Then my husband starts to kiss her and rub her breasts. After that I always wake up. Please help me have some understanding of this.

We were having problems with our marriage and were split up when the dream started. We have since gotten back together and gone to marriage counseling. We have had a great relationship since then—about one and a half years now. This is probably the best our relationship has ever been and I still have the dream. The feelings I have in the dream are calm, yet disappointed and lonely.

–*Heidi, Age 28, Married, USA*

We do not know from Heidi's dream report if her husband ever was unfaithful, but it is clear from her dream that she felt shut out of her husband's life for a while (difficulty opening the door) and that she was concerned about the possibility of another woman.

Heidi's recurring dreams are nightly testimony to the wisdom that it is very difficult for relationships to recover from separations and affairs. Fundamental levels of trust often are lost forever. The faceless woman informs us that Heidi does not know the identity of the other woman—whether she existed in reality, or was only a suspected presence.

"Laughing at Me"

My fiancé and I are engaged but that is as far as it has gone. We've not set a date, and sometimes he jokes that we are already living as if we were married, so why rush it? He doesn't care if we wait until we are forty. He has never cheated on me, but my ex-husband did and he was also abusive, another thing my fiancé would never be.

But lately I have been having dreams in which my fiancé is either leaving me or cheating on me. Some of the dreams are vague, even almost funny at times, and don't bother me. Then there are dreams like last night's—so vivid and real that I was actually still feeling angry with Kevin (my fiancé) when we got up in the morning.

The dream starts off that I am at "my apartment"—which seems to be a loft-type apartment above a boathouse of some kind, near the water. It is set at the base of a hill, with a very steep driveway that goes to the road at the top of the hill. My "best friend" is there. I put that in quotes because she is someone I have never seen or known in my waking life, yet she is very obviously my best friend in this dream.

She is blond, blue-eyed, very pretty, and smart. She dresses very stylishly and seems very personable. This is exactly Kevin's ideal woman in real life. (Oddly enough, I have brown hair and eyes.) We are talking about Kevin and how he has seemed distant to me lately. I ask her if she thinks he is pulling away from me, or even just afraid to commit. She reassures me that he loves me very much, and says that they have been talking lately, and that he confides in her that he loves me very much. I tell her how glad I am that he'll talk to her, because he won't talk to me.

I tell her she is truly a great friend and how nice it is to have a friend who can be that way without betraying me and trying to steal him away or sleep with him. Then she laughs and says now she feels guilty, so she must confess that the night before, when he said he was at his cousin's, he was really sleeping with her. I am so hurt and betrayed it's like someone punched me in the stomach. I am devastated.

Then Kevin gets home and figures out pretty quickly what's up. I scream at him how could he do this to me!!! He *laughs* and tells me it's been going on for a while. Didn't I realize that when she was over to visit, anytime I left the room they were making out? He tells me that I am an idiot and they both laugh.

I run down the stairs to the outside and try and leave in my car but it won't start. So I start up the driveway, running, but it has started to rain hard and I can't climb up because it's too slippery. I am getting soaked and covered in mud and finally I give up and collapse, crying in the muck. I want to sink into the earth and disappear. I hurt so much emotionally and physically from the climb attempt. I look over my shoulder and they are standing together, arms around each other, smiling smugly, and they laugh at me again, then turn and walk back toward the house, apparently untouched by the storm. I wake up.

Kevin is very good to me in reality and would never do anything even remotely close to this. Why would I dream something so horrible? Why does this dream seem so real and so vivid? I actually had to take some quiet time to get over it when I first woke up, almost to heal from the pain I felt and to not be angry at Kevin for something that had happened in my own dream. Can you help me understand this?

–Sharon, Age 27, Engaged, USA

In agonizing sequence, Sharon's dream leads us through realizations we are often forced to confront in a genuine scenario of violated trust: that the person with whom the betrayal was committed actually was a close friend, that it was going on for a lot longer than we ever imagined, and that, "Boy, were we naive."

Kevin's casual approach to setting a wedding date, coupled with Sharon's recent history of a failed (and abusive) marriage, has sounded alarms of doubt in Sharon's heart. What is her fiancé waiting for? Is there a reason he doesn't want to get married? What is the significance of an engagement ring, if it is not followed by the more binding commitment of marriage?

Significantly, Sharon identifies the woman in her dream as "exactly Kevin's ideal woman in real life." This observation informs us that Sharon's dream, most likely, is concerned more with her own self-evaluation—compared to an imagined ideal—than it is with actual concerns of infidelity.

As Sharon herself states, "Kevin is very good to me in reality, and would never do anything even remotely close to this."

Sharon feels inadequate to compete against this "ideal woman," and as she retreats from the relationship, familiar metaphors for feelings of powerlessness soon appear. Sharon runs to her car (symbol of the self) but is unable to get it to start. Next she attempts to flee on foot, but she is unable to ascend a now very muddy, and slippery, driveway. Throughout her dream, the symbol of water—an archetypal symbol for emotions—is conspicuously present. Her apartment in the dream is in a boathouse "near the water," and a rainstorm strikes as the dream builds to its emotional climax. Sharon's feelings of low self-esteem, and her fears of rejection, both are unleashed in this downpour.

Contrary to its surface appearances, Sharon's dream is not a warning about an unfaithful partner. Rather, her recurring dreams reflect doubts about her own desirability and self-worth—normal concerns for anyone—but heightened, in Sharon's case, by a previous abusive relationship. As Sharon works to repair her self-esteem, she can expect to hear, like a faint and distant echo, old voices in her head that tell her she is "no good," or "an idiot." Sharon's job is to identify the source of these voices (her ex-husband) and learn to treat her former abuser with forgiveness, and compassion borne of strength. Simultaneously, Sharon must evaluate, as objectively as possible, the progression of her relationship with Kevin. Her questions regarding a marriage date, however, are reasonable and fair. If Kevin's intentions are sincere, there is no reason to prolong his fiancée's insecurity.

"Ocean of Betrayal"

I was having an affair with a married man who was a very good, long-time friend of mine. He was also seeing another woman at the same time that I thought he no longer was involved with. My dream was of my friend/lover, his other mistress, a mutual good friend, and myself. The scene was at a beach. I was in the water, being pulled under, and I could see my lover standing in the water with his other mistress at his side. Neither one of them had any expression on their face. I kept reaching up through the water to have him help me and pull me up from drowning. He did not make any attempt. He just stared at me.

My other friend was back standing on the beach, at the water's edge, and he knew I was drowning, but he made no move to save me either. I eventually went deeper and the dream ended in total blackness. Two weeks later my lover informed me that he was indeed still involved with the other woman, and that he had told her about our relationship.

–Janet, Age 44, Divorced, USA

It may strike us as odd that Janet, who lives in a waking world "swimming" with deceit, is surprised to learn of her own betrayal to "another mistress." Janet knew her lover already was cheating on his wife. Did she really expect his behavior would change for her?

Janet's dream is an excellent illustration of the use of drowning to symbolize feelings of emotional helplessness. As she is swept away and pulled under by a strong, sinking current (her intuitive, subconscious awareness of betrayal), Janet searches her lover's face, and the other mistress's, for a clue to her already felt predicament. "Neither one," she writes, "had any expression on their face." Paradoxically, the expressionless faces hold the clue that Janet seeks. Her betrayal, already in progress, is shrouded by a conspiracy of silence.

Janet feels betrayed because she is the odd person out—the last one to know—in her love triangle. As is often the case, a "mutual good friend" (who stands significantly outside the waters of the immediate triangle) is also identified as a coconspirator in the betrayal. Will Janet be surprised when she learns her "good friend" knew all along?

Bird

Bird: Birds in dreams are broadly associated with freedom, romance, and with plans and hopes for the future "taking flight." If a bird is caged, it suggests goals that are constrained, or hopes for a romance that feel trapped. Rising and falling birds can symbolize rising and falling expectations, respectively. Dead or injured birds can symbolize the end of a romance or project, or the passing of an illusion. Attacking birds can represent feelings of conflict in a romantic relationship. Vultures and ravens in dreams, because they eat dead flesh and, in turn, give it life, are associated with themes of death and rebirth. Hawks and eagles are associated with perspective—the ability to see a great distance.

◆ **Interpretation tip:** Two birds together often represent a romantic couple (a pair of lovebirds). If a bird is dead or injured in your dream, have your hopes for a romantic relationship "died"? Caged birds often represent the dreamer. Can you identify where you feel emotionally stifled?

* * *

The birds that appear in the following dreams all hold symbolic import. In "Dead Bird," a dreamer's hopes for a romantic union and for childbirth both appear to come crashing down to Earth. In "Birds of Flight," another dreamer's desires for a romantic union, represented by small birds that she holds in her hands, never rise to completion. Our final entry, "Forgotten Bird," is a painful tale of neglected romance. No love can survive untended, or compartmentalized within a cage.

Bird Dreams

"Dead Bird"

I had a dream that things were falling through the skylight that is over my bed. I actually woke up after dreaming that a dead bird fell down onto my back through the skylight.

When I went back to sleep, I was dreaming about being three months pregnant. At first I was excited and curious about having formed another life, but after watching a group of women tend to their own children without any male help, I became incredibly frightened and wanted to end the pregnancy.

I was afraid of having the responsibility of raising a child and the man I was with in the dream was only a casual partner. I told him that I wanted to end the pregnancy and he said I would be a fine mother and not to worry. But he didn't make any indication what his role would be in the raising of the child. I concluded that he would be absent.

In real life I am going through a job transition and having a casual relationship with a man for the first time in two years, whom I know I don't want to be serious with.

–Pamela, Age 26, Single, USA

Pamela's dream report is an excellent illustration of how a highly symbolic dream image (the dead bird falling on her back) often is explained by a subsequent dream. Is Pamela able to see how her first dream, of falling objects, is related to her second dream, of falling romantic expectations? In both dreams, hopes and expectations are being grounded in reality.

Birds in dreams are associated with freedom, because they are able to fly unfettered above the Earth. Because of their association with flying, birds also symbolize hopes for the future: projects and plans we want to "get off the ground," and goals that we hope will "take flight."

The dead bird that falls through Pamela's skylight, accordingly, reflects the "end" of a recent "flight of fancy." Is it a coincidence that the disturbing image is followed by her dream of the new man in her life—with whom she knows she does not want a serious relationship? Have her hopes for a long-term relationship come "crashing down to Earth"?

Pamela's second dream reflects her awareness that her current lover is not committed to marriage or family. Although babies in dreams often carry symbolic meanings, Pamela's concerns, in this dream, appear to be concrete and literal. Specifically, an unplanned pregnancy with this man would make a casual relationship complicated. Despite her excitement at being three months pregnant, Pamela's dream shows she is keenly aware of the difficulties of raising a child as a single parent. The dead bird symbolizes the death of her hopes for this relationship, but it also may be a disturbing allusion to her fears of aborting a child.

If Pamela can already recognize that this man is not the one, her dream is an encouragement that it's time to move along. When she does meet Mr. Right—a man who is interested in marriage and family—her dreams will show her soaring on wings of love again, with her "little birds" safely in a nest.

"Birds of Flight"

This is the first dream that I have had about men in a long time, and involvement with men has been absent from my life for several years. I feel this dream is very important.

My dream begins with me being in a place that resembles a campus. I am lying down by a muddy pond that is filled with birds of many species, sizes, and shapes. All of the birds are very small. Some of the birds will come on my fingers and allow me to pet them.

After a time a young man appears. He tells me he is fifteen years old, although he looks to be around thirty. We talk for a while when suddenly he is holding a big box. He opens the box and inside there are many smaller boxes, which look very much like ring boxes. He starts looking through them.

All of a sudden he announces that some important person is about to speak. The two of us walk on a paved pathway that goes up and around in a spiral until we are seated upon a high ledge, waiting for the speaker. We are seated with our legs dangling over the ledge. All of a sudden the young man lets himself drop off the ledge. There are no screams, in fact, no sound at all.

Next, I find myself in a big crowd of men of all ages. I see no other women. I am the only woman there. Several of the men grab me, either by the hand or by the arm, and start talking as if we were good and old friends, although we are total strangers to each other. All of a sudden the original young man reappears completely unharmed from having dropped off the ledge. He says to me, "I am fifteen and you are forty." "I am older than that," I reply. He disappears, not to be seen again.

Then I am back at the pond again where the dream began and I start walking with a man along the same spiral path to hear the speaker. Suddenly I become aware that I am dressed in nothing but a bathing suit and a pair of heavy leather boots—as one would wear in snowy, winter weather. Then I am in the crowd of men once more. The dream keeps repeating itself, going around and around as if looking for an ending, and not being able to find one for itself. Finally I wake up.

In real life I am a fifty-one-year-old woman who has never been married. Although I feel much younger than my actual age, I have always been rather uncomfortable being involved romantically with younger men. My relationships with men have been disappointing. Many is the time I have thought a relationship was really going somewhere, only to see it drop away and leave me hanging. After several years of not trying at all, I am now starting to feel somewhat ready to try again. But this makes me rather nervous. I have mixed emotions about men.

I know that birds are a symbol of freedom in dreams. In real life, I am a bird watcher, as were my mother and grandmother, and I get much pleasure and comfort from them. Birds appear in my dreams often. Does the size of the birds (they were small) have significance?

—Stacy, Age 51, Single, USA

If we ask ourselves the right questions, and have the courage to face our fears, most dreams have no choice but to faithfully unfold their riddles. Stacy's dream is highly metaphoric, but the honest background she provides contains all the clues we need to understand its poetry.

The young man who reminds Stacy of his age in the dream (twice) also disappears twice in the dream. The first sudden exit is when he drops off a ledge. Significantly, there is "no sound at all" as he falls. The second time he disappears is after he politely guesses Stacy's age to be forty, when in fact she is fifty-one. Stacy writes that men have "dropped away" and left her "hanging" in relationships before. Can there be any mistake that Stacy suspects the age difference—between herself and some of her younger partners—is responsible for their sudden disappearances?

The spiral pathway that Stacy and the young man walk up together represents a progressing relationship. (It leads up.) The ledge she sits on represents an altar. The important man she came to hear speak? This appears to be a pastor or clergyman. How can we be confident in our marriage metaphor? The clue is provided by the young man. Before Stacy walks up the spiral path beside him, he opens a carton that contains numerous small ring boxes inside. The hope of a committed relationship is presented before Stacy, but significantly, she does not receive a ring, nor does she ever hear "the important man" speak.

Once we understand that the spiral path represents Stacy's hopes for a committed relationship, several other dream metaphors fall easily into place. The crowd of men (who act like they know her) are casual suitors interspersed between steadier relationships. The bathing suit worn above snow boots suggests an attempt to place an appearance of sexuality and attractiveness on top of feelings that she is trudging along—through an emotional "winter." Or does the bathing suit signify a period of spring and rebirth—emerging from a cold spell? Stacy tells us that after a period of not trying, she is now willing to try again.

Stacy tells us that she derives "pleasure and comfort" from her birdwatching hobby, as her mother and grandmother both did before her. Accordingly, the birds in her dreams represent a comfort Stacy feels with the natural world, and with her feminine heritage, that is being juxtaposed with her difficulty finding a lasting romantic relationship. The presence of a pond nearby (water) indicates that the birds hold emotional meaning.

In her dream, it is significant to Stacy that all the birds, despite the fact that they are "of many species, sizes, and shapes," are very small. Smallness in dreams is a common representation for hopes and plans that are not fully grown or developed. If the birds represent her romantic aspirations, we can see that Stacy, after a series of disappointments, is just allowing her fledgling hopes to grow. If the birds also represent freedom, as she suggests, then her dream is a reminder that her freedom to create her future, truly, rests in the palm of her hands.

"Forgotten Bird"

Background information: I fell in love with my roommate. He said it was mutual and we began an affair. After six really good months and plenty of reassurances from him, he told me he is moving in with his old girlfriend.

In my dream I was in a large apartment with my boyfriend and a good friend of mine (a girl). We were sitting together on the couch, with him in the middle. I walked into another room and when I looked back I saw my boyfriend had slid over to my friend and had begun flirting with her.

I turned around and said good-bye to him (my boyfriend), and we all understood that the relationship was over. I walked him to the door, where there were several boxes of his stuff. When I went to pick up one of the boxes, thousands of roaches came pouring out. I grabbed a roach spray and started killing them. Once we got the roaches under control I opened the box where they had come from and found a dead bird in a cage. I asked him what had happened and he said, "Oh, I packed the bird and forgot about it."

He then took my hand and walked me over to the couch. He said, "You were compassionate in the past. Why can't you be now?" I said, "I am compassionate, but I don't want you."

That was the end of the dream. My roommate continues to live with me while planning to move in with his girlfriend.

–Heather, Age 30, Single, USA

Something is clearly "bugging" Heather, and given the background she provides, there's only one answer: Her boyfriend is a cockroach! While Heather has every reason to be "bugged" by his "creepy" behavior, she also may have learned a valuable lesson. In the future, Heather can keep her distance from romantic love triangles.

As the dream begins, Heather's romantic predicament is clearly defined. Her boyfriend sits between herself and another woman (a friend) on a couch. As soon as Heather is out of the room, though, her boyfriend begins flirting with the other woman, which is a representation of the events that occurred in real life. Heather's boyfriend was seeing two women at the same time.

Once she learns of his actions, Heather promptly tells him to leave, and begins helping him to move out. The box full of roaches is a reflection of her feelings about her ex. He acted low—like a roach—and Heather can't wait to get the pest out of her house!

Birds in dreams are associated with romance, and with plans that we hold for the future "gaining altitude" and "taking flight." Heather's hopes for a future with her boyfriend—symbolized by the neglected bird she finds

dead in a cage—clearly are over. Her boyfriend was able to compartmental-
ize the feelings he held for Heather (put them in a cage, while he dated another woman). Without love and attention, the dreams they shared
together died.

As Heather's dream ends, her boyfriend senses her anger, and asks for
her compassion. Heather tells him that she is compassionate, but that she
doesn't want him anymore. Her dream reveals that Heather is already emotionally over this man—who treated her love carelessly. Heather's decision
to move on is a positive reflection of her self-esteem, which lets us know
that, in the future, her dreams of love will soon take flight.

Blood

Blood: Symbol of pain, emotional injury, and the life force. Blood can also symbolize feelings of guilt, especially if it is on our hands (an act we have committed) or feet (leaving a trail of deceit). Rooms full of blood, rising like water, suggest areas of intense emotional pain. If a dreamer is bleeding, it is a metaphor for emotional injury and draining strength.

Recurring dreams involving large amounts of blood reflect past traumas. When did the recurring dreams begin, and what life events occurred at the time? Menstrual blood is a symbol of fertility. In teen dreams, the drawing of blood often represents the loss of virginity. (Please see: "Vampire.") Dreams about having one's blood sucked out by a friend or acquaintance reflect a "draining" relationship emotionally. Uncomfortable dreams of giving blood reflect feelings that "too much" is being asked for in a relationship.

♦ **Interpretation tip:** What painful situation in waking life has wounded you, emotionally, and is sapping your strength? Dreams about blood should not be interpreted as precognitive.

* * *

The dreams in this chapter hurt to read. As our dreamers are stabbed (ouch!) or wade through rooms flooded with blood, we cringe at the visceral images and recoil at the vicariously shared pain. Blood in dreams is a symbol of emotional injury and anguish. Will our dreamers recognize the warnings contained in their dreams, and heed their self-delivered pleas for an exit from life-draining behaviors and relationships? Or will the nightly bloodletting continue, with ultimately devastating consequences for the emotionally involved?

In "A Bloody Affair," a young woman is stabbed repeatedly

by an adulterous suitor. Is the love they share really so "undeniable"? In "House of Pain," a young man's dream life is drenched in blood. Will he decipher the urgent message written in his dreams? In "The Right Type," a woman's flirtation with betrayal causes her to wonder if she is the "right type" for marriage. Finally, in "A Willful Death," we see a dreamer's life force steadily draining, as she struggles to recover from a romantic separation.

It is important to observe that none of our dreamers actually suffers from any physical violence in their waking lives. On the contrary, the wounding they feel is emotional, the pain, crippling.

Blood Dreams

"A Bloody Affair"

I've been having the same dream now every night for about a week. Here is my background information. I'm a twenty-five-year-old single female living alone. For a year now I've been having an affair with a married man. Yes, I know it's wrong, but our attraction for each other is undeniable. We've tried to stop in the past without success.

Now, on to the dream. It's night and I'm asleep in my bed. I awake to knocking on my front door. From the position of my bed, I can see the front door, which has frosted glass panels all over it. I can make out the shadow of a man standing there. I'm a bit frightened because I live in an apartment building where you must be buzzed in to enter. I'm not friendly with anyone in the building, so I don't know who this could possibly be at my door.

I get out of bed, wearing a very beautiful white satin and lace nightgown, and walk over to the door. I look out the peephole, but I can't see anything. Cautiously I open the door and there stands my (married) boyfriend. Seeing that it's him, I relax and open the door for him.

He stands there, looking at me for what seems like an eternity, not saying a word. I ask if he's okay and he mutters, "I love you," and pulls out a very sharp, very long knife from his leather jacket. He then proceeds to stab me in the abdomen repeatedly.

I keep pleading for him to stop, but he doesn't. I can vividly recall the brightness of the red blood all over my gown, dripping down my hands and onto the floor. I look up at him and he finally stops, steps back, says he's sorry, and then leaves. I just start crying, fall to the floor, and everything fades to black, except for the red blood on the floor. This is where the dream ends and I wake up.

–Rita, Age 25, Single, USA

The sex Rita is having with a married man, while it may be "undeniable," appears to be coming at a greater cost than she currently recognizes. Aside from the moral questions that participation in such a relationship entails, Rita has chosen to invest her heart in a man who is unable to fulfill her needs and desires in any semblance of a healthy relationship. Is it any wonder Rita feels the life force draining steadily from her?

Given the context of her relationship, the repeated stabbing into Rita's abdomen with a long, sharp knife is a clear sexual metaphor. The bright red blood that spills over her gown, dripping through her hands onto the floor, symbolizes not only the emotional damage the relationship is causing, but also, most likely, the guilt Rita feels for allowing it to continue when she knows that it is wrong.

Rita's dreams would not choose repeated metaphors of attack and wounding if these symbols did not accurately reflect her current emotional state. Her dreams are communicating with her! Does she hear the message? If Rita wants these debilitating dreams to stop, she needs to end the relationship, and set her romantic sights several notches higher.

"House of Pain"

I'm in a dark gray hallway with doors on either side, going all the way to the end of the hall. I walk toward the first door and open it. My girlfriend is sitting in the middle of the room, naked, and I can see myself naked, crouched in the corner crying. She doesn't see me or care to listen. I shut the door and go to the door opposite it.

I open it and I'm in the same position, but my girlfriend is cutting her arms and there is about a foot of blood on the floor. She still doesn't notice me crying in the corner. I shut the door and start to go to the next door but I see my girlfriend up against the wall, having sex with Trent Reznor (lead singer of the band Nine Inch Nails). She looks at me and says, "I love you." I pull a gun out and shoot Trent Reznor in the face.

She falls down and I go to the next door. In there she is receiving oral sex from an older guy she told me about once. I kill him and then go to the next room. In there she is having sex with my best friend. I kill him.

This goes on for another few rooms, all of which she is having sex in and I'm in the corner with my back to them crying. At the last door, I stumble onto the floor at the end of the hall and cry. I can hear her having sex in every room. Then she comes out of every room and all of her melts into one of her and she kneels down next to me. She says, "I love you" and I say, "I know." Then I put the gun in my mouth and pull the trigger. I scream and wake up and cry for twenty minutes. This happens three to four nights every week.

I know she still talks to some of her old boyfriends on the phone, but she never meets them. She used to be a "slut" (her own words). She is my first girlfriend and the first person I've ever had sex with. We have been together eight months.

–Carl, Age 18, Engaged, USA

At a tender age, Carl is highly invested in his first sexual relationship. He signs his name "Engaged," after only eight months of dating.

Carl's girlfriend has confessed to several lovers in her past. Unfortunately, these old loves are now starring in Carl's dreams, even after he and his girlfriend have made a commitment to marry. The rooms full of blood in Carl's dreams are a powerful symbol for intense emotional pain. The murders that he commits as he shoots a series of his girlfriend's lovers reflect the anger and frustration he feels as he confronts these ghosts from her past.

Does Carl find it curious that his girlfriend tells him she loves him—while she continues to have sex with a houseful of men? This is a very clear representation in Carl's dream of a mixed message—when a person says one thing but does another. In real life, his girlfriend's insistence on calling her old boyfriends on the phone, when she knows that this disturbs Carl, is also a mixed message. If she really loved him, would she continue to contact her former lovers, and cause him so much pain?

Carl's dream is a warning that he is engaged to a woman who is unprepared (or unable) to make a commitment to him. The fact that his dream recurs, and that he winds up killing himself in it, attests to the extreme pain this relationship causes him. The writing is on the walls—written in red ink (blood)—so that Carl will be sure not to miss it! Instead of chasing this girl through blood-soaked rooms at night, it's time for Carl to use the front door, and leave this house of pain behind.

"The Right Type"

I have a great relationship with the man I'm planning to marry. He's thirty-three years old and owns his own factory, works a lot, and loves me very much. I love him, too, but three weeks ago, someone I hadn't seen for years just called me and came to see me. . . . He was a friend, we never even kissed, but when we first met something was in the air. He was handsome, older than me by almost twenty years, but very interesting, with all that knowledge. I was enchanted, but nothing happened and we had lost touch since then.

Since he came back I have almost the same dream once or twice a week: My future husband becomes sick and is in the hospital. He needs some blood, and I immediately say, "Take mine." (We have the same blood type.) But when the doctors and nurses begin to put my blood into his veins, he dies, and everybody looks at me saying, "Look what you've done!" After that, at the funeral, all my friends and family look at me with that cold eye, like wanting to tell me "You did it!" I wake up crying and feeling guilty, but I didn't do anything!

I love him and couldn't ever do something to hurt him. Do you think my dream and my old friend coming back have any connection?

–Teresa, Age 27, Single, Brazil

Teresa is right. She didn't do anything. But her recurring dreams show that she is feeling guilty, nevertheless, about some thoughts she has had.

We can tell from Teresa's dream report that she finds this older man attractive. They have chemistry together—that's the electric feeling that's in the air when they are with each other. Naturally, the thought of becoming romantically involved with him has crossed Teresa's mind.

Teresa's dreams are connected with this other man's reappearance in her life. But in an interesting twist, instead of focusing on the attraction that Teresa feels for him, her dreams instead concentrate on the consequences (none of which are positive) of such a liaison. Is Teresa hearing the message?

If Teresa were to have an affair with this other man, it would hurt her fiancé very much. In the dream this "hurt" is represented by her fiancé becoming sick and needing to be hospitalized. Similarly, the dream's subsequent concentration on blood types is almost certainly an allusion to Teresa and her fiancé's wedding and family plans together. Teresa's future family needs her blood to survive, but in the dream, although Teresa and her fiancé share the same blood type, her blood for some reason is no good, and kills her fiancé. The final scene of the dream, which shows Teresa at her fiancé's funeral (instead of at her wedding?), symbolizes the death of their relationship. The "cold eye" given by Teresa's friends and family shows how they would perceive such a betrayal of trust.

These are warning dreams! Judging from her report, Teresa has a wonderful life ahead of her, and is the envy of millions of men and women, who wish their futures were so promising. The appearance of her "old friend," however, is causing Teresa to question what "type" of woman she is. Will she hear this dream's message and make the right decision? If her "old friend" is encouraging her to have an affair—he's not really a friend.

"A Willful Death"

I dreamt that I saw my ex-husband in a shopping mall with a woman. They were holding hands. He told me they were getting married (we've only been divorced for approximately four months). Anyway, he called me later to talk about it. I invited him over to my house. We went out to my hot tub and got in. . . . I had a knife and slit my wrists! The blood just started pouring out . . . then I woke up.

Background information: I haven't had the dream before. My husband and I are recently divorced. He had an affair; however, he is no longer with the woman involved. We have been separated for three years. Recently I asked him not to contact me anymore. I couldn't be his "friend."

—Sandra, Age 48, Divorced, USA

Sandra's dream reveals that the pain of her divorce is still very much alive. Her dream references her real-life betrayal by showing her husband holding hands with another woman at the mall. As if to rub salt into an already too-fresh wound, her ex promptly announces his new wedding engagement. His "mourning period" lasted only four months!

Sandra's recent decision to limit contact with her ex shows that she knows she needs to move on from the relationship. At this point in time, the presence of her ex simply brings back too many painful memories.

Hot tubs in real life hold associations with romance and relaxation. In dreams, hot tubs, swimming pools, lakes, and other bodies of water are consistent metaphors for emotions. When Sandra invites her ex into her emotional body, she can only express herself by slitting her wrists and allowing her blood to spill. Sandra is in pain, and she experiences her former husband's new life as her death.

Sandra's dream does not reflect a desire to hurt herself. On the contrary, her dream is simply echoing an awareness that her daytime decisions show she understands; a phase of her life is over, and it is time to move on. Today, Sandra's mind is occupied with the spilled blood of a sacred bond pulled asunder. Tomorrow, her gaze will be lifted from these troubled waters. Death in dreams is a symbol of change and separation. Sandra's willful death shows she is ready to embrace this change.

Bridge

Bridge: Symbol of transition. Bridges lead us from one location to another, often over an (emotional) body of water. Bridges suspended high above the ground frequently represent lofty career goals or intimidating personal aspirations. Bridges that are of poor construction, that sway, or that have missing planks symbolize doubts about one's ability to reach a destination, and obstacles along the path to completion. Fallen bridges represent hopes for a relationship or transition that have not been realized. Missing bridges indicate disappointed expectations; the dreamer believed he or she would be able to cross. Bridges on fire represent urgency to reach a goal. A burned bridge suggests a past that cannot be revisited. Long bridges denote a "long time" that is required to achieve a goal. Bridges can also symbolize the transition between life and death.

◆ **Interpretation tip:** If you dream about a bridge, ask yourself what destination or goal you are trying to reach. Are you able to cross the bridge?

* * *

Bridge dreams offer valuable feedback on our progress toward goals. Does the bridge that once appeared stable now sag and sway (not as easy as we thought), or does the destination recede perpetually before us (will take longer than planned)? Do we succeed in crossing the bridge, or are we left forever stranded on the near side of our destination, intimidated by a crossing that now looks insuperable?

The dreams included in this chapter show dreamers attempting to reach specific destinations. In "Falling Bridge," a young man's hopes for a committed relationship collapse before his eyes. In "Missing Bridge," a stretch of highway that is required to carry our dreamer to her life's true destination is missing. In "Bridge of Love," a dreamer surmounts repeated hurdles of insecurity as he adjusts to a new social status. Our final entry, "The Other Side," shows a bridge that can only be crossed in dreams—until it is crossed once, and forever, in our waking life.

Bridge Dreams

"Falling Bridge"

I just asked my girlfriend to marry me, but things are not as smooth as I would like. I don't really know if it is what I want, or if it will work, but we were at a crossroads, so it was either marriage or walk away. Oh, I live in Illinois and she lives in Missouri. I think that is a factor.

In my dream I was standing on a wooden deck that was overlooking the Mississippi River. The deck was just above the water and I think I was alone. I was watching the water and all of a sudden I felt a rumbling and saw people scattering around me. I heard someone say, "The bridge!" I looked over. The bridge was falling and cars were driving off the edge. I stood and watched but I didn't move.

Then I saw these waves, like tidal waves, coming toward me—one after another. That is when I started to move. I never got scared. I just knew I had to move. I started climbing up a dirt embankment that seemed to go on and on forever, and I just couldn't get up.

Then I saw this family, a mom and her small children. The littlest girl was young—two or three—and very small. She was struggling so I picked her up as I was climbing. That is when the water hit—wave after wave—but I was never scared. I couldn't reach the land to get out of the water. I grabbed the little girl and began swimming with her. Only then did I reach the shore.

When I got out I looked over my shoulder and saw that the Illinois half of the bridge was gone, only that half. All that I could think about was how were people going to get across—and that I had lost my cell phone in the river. The whole time I never got scared but I knew I should have been.

The woman that I am seeing (in real life) can no longer have children, but she has children from a previous marriage. The girl did not resemble any of her children. In my dream she had long blond hair and very pale skin. She was almost angelic.

—Matthew, Age 35, Engaged, USA

In an attempt to rescue a troubled relationship, Matthew has extended a proposal of marriage to his girlfriend from Missouri, though he has done so, admittedly, with reservations. The doubts he holds for the relationship are expressed as rumblings from a falling bridge. When Matthew looks to determine the source of the noise, he realizes a bridge that connects Illinois to Missouri is collapsing—significantly—from the Illinois side. The location of the collapse (Matthew lives in Illinois) suggests that Matthew's doubts about the relationship are stronger on "his side of the bridge."

The collapse of the bridge causes tidal waves (large waves of emotion) to engulf Matthew, who is standing on a deck just above the water. Matthew's subsequent climb up a steep, dirt embankment that seems to go "on and on forever" is a common dream metaphor for feelings of power-lessness. Will he escape this rising tide of emotion? Similarly, his swim in turbulent waters represents his efforts to "stay afloat" during a volatile emotional period. The angelic child whom Matthew rescues is a symbol of innocence. Is Matthew sympathetic to his girlfriend's plight as a single mom, and has he grown attached to her children, who need his help?

If Matthew's marriage proposal was made in haste, his dream reflects reservations that his "bridge to the future" is built on a shaky foundation. Matthew's dream is a clear message that it is time to withdraw the wedding proposal—until his relationship demonstrates itself capable of building, and sustaining, multiple bridges of intimacy and trust.

"Missing Bridge"

My recurring dream has been going on for two and a half years. I don't dream the same thing every night, but I would say once a month this dream wakes me up.

I am driving on a long highway that is over water . . . like the kind you see in Louisiana. (That is where I lived for eight years before moving back home to the Midwest.) I am always trying to get to my mom, and have no luck because there is a gap in the road that cars can fall through. It is kind of like the road curves up—like it is going to make a loop-the-loop—and then there is a gap in the road, without any bridge.

I am in a big vehicle, like a Bronco or a Yukon, and I am always frightened about not being able to get over the gap in the road. I have never made it across, since I always wake up first. One time I tried to jump the gap, but I started falling toward the water. I never hit, because I woke myself up out of fear.

My mother and I have a great relationship. She has had some health problems recently, but nothing serious. The only thing I can think of that started two and a half years ago is my relationship with my boyfriend (he lives in New Orleans). My parents really like him, so I don't think that is an issue. So far, we have no plans to get married. We just have a commuting relationship. Do you think that my dream has to do with my relationship with my boyfriend, and what we are lacking?

I love being in a committed relationship, and I do want to be married and have babies. The funny thing is that I never used to feel that way. I pushed my career very far for the age I am (twenty-five) and always kept that in front of everything else—except my immediate family. Not too long ago I was sitting with a group of my friends and told them that my great city loft and great job wasn't everything I wanted anymore. I want the whole thing: marriage, family, and kids. So, maybe that is why the dream is coming up again?

–*Claire, Age 25, Single, USA*

If Claire wants this dream to stop, she needs to start driving on a different "highway." Claire is trying to reach a destination—her mother—yet she fears she will be unable to complete the trip, due to a gap that appears in the road—"without any bridge." Is it possible the destination Claire is trying to reach, represented in her dream by her mother, is in fact motherhood itself? A committed relationship, with "marriage, family, and kids" in her future?

Claire's commuting relationship with her boyfriend is symbolized by the highway over water, which reminds her of the overwater highways in Louisiana, where her boyfriend still lives. As she tries to reach her mother (motherhood), she sees a gap in the road—without a bridge to carry her to the other side. The metaphor is clear. Claire foresees a significant obstacle on the road to motherhood in her life, and realizes, with a fright, that she will not make the trip.

Significantly, Claire's dreams began two and a half years ago, which is the same time that Claire began dating her boyfriend. Ironically, her dreams show that Claire recognized the limitations of her long-distance relationship ever since it began. Claire's drive to pursue her career has kept her desire for a family at bay temporarily, but her recurring dreams are sending an important message: Becoming a mother is important to Claire. Her dreams are asking: Why am I traveling down this road without a bridge—when I know that it will not lead to my future? The message of this dream is clear: It's time for Claire to consider dating someone new—who lives closer to her—and who shares her values and goals.

"Bridge of Love"

I was walking over a white stone bridge with my wife, but it was like an old rope bridge with missing planks, and I was having trouble with the walk because I'm afraid of heights. I kept tripping on the missing planks. Then my wife would be uncaring and pulling my arm and saying, "Come on, hurry up, let's go." This is not her in reality.

Then suddenly we were in an airplane going somewhere, and I had a window seat and some stranger was in the middle of us, and she was only talking to him. And when I would say something like, "Yeah, hello, thanks a lot," she would just do it more.

Then my dream changed settings again. All of a sudden I was in my kitchen with my teeth falling out and blood was everywhere. I didn't know what to do, so I put my teeth in a cup of milk.

—Simon, Age 18, Married, USA

As Simon's dream begins, he and his wife are walking across a white stone bridge. White is a color that we associate with weddings, while stones are associated with sturdiness and durability. Is it difficult to recognize this bridge as a metaphor for Simon's very young, and very recent, marriage?

Soon, however, obstacles are encountered. The white stone bridge becomes "like an old rope bridge with missing planks," which causes Simon to lose his balance. The metamorphosis of the bridge, from solid to becoming unstable, suggests that the road to married life is more challenging than Simon originally imagined. Similarly, losing his balance suggests occasionally confusing emotions as he pursues this transition with his young wife.

Like bridges, airplanes in dreams are also metaphors for desires to reach new destinations. As his marriage to his new wife "takes flight," Simon experiences difficulty getting his wife's attention. She keeps talking to someone else on the plane. Simon needs attention, and reassurance, from his wife.

Finally, Simon arrives home with his teeth falling out and blood everywhere. (This has not been a good day!) Teeth-falling-out dreams are common metaphors for concerns about our appearance and desirability (we lose our smile). The blood flowing from his mouth is another dream metaphor for pain and loss of power—the vital force is draining away.

Because Simon writes that his wife's behavior in the dream is "not her in reality," his dream indicates a simple need for increased support. Given that Simon and his wife are a young couple, it's natural to wonder about the direction they are headed—and about whether or not they actually ever will arrive. The solution for Simon's dream is straightforward. Simon and his wife need to talk, to confirm their love and commitment to each other, and they must show each other consideration and attention—as they cross a bridge of love together.

"The Other Side"

I think I already know how this needs to be interpreted, but it would be nice to hear a different opinion as well as any insight into the symbolism of the dream.

My daughter was murdered and I was going through a traumatic time and was very depressed, almost to the point of self-destruction. I started having dreams that I would see her somewhere, either in my house or in her grandmother's house or on the street. When I would see her, she would see me, too, giggle, and start to run away. I would call her and chase after her. Miles and miles would pass and she was always running just beyond my reach.

Toward the end, she would run up a steep concrete bridge that rose up into the sky. About the time I would catch her, the bridge would abruptly end and she would sprout wings and fly just a little further ahead. She would then turn around and say, "You can't go, Mommie," and wave good-bye. At that point I would wake up, usually in a cold sweat from exertion. I think this was my psychic attempt to deal with my depression over the loss of my daughter.

–Jennifer, Age 34, Married, USA

Jennifer's dream represents the feelings that she is experiencing transparently. Jennifer wishes she could be with her daughter, but as her daughter says in the dream, "You can't go, Mommie."

The bridge rising into the sky represents the transition between the living and the deceased. In Jennifer's dream, only people with wings can cross to the other side. We will all cross that bridge one day. Perhaps Jennifer will catch up with her daughter then. I like to believe that she will.

Car

Car: Symbol of the self in dreams—of the direction we are headed in our lives. Cars with no brakes, poor steering, or limited visibility are warning dreams that indicate we feel out of control in our lives and are experiencing difficulty seeing the road ahead. Cars driven in reverse indicate failure to advance in our personal or professional lives, or a backward movement to resume old behaviors and relationships. Dreams about racing or overtaking another vehicle represent feelings of being in a competitive struggle. Happy dreams about "hot pursuit" may symbolize the chase of romance. Dreams about driving over rivals or strangers indicate feelings of hostility, or fears of "injuring innocent bystanders," respectively.

Note the condition of the car. New cars indicate a new status in life—pregnancy, career advancement, marriage—or contemplation of a new relationship or business development. Cars with engine problems, mechanical failure, or that are low on fuel indicate feelings of depression, or of being "run-down" physically, and in "need of repair." If we dream about driving cars we owned previously, the dream suggests we are revisiting behaviors and feelings from an earlier time in our lives. Trucks and buses symbolize feelings of carrying a heavy load or moving slowly toward one's goals, respectively. Sports cars are symbols of empowerment. (We can reach a destination quickly.) Convertibles are symbols of transition.

Dreams about car accidents, as a rule, should not be considered precognitive. They are reflections of emotional losses of control, however, which reflect and foreshadow erratic decision-making in waking life. Dreams about cars out of control are *always* important dreams, encouraging the dreamer to regain emotional balance in his or her life.

♦ **Interpretation tip:** Who is driving the car? If you are a passenger, the dream suggests you are allowing someone else to direct or influence your life.

✳ ✳ ✳

The dreams included in this chapter illuminate different aspects of the car/self relationship. In "Backseat Driver," a dreamer's mother steers a new car—literally from the backseat. It's a confused seating arrangement, but an accurate mirror of the family dynamics. More "out of control" themes are explored in "Speeding Up." Will our dreamer heed her dream, and make a commitment to take charge of her life? In "A Wrong Turn," a veteran couple's relationship is on a slippery road. Is it time to abandon ship? Our next dream reveals a woman who is romantically confused. She thinks she's moving forward, but her gearbox shows she's "Stuck in Reverse." Our final entry, "New Convertible," shows a dreamer driving in the fast lane. What is it about her white convertible that makes a watching crowd so jealous?

Car Dreams

"Backseat Driver"

My mother, sister, and I were leaving a mall after a day of shopping. We got into my sister's new car, which was actually designed to look like a shoe (a woman's shoe with a strapped back and wedge heel). In reality, she does not have a new car. I was in the driver's seat, my sister in the passenger's seat, and my mom was behind me, but my mother was driving the car. We left the mall parking lot and were driving up a steep hill. We seemed to be in a mountainous area like Colorado or something.

It suddenly became very dark (like night was falling or a storm was coming in), and I said to my mom, "Mom, are you sure this is the right way?" She said yes and just as she said it the clouds broke and a shaft of light came through to reveal that we were coming upon a curve in the road that had a cliff off one side. We were going very fast—I remember looking at the dash and seeing 60 mph. When my mom realized how fast we were going, she slammed on the brakes. We skidded off the side of the road (off the cliff) and were heading down into the canyon.

I was in shock and disbelief at first, thinking in my head, "This can't be real," and "Rewind, rewind this." Then my mom said, "Oh, my God, we're going to die." When she said this I put my hands over my face and we crashed. Next I woke up (and was surprised that I had woken up), but I was lying on the bottom of the canyon. My whole body was crushed, but I was alive. I could move my head and one arm. I looked for my mother and sister, but all I could see was a green, thick liquid flowing by me with blood in it. I assumed they were killed, but wasn't sure. I did not call out to them. I remember wishing that I had died, because now I would lie here and suffer prior to dying. Then I woke up.

Throughout the dream I felt every emotion I would imagine feeling in this situation: disbelief, resolution that it was actually happening, and then curiosity about what it was going to feel like. . . .

The following night I had another dream about driving, but it was not tragic and more along the lines of a journey home. I was with childhood friends whom I haven't seen in years and the car was extremely crowded and small. We were actually driving *home*—to the town I grew up in. We made a few stops along the way, but nothing eventful. I just thought it was interesting that I'd have another dream about driving the day after this one.

Recent events in my life are the following:

My parents just moved to the town where my sister and I live. They drove here from the East Coast and moved themselves. Both of them are extremely afraid of heights and will not drive in a mountainous area. They have only been living out here two weeks, but I already feel that my life is out of control. They have expected us to spend time helping them, and guilt has been driving me to do it.

My sister and I agonized about our parents moving out here. We love them very much, but they can both be very judgmental and overbearing. As an adult I have noticed some major issues and dysfunction in my parents' relationship—things I never noticed as a child, but now can see how they have impacted my life. My sister and I are adamant about not having these attitudes inflicted on our children. Also, my sister is pregnant. I want a child but have not been able to conceive yet.

—Kirsten, Age 35, Married, USA

New cars in dreams are associated with new statuses in our lives, and high-heeled shoes have associations with dressing up, and with looking sexy. Given this information, can we deduce the symbolism of Kirsten's sister's strange new car, which Kirsten writes is shaped like "a woman's shoe with a strapped back and wedge heel"? The new car reflects her sister's change of fertility status, at a time when our dreamer would like to become pregnant herself.

In the dream, Kirsten is in the driver's seat, while her sister, whose car it is, is in the passenger seat. This driving arrangement suggests Kirsten is the dominant personality in the relationship. (Is Kirsten the older sister?) Surprise, though. Kirsten's mother, seated in the backseat, actually is the one who is driving. Kirsten's mother is literally a "backseat driver."

The location of Kirsten's mother, and her subsequent reckless driving and accident, indicate that Kirsten is concerned about her mother's influence on her life. The rapidly approaching storm that causes the way to become dark is a common dream symbol for uncertainty about the future; Kirsten is unable to see the road ahead. As Kirsten questions her mother's sense of judgment (direction) in the dream, her mother loses control of the vehicle and drives off a cliff. The death Kirsten fears symbolizes her doubts about whether she will be able to "survive" this difficult period in her life. The accident is a strong warning that Kirsten feels her life is out of control.

Kirsten's second dream, though it appears to be mundane, echoes issues explored in the first. Kirsten is traveling in a car that is "extremely crowded and small," and that is full of childhood friends whom Kirsten hasn't seen in years. What is the connection? Kirsten feels like a child again, and her space is crowded. What is the larger connection? Kirsten feels oppressed by her mother's arrival in town.

Kirsten's dreams are warnings that she needs to set clearly defined boundaries between her parents' and her family's lives, which suddenly have become geographically much closer. Kirsten's family needs physical and emotional space to grow and develop as a unit, and Kirsten needs to feel that she is in charge of her family's life—and not her mother. In future dreams, Kirsten wants to be behind the wheel of her own car, and driving in control.

"Speeding Up"

I have been having the same dream for almost ten nights in a row. I am driving a car, all is peaceful, then suddenly and abruptly, I am speeding into the car in front of me—about to rear-end it. It is always a different car and I never crash. The force of the speed and near collision actually physically awakens me, every time.

As for my background: In January I discovered that my husband was having an affair, when I was seven months pregnant. In March I gave birth to my son. It was a thirty-hour-long, hard labor. During all of this my alcoholic/drug addict father went over the deep end and lost everything he had and got very ill. And one month ago we moved to a totally new city where we know no one. Is my subconscious telling me that my life is *way* out of control right now?

—*Ruby, Age 28, Married, USA*

Ruby's dreams are using the metaphor of a car crash to reflect her current emotional state. And from what Ruby tells us, it's not hard to see why. Ruby has been through a lot lately, and in the back of her mind she's wondering what's next. What's the next disaster out there waiting to strike?

Ruby has accurately determined the cause of her nightmares. Car-out-of-control dreams are one of the most common—and clearest—indicators that we have lost control over the direction of our lives. If the car is being driven recklessly, too fast, if the brakes don't work, or if we have difficulty seeing the road ahead of us, the message always is the same. We are advised to open our eyes, immediately, to the behavior or relationship that is pulling us emotionally off balance. Once we identify the source, we need to take concrete steps in our waking lives to resolve the issues. In Ruby's case, she needs to set new boundaries with both her husband and her father—both of whom are "accidents waiting to happen."

"A Wrong Turn"

I have been divorced from my ex-husband for over twelve years. We have two teenage children. One of the reasons we divorced was his hoarding obsession.

In my dream my ex-husband is driving a car that we owned when we were together, and I am in the passenger's seat. He takes a wrong turn and we end up on a muddy incline. Straight ahead is the ocean. It's impossible to control the car, and we slide into the water.

I start rolling down the window so it will be easier to get out. The seawater is rushing in. My ex is busy trying to retrieve things from the backseat, and won't get out of the car. I want him to save himself, but he won't come. I tell him that I am pregnant, and can't raise another child by myself. (I am definitely not pregnant.) He seems to listen to me, but I get out. That's all I remember.

–Kimberly, Age 50, Divorced, USA

Whenever we find ourselves in the passenger seat of a car in a dream (instead of behind the wheel), it's a sign that we are allowing someone else to "steer the course" of our lives. The "wrong turn" Kimberly's ex-husband makes is a reference to problems Kimberly and her ex experienced in the past, that led to their divorce. Soon after the "wrong turn," Kimberly's ex-husband loses control of the car, and it plunges into the ocean.

Oceans in dreams represent emotions, and often hold broader associations with the subconscious mind. Judging by Kimberly's dream, it is evident she feels her ex-husband's compulsive (subconsciously controlled) hoarding behavior is ruling his life, and threatens his survival. He would rather drown in the waters of his subconscious compulsion than save himself and leave his behaviors behind.

Kimberly's pregnancy in the dream is a symbol of hope for the future. Kimberly is "pregnant with expectation" and wishes her ex-husband, if he could change his ways, might be able to join her. Unfortunately, Kimberly's dream suggests she already knows the answer to this pressing question. Even though her ex appears to hear her, he will not stop hoarding, and she is forced to leave him behind.

Kimberly stepped out of this car a long time ago. Her dream suggests it would be a mistake to get back in—to take another ride. Kimberly's pregnancy, on the other hand, indicates excitement and confidence for the future, and a new period of growth and development within herself. If Kimberly wants a partner to "share the ride," her dream suggests it's time to look to the future, and not to the past.

"Stuck in Reverse"

I had a dream last week that my former boyfriend's new girlfriend, whom I have met, was coming after me with a golf club. I was trying to get in my car to get away.

I got in the car, thought I was putting the car in drive, and wound up putting it in reverse and backing over her. Then I got out of the car and I could see her lying on the ground. Her legs were broken and there was blood on her face.

I started to panic and called my ex-boyfriend to explain what happened. He was saying, "I know, I know. I heard all about it. She's crazy." And that was the end of the dream.

He and I have been broken up for about five years now, but we have mutual friends and have always maintained a close relationship. Recently, I heard that his new girlfriend resented the fact that we were still friends after so many years of going our separate ways.

My ex and I have been together many times after we split up, as recently as last month. What do you think this dream means?

–*Molly, Age 31, Single, USA*

It's an interesting dream—but there's only one problem with Molly's story. Molly and her ex-boyfriend never did "go their separate ways." Molly tells us that she and her ex "have been together" (had sex?) just last month.

Molly writes she is moving on with her life, but her dream shows her moving decidedly in reverse. (Surprise!) Not only is she failing to move forward, her behavior is injuring innocent and unknowing people.

If Molly really was moving on with her life, she would not begrudge her ex's new girlfriend, nor would she enjoy the hollow spoils of a petty territoriality match. The message of this dream is clear: If Molly really does want to move forward, she needs to study the gearbox, figure out how to get her car out of reverse, and drive herself away from this mess.

"New Convertible"

I am driving a beautiful white convertible car. My best friend is next to me. I'm going really fast but I'm totally in control. I'm laughing and screaming out of joy. I'm extremely happy. My hair is flying in the wind. Everything seems to be so light and easy.

Then I noticed some ex-girlfriends of my husband's around the car. They are all very jealous. I explain to my friend that they can't stand that I'm driving this beautiful convertible car. The fact that the car was a convertible made them so jealous.

Background about me: I was just married last week. I understand the ex-girlfriends are jealous, but what does the car symbolize?

—*Antonia, Age 30, Married, USA*

The last few weeks (before and after her wedding) have been fast and hectic for Antonia. Her dream shows, however, that despite the rapid pace, she still feels totally in control. In fact, her new car signals an unmistakable surge of empowerment. As Antonia observes, "Everything seems to be so light and easy."

Given the context of her dream, it's no accident the car she is driving is white (think wedding), or that she happens to "pass by" some of her husband's ex-girlfriends. Antonia won the race to her husband's heart, and her victory lap is deserved. As the dream ends, a great deal of significance is placed on the fact that the car she is driving is a convertible. Can we decipher the meaning of this (not uncommon) dream metaphor?

Convertibles are cars that can alter their function and appearance. Accordingly, they often symbolize periods of transition in our lives. Now that Antonia has "converted" her status from single to married, can we think of a more appropriate vehicle for her to drive?

Cat

Cat: Feminine symbol highly associated with babies, the desire for children, and female sexuality. During pregnancy, first-time mothers often dream of giving birth to cats. If a cat is aggressive, scratches you, or jumps on you, it may indicate difficulty with your sexuality, or mixed feelings regarding your desire for children. Lost cats may represent fears that time to raise a family is running out. Cats may represent the anima or feminine aspects of either a man or a woman's personality. Cats are holy animals in Egyptian, Persian, Scandinavian, Greek, and Japanese cultures.

Among cat owners, literal dreams reflecting concerns about a cat (feeding, safety, fears of getting lost or attacked) are common.

♦ **Interpretation tip:** If you dream about losing your cat or about caring for a kitten, be open to the possibility that your dream reflects a desire to nurture children.

* * *

Who would think that cats in dreams would be so highly identified with the feminine, and with babies especially? Is it the inherent elegance and sophistication of the cat, when compared to the obvious masculinity of the dog? The dreams that follow make a convincing case for cats as symbols of babies, and of feminine sexuality more broadly.

In "Attacked by Cats," a young woman is plagued by recurring dreams of attack. Significantly, the dreams began when she started brooding about possible names for babies. In "Swallow My Cat," a fifteen-year-old girl is curious about her mother's recent dream. "What does it mean," she asks, "if my mother dreamed I swallowed a cat?" The next dream, "On Vacation Without My Cat," tells the story of a woman who dreams repeatedly of being on holiday, only to be frantically concerned about caring for her cat. Our final entry, "Resurrected Kitty," explores a broader relationship between cats and creativity. Is it time for our dreamer to brush off the moss and allow her creative spirit to flow?

Cat Dreams

"Attacked by Cats"

I'm a twenty-seven-year-old female, happily married and working as a nurse. Over the last few months I have had rather disturbing dreams about being attacked by cats. (I have never actually been attacked.)

I have had the dream about ten times, and each time the scenario is slightly different, i.e., time and place. The similarities are that the cat is viciously trying to bite and scratch me whilst I try to strangle, beat, stamp, or crush it—just to stop it. The cat seems to be unstoppable and continues to attack me.

Each dream puts me in a setting surrounded by people who seem to be oblivious to my distress and carry on about their business as if nothing is happening.

As for my background: On the home front, my husband and I have no children, and during our three years of marriage the subject of a family has never seriously been discussed. We like the freedom of having a good income and no kids. I have never really had a maternal instinct, but over the last few months I have found myself becoming more and more broody. I find myself thinking about which names are nice, or what color I would paint the nursery. This really is not me! My hormones seem to be considering a "yes" whilst my head is still saying "no way"! (By the way, my husband is definitely still saying "no way"!)

I have always had an absolute dread of childbirth and cannot imagine putting myself through all that pain and suffering. In fact, during my nurse training I could not bear to see a child being born, and refused to participate in my three-week maternity placement.

In my most recent dream, the attack happened while I was inside a huge glass display cabinet inside a shopping arcade—with people glancing at me as they passed by. The people in the dreams are not necessarily people that I know, although I can say for certain that my husband is there somewhere. We have a good relationship and he is always concerned about my problems and troubles, and would be very quick to defend me if I was ever attacked or threatened. However, in the dream he does not intervene at all, and just like the passersby, he does not seem to acknowledge my distress.

One last point is that my dreams do not seem to have a finishing point, and by this I mean that I don't recall who wins the fight, or what happens next. I have never had a dream where anything happens beyond the fight. I guess, perhaps, the fight is still in progress?

–Maggie, Age 27, Married, United Kingdom

If we read Maggie's report carefully, we note that her recurring dreams of attack by cats began about the same time as her brooding about children. The other information that is unusual is her admission that, as a nurse, she refused to watch live childbirths—and even had herself removed from a three-week maternity placement. Both these responses to childbearing by a woman are unusual, yet they are doubly unusual in the context of Maggie's profession.

If Maggie is accurate when she surmises that her biological clock—her hormones—are beginning to catch up with her, then her dreams suggest that babies are knocking at the door, but neither she nor her husband is ready yet to let them in. The detailed background Maggie provides confirms the presence of a phobia about childbirth, which in turn makes the thought of children all the more anxiety-ridden, and even confrontational. Thus, the "attacked by cats" theme in her dreams is explained.

Cats are associated with babies in women's dreams for many reasons: They are about the same size and weight as newborns; we typically carry them cradled in our arms or draped across our shoulders like newborns; and we usually raise them from being "baby" kittens to adult cats. We are also responsible for their care: feeding them, letting them in and out of the house, and making sure they don't get lost or hurt.

Despite the similarities, the question still remains: Why cats? In other words, why wouldn't Maggie's dream simply show a confrontation between herself and babies? The answer is because the issue of having children, at this point in time, is still emotionally charged for Maggie. Because of her anxiety regarding childbirth, her emotions toward children are expressed indirectly in her dream. And cats, for the reasons mentioned above, often are the next best, neutral symbol we think of.

It is significant that Maggie's husband is always present in her dreams but that he does not notice her distress. This aspect of the dream reveals that Maggie's struggles, so far, are interior.

The dream that places Maggie in the shopping arcade display window indicates that Maggie feels social pressure—people are watching her—to start a family. In three years of marriage, however, the subject of family has not been seriously discussed.

Maggie's phobia about childbirth is causing her to resist (fight against) social and biological pressures to bear children. Is it time for Maggie to break the ice with her husband about her desires for a family? Because she works in a hospital, it should be easy for Maggie to find information on maternity counseling, which will dramatically reduce her fears of delivery, and help prepare her for motherhood.

"Swallow My Cat"

The dream I'm writing about is not one that I had. My mom had it last night, and she told me about it because it had to do with me. I am just wondering what exactly it means because it's really weird.

She said that I was standing in a room with her, holding my cat in my arms, when all of a sudden my cat started jumping down my throat. My cat is full-grown and a little big, so it wasn't like an object that would normally fit in someone's mouth. She said my cat crawled all the way down my throat until only the tip of her tail was sticking out of my mouth. I was choking, not able to breathe at all.

My mom said that she felt my stomach and she could feel the hardness of my cat's body inside me. She bent me over while she pushed up on my stomach to get my cat out. During the dream she was worried about my cat's hind claws scratching up my insides. She knew as soon as she got them out of me that the rest would come out easily. She pulled it out like a baby being born, she said. Then she finally got my cat out of me and I was fine, like nothing happened; but my cat was slimy and covered in saliva.

I asked her what it meant and the only thing she said was that cats mean change, or good or bad luck, and that I was undergoing some sort of change in my life and dealing with it. Can you tell me what you think it means? Thanks a lot!

–Julie, Age 15, Dating someone for 10 months, USA

It's clear that Julie's mother is associating Julie's cat with a baby. When she touches Julie's belly, it feels hard, as if Julie were pregnant. When she pulls the cat out of Julie's stomach (by its hind legs), her mother said it looked slimy and wet—like a newborn. Her mother also felt that her dream was about changes occurring in Julie. Are we able to see the connection yet between Julie's cat and her mother's dream?

Julie tells us she has been dating a boyfriend now for ten months. If Julie's relationship is starting to turn sexual, this may be the change her mother senses the dream symbolizes. Her mother is concerned Julie might accidentally become pregnant (swallow a cat).

Is Julie's mother a savvy enough dream interpreter to recognize the signs appearing in her dreams? Will she initiate the conversations with her daughter about sex, which her dream is requesting? Her daughter needs her help.

"On Vacation Without My Cat"

I have been divorced for six years and am currently in a relationship with a much younger man. I live alone, am financially independent, and a very strong woman. I also have a cat that I am very attached to—probably because I am not close to my family.

I have been having recurring dreams that all have the same theme. The dream is as follows: I am away on vacation when I remember that I forgot to have someone watch and feed my cat. It's the middle of my vacation and I am afraid something has happened to her. I begin to panic. I frantically try to get a flight home but there are none until the following week. I call to rent a car but it's too expensive and I can't afford it.

I wake up from this dream extremely upset and emotional. I have this dream at least once a week, and I don't understand what it is about. Is it just that I am very attached to my cat? Or is it something else? I would really like to stop having this dream. Thank you.

–Elizabeth, Age 32, Divorced, USA

This is one lucky cat—to have a "mommy" who wakes up at night worrying about it!

If Elizabeth is an especially zealous cat lover, her dreams may be simple reflections of anxiety she feels when occasionally she is forced out of town, and must leave her cat behind. Because she has the dreams when she is not on vacation, however, and because the dreams cause her to awaken "extremely upset and emotional," intuitively Elizabeth has grown suspicious. Do her dreams hold a deeper meaning?

Elizabeth's recurring dreams contain specific references to time, and to feelings of urgency. If her cat is indeed associated with her desire for a family, then is the true meaning of her dream that Elizabeth feels time is running out—to bring this family to life? Elizabeth is also currently dating a "much younger man." As her bio clock ticks softly in the background, does Elizabeth feel her time with this man is like "being on vacation"—a bit too far from the responsibilities of the real world?

If Elizabeth has been taking a vacation from her desire to begin a family (natural in the aftermath of a divorce), her recurring dreams are directing her to recognize the value that she attaches to this goal. If she knows the man she is dating is not a realistic partner with whom to build a family, the dream's warning is to gently move on from the relationship. Then she can allow a more appropriate mate, who also is family-minded, to enter her life.

"Resurrected Kitty"

I am working in a large art museum warehouse, where artworks that have recently been purchased by the museum are being processed— sent out to be restored if necessary, or to be stored for later exhibition. After processing some paintings by a well-known artist that are to be restored, I notice three drawings of mine (that I had done years ago, in college) being brought into the storage area of the warehouse.

When I go back to see what is going on, I find a box full of stuff from my past. In the box is the body of a dead cat. In the dream I think this is a cat that some friends and I had that died while living with us (over ten years ago). I think to myself, "I can't believe we kept this."

When I pick the cat up it starts to shake and I realize that it is coming back to life. I put it down on the floor and after staggering around a little it starts to play with some string on the floor. Since it really is alive I decide to feed it and take it to my parents' house. I find some food, and then take it into the bathroom, close the door, and give it food and water. The cat eats and drinks with gusto.

As for my background . . . I am an artist, although I have only recently begun working at it again after a fifteen-year hiatus. I have had many health problems recently and have been trying to get my life together.

—Skylar, Age 38, Single, USA

Cats often represent newborns in dreams, but they also function as broader symbols of feminine creativity. In Skylar's dream, the cat she is nurturing represents her art and her passion for drawing.

Skylar's dream, at one level, reflects her commitment to bringing her artwork "back to life." In the dream her artwork is being moved from "in storage" to "on display," a clear sign that, after a long hiatus (fifteen years), Skylar is ready to begin working again. The fact that Skylar's art is to be displayed in a prestigious museum, no less, indicates a positive self-assessment of her previous artistic efforts.

When Skylar notices the cat is alive, she brings it to her parents' home to give it food and water, and to allow it to recover. Is this another dream clue that assists our understanding of the cat's true identity? Skylar is nurturing the recovery of her artistic goals, but like the cat, Skylar is also gathering her strength after many health problems. Has Skylar received support from her parents, as she has worked to "get her life together"?

If Skylar chooses to draw the cat that appeared in her dream, it will be a drawing imbued with a wonderful energy—mysterious, feminine, and twice-born. The twice-born metaphor applies both to our dreamer's art and to herself. Skylar is feeling better—back safely from the brink of illness. Long live the creative spirit.

Celebrity

Celebrities: Dreams about celebrities and other public luminaries rarely reflect literal desires for contact with the famous. Instead, the dreams function as mirrors in which our own self-esteem is measured and evaluated. Does the celebrity receive you, treat you like an equal, or find you romantically attractive? Congratulations! Your dream reflects feelings of self-confidence and high self-esteem. (A celeb treats you like one of them.) Significantly, it doesn't matter if you like the celeb or not. What counts is their status, and the fact that they are talking to you—a person moving up in the world, who can feel the gears of recognition tumbling in your favor.

Dreams about celebrities also reflect desires for power and recognition in our personal lives. Difficulty making contact with a celebrity signifies frustration in our effort to achieve a status or approval we desire.

♦ **Interpretation tip:** If you dream about being involved with a celebrity, ask if your status is "moving up" in your personal or professional life. Did you recently get a raise, promotion, or other recognition for your talents?

* ✳ *

Dreams about celebrities reflect concerns about power, status, and attention. What we may find curious about these dreams, however, is that our motivations in them are always so selfish! To assume that celebrity dreams are about celebrities is to miss the point entirely. Instead, celebrity dreams are all about us, and about whether or not we measure up to the lofty stature that celebrity represents.

In "A Powerful Man," a woman's desire to compete in a male-dominated business environment is dramatically represented. Her new job position is intoxicating—fabulously so—

but will it turn her into a person whom she does not like? "High Expectations" also shows a woman whose career has just made a significant leap. Her dreams of romance and of being a celebrity herself show she has begun a new relationship—for the first time—with status and power. Our final dream, "Singled Out," shows a woman reveling in the attention of a famous rock 'n' roll star. She doesn't even like the celebrity, but she certainly does enjoy the attention she is receiving. Unromantic boyfriend—are you listening to your lover's dreams?

Celebrity Dreams

"A Powerful Man"

I'm forty-five years old, single, and not sexually active (in other words, no husband or lover). Last night I had a really vivid sexual dream that was both pleasant and disturbing.

In the dream, I have very hot, steamy, and satisfying sex with a man. My feelings during the dream were very intense—it was very satisfying because of the intimacy and sexual release, but it was as if I were being absorbed into this guy, becoming part of him. Although some of those feelings were very positive (being loved, wanted, accepted), I was somewhat uncomfortable with the feeling that he wanted to "possess" me. He loved me so much that he wanted to "mark" me as one of his possessions. There was real conflict here; I was with the man of my dreams (literally!)—someone who I believed to be a perfect match for me—but I didn't like the way he thought of me.

The man in the dream is a real person—a public figure. In reality, I don't know this person; in fact, I dislike him intensely. He is a politician whom I have no respect for. It was Jesse Ventura, the governor of Minnesota. I can't stand the guy. I think he's an idiot. I occasionally have sexual dreams in which I actually have an orgasm. This was one of those dreams.

As for my background: I've just received a promotion at work and have joined the ranks of the "executives" in the company, all of whom are male except me. I'm struggling to fit into this new role and find a way to make my voice heard, play a role in the high-level decision making, and not get run over by a few of the more power-hungry execs in the group. So far, I haven't been successful in doing that. In fact, I'm questioning whether I *want* to do what it takes to fit into this executive role. Can you decipher the clues?

—Erika, Age 45, Single, USA

In her waking life, Erika has begun a new relationship with power. A recent promotion has caused her to become the only female executive in her company. As she assumes her elevated status, Erika acknowledges that she enjoys the acceptance and validation that her new position accords. She is concerned, however, that many of her coexecutives appear to be power-hungry and obsessive. Will she soon become just like them?

Erika's "courtship with power" is represented in her dream as a sexual tryst with the governor of Minnesota, Jesse Ventura. As governor, Mr. Ventura is indeed a powerful man. As a former professional wrestler, he also holds strong masculine associations. Erika's dream reveals that she finds her new relationship with masculine power intoxicating—so intoxicating, in fact, it is represented as an orgasmic encounter.

In her dream, Erika is uncomfortable with her suitor's dominance. The governor wants to "mark" her, and make her one of "his possessions." Is it so difficult to identify the concerns she holds? Erika wants to know to what extent she will have to sacrifice her identity, and her independence, to satisfy her desire for power. Is it a coincidence that her dream frames her new position in a political context? Erika needs to master the "politics" of her new executive position, to find the balance of power she desires.

"High Expectations"

I have had two dreams in the same week that have been very unsettling. In the first I was a famous music producer at an awards ceremony and one of the artists decided that he was interested in me. It was funny because this man is much, much older than I am.

At first he made slight advances toward me while his wife's back was turned. Then my dream cut to me in what seemed to be my apartment or something. He was at the front door. We ended up in my room, on my bed, just kissing. Then we actually had sex, but it was in slow motion.

For some reason, during the middle, I told him that it was my first time. He gave me a puzzled look like he didn't understand, and I continued as if to advise him that it was all right. After we were finished, I was taking a shower. After what seemed like a long time in the shower, he joined me. And then we again had sex.

The strange thing is the next night I had a dream that I was pregnant, but not by him. It was another guy and this guy had gone away to what seemed like a farm. I was trying to contact him by phone. I was holding the phone during the whole dream but the phone number he wrote down kept changing. I would look at the paper he gave me with the phone number and I would start to dial, but it would be different when I looked at it a second time.

In real life I actually just started a new job at the world's second largest bank. It is very professional and is considered an extremely respectable job. People try for years to be a part of this bank, or at least that is what I have been told.

–Lillian, Age 21, Single, USA

Lillian's is a celebrity dream with a twist. Not only is Lillian romanced by a celebrity, she has also become one herself.

In her dream Lillian is a famous music producer attending an awards ceremony. (Does Lillian feel like she just received an award herself—her new job title?) At the ceremony, a celebrity is interested in her romantically, which is a consistent metaphor in dreams for high self-esteem. (If a celeb finds us attractive, we must be "celeb" material ourselves.) Lillian's new position with the world's second-largest bank has clearly given her confidence.

Significantly, the person with whom Lillian has sex is not a physically desirable partner. (She writes that he is "much, much older" than she is.) Accordingly, Lillian's sexual relationship with him is a metaphor for her "attraction" to the qualities he represents (status and power) and a reflection of her desire for security (he is older). The fact that their lovemaking occurs in slow motion is yet another clue to the symbolic nature of the act. Did Lillian pursue her position over the course of several months or years?

Lillian's dream suggests relief that she has attained a position of status and financial security. As in Erika's dream of sex with the governor, however, it is evident that Lillian finds her swift upward ascent in status somewhat destabilizing. Her observation that it is her "first time," when she is making love with the celebrity, is an allusion both to the magnitude of the transition and to her sense of initiation.

Lillian's second dream, of pregnancy, indicates the high expectations she has for her new position. It also shows her desire to communicate her new status to a mysterious dream man. The rapidly changing phone numbers indicate this man is inaccessible. His location on a farm suggests he is a great distance from her—or perhaps even deceased. (Is he her father, or an ex whom she would like to impress?)

Can Lillian identify this mystery man in her waking life—who would be very proud to learn of her new status? Now that Lillian has closed the deal with the bank, it is natural that she wants to share the news with her friends.

"Singled Out"

I have been dreaming a lot about famous people lately, and I want to know why. I had a dream that I was back at my home in Cleveland, Ohio, and I met the lead singer, Justin, from the group 'NSync. He then came over to my house and we hit it off really well, which led to us kissing/making out most of the time in my dream.

My whole family was there, as were some people from my workplace. Justin and I spent the day together and took pictures. It was great, and we got along fine. In my dream, I felt like I could talk to him, even though he was like a teen idol. He invited me to come see him on tour and he would buy me a plane ticket. In my dream I had a sense that he was kind of stuck-up in a snobby kind of way. I do think he is kind of cute, considering he is younger than me.

At the end of my dream we took a walk in the park and he said he had to go—that he would see me soon. I knew in my dream I would never see him again. I am twenty years old and dreaming about a teen idol! What is wrong with me? I recently won 'NSync concert tickets and decided to take my cousin for her birthday. Would that have anything to do with my dream?

The night before, I had a dream I met the Beach Boys at one of their concerts. I took pictures with Mike Love, who is my favorite Beach Boy. I started crying I was so happy.

I felt really good when I woke up from those two dreams. I wasn't sleepy; it was like I was excited. I think I want to feel important or special. My boyfriend is kind of controlling and never makes me feel very important. In my dream I felt like I was free, like nothing could make me feel bad.

When I was little, I always wanted to be famous, and some of me still does. Either that or meet a celebrity and befriend them. I think I just want people to know who I am. I want to feel free and wanted at the same time. Does that make sense?

–Crystal, Age 20, Single, USA

The fact that Crystal won concert tickets to the 'NSync concert has a lot to do with her recent series of dreams. It's exciting to win things. We feel lucky and singled out. Not unlike . . . being a celebrity for a day.

Like all dreams about celebrities, Crystal's dream reflects more brightly upon her own life than it does upon the celeb about whom she dreams. As Crystal says, she is not especially attracted to Justin of 'NSync. What she does enjoy in the dream, however, is the attention she receives. Her dream shows her being accepted and liked by the lead singer. In fact, she is even intimate ("making out"), and she has a brief relationship with him—which she knows will not last.

One of the forces that makes celebrity seductive is the attention that celebrities receive. Most of us fight for attention all our lives: first from our parents, then from our friends, then in our love relationships, and then from professional and social peer groups. We all share a basic need to be recognized and validated. Crystal's dream is happy and exciting, because it shows this desire being fulfilled.

Crystal informs us that her boyfriend, at present, does not make her feel especially important. Accordingly, is it possible that the true message of this dream is that Crystal wishes she were appreciated more—by someone who is close to her heart? By showing her the thrill of attention, Crystal's dream may be informing her of a quality that is painfully absent in her real life. Is it time to trade her boyfriend in for someone who makes her feel special and desired?

Chase

Chase: Common metaphor for feelings of being "pursued" by disturbing fears and emotions. Typical chase themes include pursuit by attackers who will hurt, rape, or possibly kill the dreamer, with the dreamer then experiencing all the commotion of running away, hiding, and outmaneuvering the potential attacker. Chase dreams often end with the dreamer waking just before being caught or found. Because we awaken directly from them, chase dreams are commonly described as nightmares.

Successful confrontation of a pursuer indicates confidence in one's ability to face challenges in life. Chase dreams may reflect literal fears of attack, especially in a sexual context among young women. Chase dreams should not be interpreted as precognitive.

Please also see: "Attacked."

Faceless attackers indicate that our pursuers most likely are not real persons (with whom we have a conflict) but instead represent unresolved fears, feelings of guilt or shame, or emotionally painful memories. Recurring dreams about chase and attack by faceless men or women may reflect repressed memories of physical, sexual, or emotional abuse.

Escape: Repeated dreams about escape, involving exits through numerous doors and trapdoors in a house, may reflect the operation of repression (habitual avoidance of disturbing feelings and awarenesses) in the dreamer's life.

◆ **Interpretation tip:** What disturbing feelings are pressing upon you that you wish you could avoid? Are you procrastinating a decision in your life?

* * *

Chase dreams are strong messages that we need to turn and face our fears. In "The Child Catcher," a teen experiences recurring nightmares about a character from a movie. Can she identify her real-life concerns that have surfaced in her dreams? "Chased by Lions" shows us the pursuit of a romantic relationship in classic dream style: A suitor's "animal nature" is revealed. In "Stalker," a young woman is subjected to repeated advances and harassment. Our final entry, "Chased by a Wolf," shows a woman chased by a faceless pursuer. As the wolf gradually becomes identified, our dreamer confronts her awareness of a painful past.

Chase Dreams

"The Child Catcher"

I keep having nightmares about people trying to murder me. They are very frightening and disturbing. One was about a villain in the movie *Chitty Chitty Bang Bang*. He's a child-catcher in the movie and it scared me a lot when I was little. Anyway, I'm running through a deserted fair at night and the child-catcher is running after me with a big knife. I run into the house of mirrors and I can't find my way out. Then I see him in all of the mirrors and I start screaming and trying to find a way out. He grabs me from behind and I get out of his grasp for a second but then he grabs my ankle and is about to kill me. Then I wake up.

I've noticed that in my dreams the killer is always a man and he always has a knife of some sort. It's never any other kind of weapon. I've also noticed that I'm always alone in my dream. It may start out that there are people with me but they eventually fade away—I'm not really sure where they go. I could really use your help on this because I wake up crying at least once a week. They started recently and my parents are going through a divorce right now. I'm not sure if that will help you at all, but I would appreciate your time.

–Amanda, Age 16, Single, USA

It is hardly surprising that Amanda was scared as a little girl by the "child-catcher" from the movie *Chitty Chitty Bang Bang*. The child-catcher was a man who captured children and took them to prison, in a town ruled by an evil king and queen. Kids weren't allowed in this town, because the queen didn't like them.

In the movie, if you were caught by the child-catcher, you would be separated from your parents forever. The two children in the movie do get caught, and they are taken to prison, but eventually they escape and rejoin their parents. In fact, at the end of the movie, all the children escape, and all the families in the village are reunited. It's a happy ending.

The child-catcher has recently begun appearing in Amanda's dreams, though, and judging by her description, he hasn't gotten any nicer. In fact, the child-catcher now carries a big knife in his hands, and he's chasing her, trying to kill her.

Amanda informs us that her parents are currently going through a divorce. Do we see the connection between this dream and Amanda's feelings about the divorce? Amanda feels like there's a real-life child-catcher out there (whose name is "divorce") who's trying to "cut up" her family (with a big knife) and separate her from her parents. Has being a kid suddenly become outlawed?

Amanda is uncertain whether or not she will survive this transition in her family life, which is why the threat of death (symbol of change and separation) looms over her dream. Accordingly, Amanda needs reassurance that her family will not end, even if it will change shape. Similarly, it is apparent that Amanda sometimes feels she is living in "Chitty Chitty Bang Bang" land—where an evil force rules that doesn't like children. Amanda again needs reassurance that her parents love her very much. As Amanda settles into her new family shape, and is assured of her parents' love, her dreams of chase will stop.

"Chased by Lions"

I had a dream that my friend and I were at a party and we met these two really good-looking guys. At the end of the night we all went back to my flat. We all started talking and having a laugh but then the two boys turned into lions and started to chase us. Then I woke up. What does this mean? Please help me!!!!

—*Esther, Age 17, Single, United Kingdom*

Esther and her friend are having a good time—talking and having a laugh—when suddenly the nice boys Esther invited over to her flat turn into lions and begin to chase them. (Some manners!)

Esther's dream is a metaphor for the "chase" of a romantic relationship. In her dream the two boys whom she invites back to her flat are attractive. The group is getting along great, but then suddenly the rules of the game begin to shift. The boys turn into lions (show their aggressive, animal nature) and promptly begin to pursue Esther and her friend.

If Esther recently began dating, it appears she has already perceived the romantic interest that boys hold for her. Can Esther think of any men she has been talking to lately, who she thinks are "just friends"? The message of this chase dream is that they may have something more physical on their minds.

"Stalker"

I dreamed that I was a reporter, and I was at a mansion where a party was being held. My job was to write about the party. I was excited because my story was going to be put on the front page. Then I was looking for the hosts of the party, so that I could get some quotes about the party from them.

As I was looking for them, I saw a guy I didn't want anything to do with. I didn't want him to see me or talk to me, but he came up to me and asked how I was. I told him I was fine, and that I was working, and to leave me alone. He said no, that he wanted to talk to me and that he wanted to dance. I told him I was busy and to get away from me. He kept on wanting to dance and I kept on saying no.

So I walked out to my car to get my recorder because I had forgotten it. He followed me and kept on asking. Finally I got tired of him and I started to run away. He ran after me, and we ran around my car for about thirty seconds, then I ran into a building to hide from him. At that point I was terrified. I ran into the building and tried to hide, but every time I did he'd find me. (This building was a restaurant-style kitchen.) He grabbed me and started to dance some steps with me, and I was struggling to get away. Finally I hit him over the head with something and he fell to the ground. I ran out and I ran toward the party. I walked in like nothing had happened.

What can this dream mean? I know it doesn't mean that a guy or boyfriend is trying to get me back, because I've never had a boyfriend in my life.

–Tamia, Age 16, Single, USA

Tamia's dream of being attacked by a stalker holds an unwanted sexual overtone. When the stalker asks Tamia to dance—a sign of sexual attraction—Tamia tells him she is not interested. But the stalker refuses to leave her alone, and soon winds up attacking her.

Tamia has read about stalkers in newspapers, and heard stories on TV, which is why her dream, most likely, is set in a media context. The fact that Tamia outwits and defeats her attacker is a positive sign. This shows that Tamia possesses a healthy sense of self-confidence, and of her own empowerment, in the world.

After being attacked, Tamia rejoins her party in the mansion, and walks in "as if nothing had happened." Tamia's failure to acknowledge her feelings is significant. If her dream reflects uncomfortable feelings that unwanted sexual attention occasionally evokes, Tamia's response indicates she is not acknowledging the true level of her distress. Is it time to voice her feelings to a friend who will support and echo her sentiments? In her dream, Tamia proved resourceful, and was able to escape. In the real world, this dream could be a nightmare—and might not have such a simple ending.

"Chased by a Wolf"

About two years ago I began dreaming that a wolf was chasing me. The dreams occurred once or twice a month and grew in intensity and detail over the following year.

First the wolf was chasing me into a mobile home we lived in when I was a child. I was carrying a baby I had to protect from the wolf. I ran in the back door, slammed it, and climbed into the roof by sliding between the ceiling panels. I awakened just as the wolf came into the trailer and discovered my hiding place.

As time progressed, the wolf chased me through each home of my childhood and later my adolescence. Over time the wolf began to take on the form of a half-man, half-wolf. Finally the dreams ceased.

Background: This nightmare followed the death of my father by suicide (a violent one). He killed himself on the day my sister (who is now a grown woman) confronted him with the fact that he had molested her in childhood.

—Ariana, Age 37, Single, USA

Given the background Ariana has provided, can there be any doubt about who the wolf in her dream represents? The wolf is her father, who Ariana feared was going to attack (sexually molest) her sister. The baby Ariana carries in her arms (whom she knows she must protect from the wolf) symbolizes her sister. Because no one operates in isolation in a family, however, we know that Ariana's childhood, even if Ariana was not molested herself or directly aware of the abuse, was also affected.

When we experience traumatic events in our lives, our body often protects us from absorbing the full impact of the experience by filtering it through a psychological lens, as it were. For example, it is significant that Ariana's father never is directly represented in her recurring dreams. The reason, most likely, is because it would be very difficult for Ariana to see her father in this violent, attacking role. Accordingly, the dream protects her from seeing this disturbing vision by disguising her father as a wolf.

With time, however, the identity of the wolf gradually becomes revealed. In later dreams we learn the attacker actually is a half-wolf, half-man type of creature. What new information has the dream imparted to us? Ariana's attacker actually is a human being, and he is male. We know from the locations of the dream (houses Ariana lived in as a child) that the attacks occurred close to home.

In dream interpretation circles, Ariana's recurring dreams are an excellent illustration of a camouflaged dream symbol, over time, becoming less obscure (less disguised) and more transparent (the representation more accurately reflects our waking world). This transition in representation—from disguised to transparent dreams—parallels our ability to manage difficult feelings and awarenesses consciously in our waking lives.

The transformation of the dream symbol, and the eventual end of this dream, tell us that eventually Ariana was able to absorb this painful experience into her life and move on. When the dreams ceased, we know that some of the pain of this experience was released.

Clothing

Clothing: Symbol of presentation in dreams. Wrinkled suits and soiled dresses reflect hopes for the future that have "been spoiled" by disappointment. Clothing worn backward suggests role reversal. Clothing worn inside out indicates feelings that are "exposed"—for all to see. If our clothes are torn and ragged, it suggests a period of physical or emotional hardship. Wearing different shoes suggests we are pulled in two directions. New or expensive clothes indicate a new social status.

Arriving at a social function (wedding, formal party, business meeting) with an important piece of clothing missing (a shoe, hat, or glove) suggests unpreparedness for whatever event is represented. "Wedding Day" anxiety dreams (the bride's dress is the wrong color or does not fit) should not be interpreted as precognitive, or as a negative omen for the marriage. Rather, the bride or groom simply is anxious that everything "go right" on the big day.

♦ **Interpretation tip:** If you dream you are inappropriately attired, ask where you feel unprepared in your romantic, social, or professional life.

* * *

Dreams about clothes concern themes of role identity and self-presentation. Our first dreamer, in "The Wedding Dress," has a big decision to make. Will she wear her old wedding dress, with all the memories that are attached to it, or is it time to make a fresh start? In "Dresses Don't Fit," a dreamer has had a disturbing dream for years. Can she identify the decision she is procrastinating? Our next dream, "Sweater on Backward," shows an employee who keeps showing up at work with her sweater on backward. Now she wonders: Did management make the right decision? Our final entry, "Nice Pants," reflects a dreamer's concern that her husband "keeps his pants on." Our dreamer is valiantly trying to keep her marriage "on track."

Clothing Dreams

"The Wedding Dress"

I am a forty-nine-year-old woman, married now for thirty years. I have three children in school. I cared for my parents in their old age, until they died at home with us. I am also a professional seamstress. My marriage is not good, and I intend to leave it when the children are grown.

Also, I have been reunited with a lost love from my high school and junior high school years. He and I have renewed our relationship, long distance, this past year. I have told my husband I am leaving him. He does not want the marriage to end. The reason I am sending you this dream is that it seemed full of meaning.

In the dream I have been invited to a wedding at a wedding chapel. It's a lovely, clean, nice place. I go into a room where the prospective bride is supposed to be, where a lot of women are gathered. I do not know who the bride is, though. When I enter, they tell me I am the bride. I am shocked, and afraid.

They say they have my dress all ready for me. It is the dress I was married in thirty years ago. They tell me that I am remarrying my husband. I want to scream no in my dream, but hold back, feeling sick.

They bring me the dress in a large, white, new plastic bag. I cannot see the dress until they unzip it. The women seem excited about all of this. When the bag is unzipped, the dress is very old, stained, and has rips all over it, where it has been repaired. I notice the tears in the dress have been very neatly sewn—very carefully. It is yellow-looking and ugly, has not even been cleaned, and is full of patched places on it.

I walk away, leaving the room. I am looking for my parents, but can't find them. Then they are there. They look sad, but my children are happy, and my husband is excited and happy. I will not do it. I will not wear that dress. I feel sick inside. I want to run away. Then I wake up. The dream stayed with me a very long time afterward.

–Isabelle, Age 49, Married, USA

Given her background as a professional seamstress, we know Isabelle has a discerning eye when it comes to clothes. Can there be any doubt, then, about the meaning of this dream? This is one dress that Isabelle does not want to climb back into.

It would be difficult to imagine a more potent symbol for the hopes and dreams that fill our hearts as we enter into marriage than a wedding dress. After thirty years of a disappointing relationship, however, hard times have taken a toll on Isabelle's dress. The dress is dirty, ripped, and yellow with age. Though the rips and holes have been carefully sewn (by a professional seamstress?), the accumulated years of neglect are still visible.

Isabelle's decision to postpone leaving her marriage until her children are grown reflects her dedication to the responsibilities of family, as does the care she gave to her parents in their final years. Her romantic reunion with a childhood friend, however, has brought the issue of separation to the fore of her attention. Now that a door to the future is open, does Isabelle have the courage to bravely walk through it?

The significance of the wedding in Isabelle's dream, paradoxically, is not the hope that Isabelle holds for her new romance. On the contrary, the wedding symbolizes Isabelle's fears that she may be unable to escape her past. The enthusiastic crowd that encourages her to remarry her husband almost certainly represents social pressure Isabelle feels to stay together— from friends, her husband, and children. Each time she looks at that dress, however, and the disappointment it represents, Isabelle begins to feel sick.

If Isabelle truly wants to "cross the threshold" to a new chapter in her life, her dream outlines two hurdles she needs to surmount: guilt about splitting up her family, and guilt about the social stigma of divorce. Isabelle's dream is an emphatic encouragement that it is time to recapture those dreams that were lost and postponed so many years ago. When Isabelle does recapture them, the clothes she wears in her dreams, which are a reflection of her spirit, will undergo a fabulous transformation. They will be clean, vibrant, and beautifully sewn—and admired by all who cross her path.

"Dresses Don't Fit"

I have been dreaming about going to the same dress shop to buy a dress. The initial scene is always different, but at the end I'm in the same dress shop. It is closing time and I have a feeling of urgency to pick a dress. But none of the dresses fit!

I've had this dream on and off for three years. I have gained sixty-
five pounds in those years, so maybe that is the connection?

–Susan, Age 51, Married, USA

Susan's dreams reflect literal anxiety about having put on extra pounds,
and show that she genuinely would like to lose the weight. The fact that
her dreams began at the same time as her weight gain is significant. If we
are ever puzzled by a series of recurring dreams, the most illuminating
question we can ask is: "What was occurring in my life when the dreams
begin?" There is always a correlation.

In her dreams, Susan is distressed. Will she find a new dress before the
store closes, and she runs out of time? The urgency Susan feels is a reflection of her anxiety (and procrastination) about her recent weight gain. The
dream shows that Susan feels uncomfortable with her new body image.
Will she reverse the trend, and find a size that fits?

"Sweater on Backward"

I've had this weird dream about four nights in a row—it's really not a
full-fledged dream, it's more like a snapshot of me in different
situations. In each one, I'm wearing a sweater backward, with the tag
that's sewn on the neckline in front, instead of being on the back.
(Not inside out, just backward.) I'm always out in public (twice at
work, once in a mall, once in a restaurant) when I realize my sweater
is on wrong. By the way, it's been four different sweaters.

I recently received a promotion at work and that's what I think the
dream may be associated with in my waking life. My new job is more
technically oriented than I'm accustomed to, and sometimes I feel
insecure about that.

–Candice, Age 35, Single, USA

Candice's dream is a variant of the common exposed-in-public dream.
She is in a public setting, only to realize that she is inappropriately attired. In her case, Candice is not naked or without a piece of clothing—
dreams that indicate feelings of exposure and unpreparedness—but rather
the sweater she is wearing is backward. The office context in two of her
dreams alerts us to the fact that the dream is work-related.

It is significant that Candice's sweater is on backward, and not inside out, in all four of her dreams. If the sweater were inside out, it would suggest that Candice is wearing her inner feelings—emotions and intentions—on the outside, readily visible for others to see. Backward, however, suggests a sense of role reversal.

Candice tells us she feels awkward adjusting to a new technical position at work. Her dreams reflect these feelings, but as is always telling in dreams about self-presentation, her coworkers are unable to witness her discomfort. (The tag is on the inside.) What is the meaning? The awkwardness Candice feels as she adjusts to her new role is not readily visible to her coworkers. As Candice builds a new skill set to match her promotion, these dreams about role reversal, and feelings that management "got things backward," will soon turn themselves around.

"Nice Pants"

I had a dream that my husband was looking for me in a crowded nightclub. While he was looking for me, he was approached by a very attractive young girl. She told him that she liked the pants that he was wearing, and he was obviously flattered, so much so that he offered to give them to her.

She took them, and he walked around the club without his pants. I was furious. After he gave away his pants we went looking for them, as I insisted that he get them back.

Then the dream changed quickly into a dangerous train ride, in which I was trying with all of my might to keep the train on its track—but it seemed destined to jump the track.

–Jaime, Age 40, Married, USA

Jaime's husband's willingness to take his pants off for an admiring female, who, significantly, is younger and attractive, leaves Jaime feeling betrayed. Jaime then spends the remainder of her dream trying to get her husband to atone for his misstep—and to cover himself up—by trying to locate his pants. This scene closes without resolution, and suddenly Jaime finds herself behind the wheel of a large, fast-moving train, careening dangerously down a track. Jaime is trying with "all of her might" to keep the train on course, but she worries that "it seemed destined to jump the track."

The metaphors expressed by this dream, unfortunately, are all too clear. Jaime wants her husband to "keep his pants on" (not become sexually involved with another woman), and she is working hard to keep their marriage "on track." Her dream reflects significant doubts about her ability to keep this train (their marriage) on course.

If Jaime's husband is "overfriendly" in social situations, Jaime should tell him it's disrespectful. If her husband is a sensitive man, he will understand her emotions, and he will change his ways. If the train is further down the line than this, and Jaime really thinks her husband may "jump track," she needs to consider making an appointment with a marriage counselor. A good counselor will help Jaime understand her feelings and options, and will shine light on forces driving her husband. Judging by Jaime's dream, she may need some extra help to keep her marriage on course.

Communication

Communication: Dreams about trying to communicate with friends, lovers, relatives, and the deceased reflect desires to make contact or to clarify understandings with these people. Successful communication indicates confidence in the future of these relationships, and often leaves dreamers with feelings of emotional closure. Unsuccessful attempts reflect difficulty connecting in waking life, or an inability to express oneself as desired.

Common metaphors for the inability to communicate include telephones that do not work, continuing interruptions when trying to speak personally with another, inability to locate someone in a crowd, literal barriers to communication (a glass wall), or a recurring series of obstacles that prevent contact. If a dreamer is unable to speak due to an obstruction in his or her mouth (chewing gum, teeth falling out), difficulty expressing one's feelings is indicated. Dramatic metaphors for the inability to speak—tongue is removed, throat is cut—indicate feelings or memories that one is currently "unable to talk about." Speaking in foreign languages is a common metaphor that symbolizes difficulty understanding a partner or associate.

Telephone: Symbol of communication. Phones that don't work, wrong phone numbers, and disconnected phone calls are metaphors for difficulties communicating. Unanswered phones indicate avoided or missed communications in waking life. Dialing 911 is a "call for help" and reflects an emotional crisis for which a dreamer seeks guidance and assistance from an authority figure, represented in the dream as police or rescue workers. Unanswered calls for help symbolize feelings of helplessness, and lack of support from friends, family, or coworkers.

◆ **Interpretation tip:** Can you identify the communication breakdown in your life? Is it time to speak up—or change lines?

✳ ✳ ✳

Difficulty communicating in a dream reflects difficulty communicating in real life. Our first dream, "Can't Connect," shows a dreamer trying to call an old boyfriend on the telephone. Is her connection lost forever? In "Can't Speak," a man loses his jawbone and wonders if he will ever regain his voice. In "Foreign Languages," the complexity of international relations is explored: Two dreamers don't speak the same language. Our final entry, "Lost in a Crowd," shows a man searching for his date. Will they ever find each other?

Communication Dreams

"Can't Connect"

I am twenty-four years old and I had a dream about a guy that I had previously dated. Things seemed to be going very well, but then he suddenly broke up with me due to some personal problems in his life. Even though we have remained friends, I still have feelings for him. He recently moved to a different city.

In the dream, I was at my childhood home trying to call him on the phone, but different things kept getting in my way. The first time my mother calls for me. Then when I try to dial again, a female coworker walks in, which seemed weird because I was at home in Delaware in the dream, and I now live in Arizona. She walks in and we start talking, and I didn't want to call him with her in the room, because I felt jealous of her.

Then she finally leaves, and just as I try again, someone knocks at my window, which is on the second floor. I look up and see a man with a helicopter propeller strapped to his back floating there. He asks me if I want a snow cone. I look out the window, and there are several people there making them. In the end I never got to call him before I woke up. This dream felt very real, and I think it says that I still have feelings for him, but I am not quite sure what it all means.

–Carol, Age 24, Single, USA

Carol's dream shows that she still has feelings for her ex-boyfriend. As she attempts to contact him on a telephone, however, she encounters several barriers to completing her call.

It is significant that Carol's dream is located in her childhood home. When dreams send us back in time, we are encouraged to look for areas of our life where we may be retreating from adulthood. When confronted with the complexity of a new situation, we often regress to behaviors and strategies that were successful for us when we were younger. The strategy is logical, but it's usually not the best response we are capable of.

Carol's phone call is interrupted by her mother, and next by a coworker—whom Carol acknowledges she is a bit jealous of. The first interruption suggests Carol may be feeling like a young girl again—awkward—when she wants to be around a guy and her mother is there. The second interruption suggests she is concerned about the presence of other women in this friend's life and uncertain of her own attractiveness.

The last scene, however, is the most telling of all. Carol reaches for the phone again, only this time she is interrupted by a man floating outside her window with a propeller strapped to his back. The man offers Carol a snow cone. The entire scenario is reminiscent of an amusement park. At this point in the dream, does Carol agree that her situation with her ex has become a bit comic—and even cartoonish? The cartoon atmosphere, indeed, may be yet another allusion to childhood.

The frustration Carol feels with her ex is instructional because it reveals qualities that are important to her in a relationship. Carol wants a partner with whom she can communicate freely and easily, like an adult, and without insecurities and jealousies. (Without feeling like a little girl, and without worrying about other women.) Judging from her dream report, Carol has not found these qualities in her ex. What's the message? If Carol is looking for a love relationship, she needs to choose a connection that's clear—and easy!

"Can't Speak"

I've had this recurring dream where I lose my teeth, or in the most recent case, my entire jawbone. And thus my voice becomes mumbled and isn't understood by the other characters in the dream.

The story of the dream isn't always the same, and it's usually just a secondary occurrence in a much bigger plot. In the most recent one I ended up having to search for someone on the streets who could put my jawbone back in place, though I never actually found him or her. The dreams didn't cause any anxiety, or even much second thought, until the more recent dream.

It's mostly a curiosity issue. I'm an English major, and an aspiring writer/poet. However, I haven't been able to get much writing done lately, as I've been too busy with school and my job. And I know I want to start writing, but I haven't found the time in my schedule to do it.

If I were to guess at an interpretation (I'm no expert), I would say it was a message to me saying that when I'm not writing regularly, I lose my voice as a writer. What do you think?

–Sergio, Age 21, Single, USA

Unlike teeth-falling-out dreams, which typically represent feelings of uncertainty regarding our social presentation (we are worried about our looks or image that we present to others), several clues in Sergio's report alert us that his dreams really concern his artistic "voice." In all the dreams he is unable to speak clearly to others. And unlike most teeth-falling-out dreams, where we feel self-conscious and seek to hide our condition from others (another reference to appearance), Sergio actively seeks help. The prevailing theme is not embarrassment, but rather, difficulty and frustration trying to communicate.

Given the context of Sergio's dream—an artist's creative aspirations constrained by the responsibilities of everyday living—the dream's reference to voice becomes clear. Sergio has not been able to write recently, and is worried about losing his connection with his audience. As a writer, Sergio understands that his voice, though literally inaudible, is heard in his readers' minds.

Sergio's dream could have chosen several metaphors to reflect time spent away from his craft. He could have dreamed about searching for a pencil, or about a computer set away from him that he never was able to reach, or of words slowly evaporating from a written page of text. In all cases, the message still would be the same. It's time to reassert the regular rhythm of creation. Sergio's muse is calling, and she wants him to speak up.

"Foreign Languages"

In my dream, I met up with a man I used to work with. In real life, he had asked me out for a drink one evening, and I agreed, but we didn't actually decide on a day. I worked with him for another two weeks or so, but then I was away for a week. I returned to hear that he had left and was moving to Africa for a year. I didn't see him again.

In my dream, I was walking down the street and I saw him. I tried to speak to him but he would only speak to me in Spanish. At first, I thought I was mistaken and that it wasn't really him, but then I had an overwhelming feeling that told me it was. He finally started speaking to me in English, but when I woke up, I could not remember what he had said. All I could recall was that I had shouted at him about standing up a friend of mine. Just a bit strange, don't you think?

–Joanna, Age 21, Single, England

There are so many languages spoken in Joanna's dream, it's no wonder she's confused. First it's Spanish, then it's English, and throughout it all—it's Dreamspeak!

In the midst of all these translations, has Joanna confused the identity of her friend who was stood up? After all, Joanna is the person with whom her former coworker made a date. She was supposed to get together for a drink one evening, but then way led to way, and before she knew it he was gone. All the way to Africa, no less.

The reason Joanna's friend appeared speaking Spanish in her dream is because she knows that he is currently in a foreign country. The different languages also suggest a communication breakdown between the two. Joanna was at least expecting a good-bye, if not the drink she was promised, before her new friend departed the country.

Joanna's dream shows that she was looking forward to her date. Given that her friend left in a hurry, perhaps she can forgive him this missed appointment. In the future, though, if Joanna finds that they still speak foreign languages, she will want to remind herself that it most likely is not a coincidence.

"Lost in a Crowd"

I have a friend who lives about two hundred fifty miles away. I have only met her once and I know she supports her local football team. We E-mail each other occasionally.

I had a dream that I went to watch her local football team and knew that she would be in the crowd, but the seats were arranged in such a way that it made it hard to see anyone. I thought I could see her but I wasn't sure.

Suddenly I found myself traveling on the same train as her, then I woke up and the dream ended. I can't make any sense out of it, but it was a really clear dream. Felt quite real.

–Tim, Age 26, Single, England

Tim has had a common missed-connection dream. He goes to meet a girl at a football game, but he can't see her, due to the way the "seats are arranged." Then he thinks he sees her in the crowd, but still they don't connect. Suddenly he is on the same train as she, but again they fail to meet.

Tim complains about "the way the seats are arranged" in the football stadium in the first part of the dream. Is this a reference to the physical distance, in the waking world, that separates this potential couple? The "arrangement," he observes, makes it "hard to see anyone." Later in the dream, Tim is located on a train. Like cars, trains in dreams represent directions we are headed in our lives. Tim's continued inability to connect reflects the difficulty he experiences getting his romantic interest headed in the same direction.

The distance that separates Tim from this woman is a formidable obstacle to the development of a relationship. If Tim wants to be closer to her, the message of his dream is that he needs to exchange more-regular E-mail with her and pick up the phone to talk. If he feels they have chemistry over the phone, then he'll need to make firmer plans than hoping to meet at a football game. Is Tim ready to bite the bullet and make a date? His dream shows this is a connection he would like to make.

Death

Death: Symbol for change and separation that should not be interpreted literally. Dreams about the death of a child, sibling, friend, or other family member symbolize change in the quality of the relationship, or a fear of separation. Dreaming about one's own death is a potent symbol of inner metamorphosis; old ways of perceiving are passing away; new aspects of the personality are developing.

Separations caused by the end of high school, college, a romantic breakup, divorce, the end of a friendship, the loss of a job—all are frequently represented as deaths in dreams. Willful deaths in dreams—suicides with guns or the slitting of the wrists, for example—symbolize intense emotional pain and frustration. Happy deaths—the dreamer dies but is not upset—indicate a dreamer's willingness to release the past and embrace the change of the future. Encounters with "the Grim Reaper" or with other representations of death (a skeleton, for example) are often caused by health problems in the dreamer's own life, or by the health problems of friends and family members—especially parents. The dreamer is encountering awareness of his or her own mortality.

Coffin: Dreams about seeing a friend or loved one in a coffin signify change or separation in that relationship. Seeing oneself in a coffin indicates the "passing" of a phase in one's life, and the beginning of a new period of growth. Coffins can also be symbols of weakness and lack of vitality.

Funeral: Funerals may refer literally to fears of death or concerns about proper burial rites, especially with seniors. Like death, funerals can also be a positive symbol indicating growth and rebirth. Witnessing your own funeral suggests a transition in your life, a break between the past and the future.

◆ **Interpretation tip:** If you dream about a friend or lover's death, don't be fooled by the literal appearance. Instead, ask what change is occurring in the relationship.

✳ ✳ ✳

Few dreams hold the immediacy of death. In "Best Friend Dies," a dreamer is worried she will lose her best friend. Is her dream precognitive, or is she just nervous about saying good-bye? "Child Dies" is a common dream that strikes fear into the heart of every parent. "I Am Dying" shows a dreamer in the grips of a terminal illness. She wonders if the end is near. "My Funeral" is an exploration of the multiple deaths, and births, that are contained in any lifetime. Our final entry, "Rebirth," shows a dreamer who is delighted to be settling into a coffin. Who would think that change could feel so good?

Dreams about Death

"Best Friend Dies"

I dreamed that my best friend died and I don't understand why. We were at the college she probably will end up going to and tons of people had died and she was one of them.

I was there in the field where the funeral was taking place and crying. Then I called my best friend's sister and was like, "She died, she died." She was like, "No, she is here and okay." Then it ended.

–Claudia, Age 19, Single, USA

Claudia's dream is not hard to figure out—especially if we remember that death in dreams almost always is a symbol of change and separation.

The location of the dream, significantly, is the college campus where Claudia's best friend will probably go to school next year. Another clue to the meaning of this dream is that her best friend was only one of "tons of people" who had died. Can Claudia figure out why she had this strange dream? Claudia is in her last year of high school. Her dream is a metaphor for the change approaching next year, when Claudia and her high school friends ("tons of people") will split up and head separate directions to colleges all across the country.

Claudia is aware that her relationship with her best friend is about to change. The funeral depicted in the dream symbolizes her awareness that a special time in her life, high school, is drawing to a close. Claudia is going to lose contact with many of her good friends.

Claudia's dream thoughtfully takes an extra step to reassure Claudia that the death she perceives is not literal. When Claudia contacts her friend's sister on the phone, she learns that her best friend is really alive, and okay. In this way the dream lets Claudia know that her friend's death is only symbolic.

"Child Dies"

I dreamt that my beloved ten-year-old daughter was dead. I was crying bitterly in my dreams and telling my sisters about it. When I woke up today, my daughter was sleeping soundly beside me. I feel very uncomfortable about this dream.

–Skyler, Age 36, Married, Singapore

It is every mother's deepest fear that she will lose a child. Perhaps something Skyler read in a newspaper recently, or saw on television, aroused this concern within her? A story of a child's abduction or a tragic automobile accident will awaken any parent's awareness of the dangers that threaten a child's safety. In this scenario, Skyler's dream may be a simple representation of the fear that all parents share—that some harm or misfortune will befall their child.

In a second scenario, where death in dreams reflects growth and metamorphosis, Skyler's dream is a representation of the changes that currently are taking place within her young girl. Her daughter, now ten years old, is beginning her transition from childhood to preadolescence. Skyler may have noticed recently that a certain phase in her daughter's development is "passing away," while a new period of growth is beginning. For example, Skyler may have noticed recently that her daughter is paying more attention to friends than she has in the past, and that she may be acting more independently in her relations with Skyler. These are natural and healthy stages of a child's development.

With growth, childish aspects of the personality pass away, while older and more mature aspects come into being. Unless Skyler has reason to fear otherwise, her dream is a reflection of the many changes to come, as she watches her daughter blossom into young adolescence.

"I Am Dying"

In the last week or so I have been experiencing some very upsetting and extremely vivid nightmares—and nightmares are things I *very* rarely have. It is almost a recurring dream in that it eventually involves my imminent death—either by falling or car crash. In any case, the last moments are always the same. I know I am about to die, I know it is going to be painful, and I am simply waiting for the end, wondering how bad it will be and hoping it isn't going to be as bad as I fear. Of course I always wake up before "the end"—although it seems to go on forever. When I *do* wake up, my entire body is flooded with adrenaline, and it is very difficult to go back to sleep.

As to recent problems in my life, there are many. A job I really loved has been changed to a job I despise, both my parents have become extremely ill (my stepfather is terminal), and my boyfriend is encouraging me to move in with him, which would result in a four-hundred-mile move and an attempt to find another job. I'm in my early fifties and a little tired of this, since I just made a move a little over a year ago (divorced and moved seven hundred miles from my hometown).

My laundry list of "bad things" that have happened in the last year could fill a book, but the nightmares are very recent—in fact, they probably started at about the time I found out that my stepfather had a terminal illness. I'm wondering if these nightmares are just my subconscious reaction to all the stress or if they might be an indication that there is something physically wrong with me (as opposed to being on the road to a padded cell somewhere!).

–Carla, Age 52, Divorced, USA

Significantly, Carla's nightmares started at about the time that she learned her stepfather had a terminal illness. As is always the case with recurring dreams, the timing of their onset reveals important clues as to their origin. Accordingly, Carla's nightmares and her stepfather's illness are related—though for reasons that Carla most likely would not suspect at first.

The logic may be selfish, but Carla's dreams reflect concerns she has for her own life. Carla's experience with her stepfather—watching him slip from health into terminal illness—has caused her to think forward to her own eventual death. Is it a coincidence that Carla's condition, like her stepfather's, is also terminal? She writes, "I know I am about to die, I know it is going to be painful, and I am simply waiting for the end, wondering how bad it will be and hoping it isn't going to be as bad as I fear."

There is a great difference between awareness of mortality in an intellectual sense (we all know that we are going to die) versus coming to grips with the realization emotionally. Most of us successfully avoid thinking about death for most of our lives. Usually it is not until a parent or a contemporary dies (or becomes seriously ill) that we are forced to confront the issue. It is as if our brains finally say, "If it can happen to him (or her) then it's really going to happen to me, too."

Carla's fears of death are natural. None of us knows what will happen when the day comes. In death's shadow, however, we can all learn to appreciate the magic of life.

"My Funeral"

Background: I have known my soon-to-be ex for approximately twenty years. Our life together was never happy, even before we married. Still, I loved him deeply. Although we were very different (he is quiet and lacks friends, while I am extremely outgoing, with many friends), I always felt the need to protect him. He has hurt me numerous times due to infidelity, verbal abuse, and being a less-than-satisfactory husband or father (we have an eleven-year-old son). Although I am no longer in love with him, I do care about him.

In my dream I died, and I am laid out in a casket. There are so many people filling the room. Some are standing outside, and all are crying—except my ex. It is as though I am an unseen, outside observer. I feel the pain for everyone, yet don't feel bad that I am the one who died.

In the next part of my dream, my ex dies. He is laid out in the same place as I, but no one is there for his funeral—except me. I am the only one crying, and I am dead. Please explain this.

–Ruth, Age 40, Separated, USA

Dreams speak a peculiar language. Ruth's dream is about her and her husband both choosing to move on in their lives, but this transition is represented in her dream through the metaphor of death. Since when, Ruth may be asking, did death and divorce get to be such close bedfellows?

Death is a symbol for change and separation in dreams, and almost never should be interpreted literally. In other words, Ruth's dream is not precognitive, and neither she nor her husband needs to worry about a premature demise. On the contrary, this dream reflects the "death" of her marriage, which Ruth informs us is formally coming to an end after many years of drifting apart, and after two years of separation.

The many people who attend Ruth's funeral represent her awareness that she will receive a great deal of support from family and friends during this period of transition. The concern Ruth has for her husband is also represented. In her dream, she is the only person who attends his funeral, and even then she is only a ghost. Does Ruth worry that he will be alone again, without her there to help him, as she has in the past?

As a witness to her own death, Ruth writes that she "does not feel bad" that she is the one who has died. The meaning of her sentiment is clear: Ruth still cares for her husband, but she is ready to embrace her approaching transition.

"Rebirth"

I usually have enigmatic dreams, but the one I had last night beats them all by far. One of my closest friends (I am a woman) is Alan. Before being friends we flirted some, but nothing ever came of it. Now I consider him almost like a brother. I know I am still partially attracted to him and this has fueled many strange dreams/nightmares.

Last night I dreamed Alan and I were essentially flirting. He would come running down five flights of stairs and tease me to come get him. I would run to him, but then he would run up the stairs again. I would go up a couple of stairs, then give up and come back down. Then he would do it again and off again I would go, up to get him, only to see him running up, laughing again.

This went on about five or six times, until I grew tired of the game and just left. I think someone told me to go check on my table because Alan was there, so I walked back to the end of the stairs, where I had a table, to see Alan placing red roses on it, one by one with lots of care. He had a brilliant smile on his face. So I walked up to him and we kissed. But here comes the weird part.

As it happens, this place was some kind of passage place, and everyone went there to die and be reborn. I was a little scared but Alan took my hand. We took our clothes off and lay down together in a coffin to die together, so that our rebirth would be together. By this time I was *very, very* happy to be dying with him. And I woke. What is going on?

—*Silvia, Age 22, Single, Canada*

Who would have thought that Silvia's back-and-forth romance with Alan would wind up with both of them lying naked in a coffin, and that Silvia would feel so exquisitely happy about it! Some things can only happen in dreams. . . .

Sigmund Freud observed that stairs in dreams often have sexual associations, due to: a) the movements we make climbing them; b) the fact that we are trying to reach a destination; and c) that we often arrive at our goal short of breath.

Silvia acknowledges that she is attracted to Alan, and that she has flirted with him for quite some time. After a few rounds of a lover's dance, however (up and down the stairs), Silvia tires of the game and decides to leave. Significantly, at this point someone tells her to check her table. When Silvia does, she notices Alan carefully placing red roses on it. The symbolic meaning of Alan's act is not lost upon her. Roses in dreams—red roses especially—are symbols of passion and attraction. Soon enough, Silvia shares a kiss with her pursuer, and a magical transition in their relationship occurs.

Death in dreams is a symbol of change. Nudity in dreams, when we feel comfortable with our partner, is a metaphor for emotional transparency and intimacy. As Silvia sheds her clothes and prepares to die with her lover, she is indicating that she would like her present relationship status—as just friends—to pass away. Silvia would also like an intimate relationship, represented by her nudity, to be born in its place.

If Silvia has grown weary of "the chase" with Alan, her dream is a reminder to take a second look (or a fifth or sixth) at her good friend. Her powerful dream informs us that her relationship with Alan has reached an exciting transition. Silvia should enjoy her rebirth.

Deceased

Deceased: Dreams about the deceased are common, and should not be considered signs of paranormal activity or of supernatural contact. Dreams about visitations by the deceased often reflect desire for contact with them, and for emotional resolution. The inability to speak with or touch the deceased may reflect frustration or anger due to the deceased's departure; we are no longer able to communicate.

The dead typically appear fit and healthy in our dreams, and younger than their age at the time of their passing. They often reassure dreamers that they are okay, explain particularities of their death, and occasionally give advice. Many people believe the dead actually communicate with the living in dreams, and that the living are able to experience emotional closure, especially with someone who died suddenly. Many dream reports, if accurate, leave no option but to believe that contact actually was made.

◆ **Interpretation tip:** Try not to be frightened by dreams about the deceased. If you have gained emotional closure through a dream of contact, enjoy the mystery.

＊ ＊ ＊

Dreams about the deceased always cause us to wonder: Was contact really made? In "A Supernatural Date," a woman's extraordinary dream prompts her to take action in her waking life. Did she just have a brush with the supernatural? In "Saying Good-bye," a dreamer waits for her phone to ring, long after a family member has died. In her dream, she receives the call that was promised. Our final entry, "The Confirmation," shows a dreamer who still is wrestling with the grief caused by her husband's passing. This heartwarming dream should convince her of his love.

Dreams about the Deceased

"A Supernatural Date"

This dream occurred many years ago and has always haunted and perplexed me. The dream happened about two years after I divorced my first husband and had already married my current husband.

In my dream, I was visited by my ex-father-in-law (who had passed away the month our divorce became final). He insisted that I had to go visit his mother (my ex's grandmother), whom I had been very close to. He said she would enjoy seeing me and we should share a meal. It was very important that I visit her.

The dream didn't wake me up but I remembered it perfectly the next morning. I went to work and phoned my ex-grandmother at 9 A.M. I hadn't seen or spoken to her for a very long time. She was very happy to hear from me and I told her about the dream. She invited me over for dinner on Friday (the dream occurred on Monday night) and asked me to bring my wedding photos. I ordered a bouquet of flowers as a gift, and we had a very nice visit.

When I told her about it, she didn't seem at all bothered by my dream—just glad that it brought us together. Two weeks later I received a phone call from my sister-in-law, who said my ex's grandmother had suffered a stroke. About two weeks after that, she passed away. This has always confused me, but I've always been grateful that we were able to share that time together. Can you explain if this was some sort of psychic dream?

–*Jessica, Age 41, Married, USA*

If Jessica's dream wasn't psychic, the only other explanation is blind chance, and what are the odds of that? Before Jessica becomes spooked, however, it may help if she knows that more than 50 percent of Americans believe they have had precognitive dreams. They aren't the rule, but they are more common than one might think.

The body is in a unique physiological state when we dream. The musculature is deeply relaxed—much more relaxed than during nondreaming sleep—yet the brain, curiously, is as active (dreaming) as when we are awake. Given that so many people report psychic experiences during dreams, we are left to speculate whether the physiology of REM sleep plays a role. After all, an active brain in a resting body is the goal of most meditative disciplines. Are we especially sensitive to subtle energy when we dream?

Because her dream was extraordinary, Jessica listened to her inner voice and chose to make the dinner date that was requested. Though she is grateful she did, the entire experience has challenged some familiar assumptions, which Jessica finds troubling. Is it possible to have contact with the deceased? Do the dead know when the living are going to pass? Do the dead wait for their loved ones to join them? And just where is "the other side" anyway?

It is normal to lose our balance, momentarily, when an older worldview is replaced with a fresher one. Rather than feel destabilized by her dream (which surely is not the intent of the deceased), we hope Jessica's experience of contact simply initiates her into a heightened appreciation of life's true mysteries. One day, we will all learn the answers to these questions.

"Saying Good-bye"

I was riding in a Range Rover–type vehicle with my boyfriend and a group of his friends whom I recognized in the dream as people we share Friday nights with—for dinner and a movie. I remember a tense moment among the people in the vehicle and I asked to be let out. When I got out of the car, I walked into a house and saw beyond the front hallway my mom, my aunt, my grandmother (who is deceased), and my grandfather (also deceased). Someone else walked out of sight when I entered the room.

My mom said, "Oh, we didn't expect you to be here." My mom was very happy to see me, and everyone in the room welcomed me in. I remember walking further into the room, and at that point I was in a very bright room. The room had floor-to-ceiling French windows on every wall and was bathed in this fantastic light. The sky outside was blue and beautiful. Red and orange curtains hung from each window, billowing on the breeze blowing into the room. The images in the room—the curtains, the sky, the light—were all a surreal Technicolor. The breeze was warm and I could smell the air. I felt very comfortable.

Immediately after I entered the room I was hugging my dad, actually clinging to him, sobbing and asking him not to leave: "Don't go. Why do you have to leave?" He was hugging me and I felt such love from him. In this dream I could actually feel his hug. (Historically, in dreams I've had where touch was involved, I only had a thought that I was being touched. But in this dream, I actually felt my dad hugging me and comforting me).

I asked my dad if he would ever come back and he looked around the room and said, "No, Margot, I don't think I'll be back here again." My dad continued to hug me for what seemed like a lifetime, until I regained my composure and stopped crying. I don't remember leaving the room, but then I was back with the people from the beginning of my dream. I was walking to my boyfriend. I wanted to tell him what had just happened, to let him know that I'd just talked to my dad, and that I was sad that I might never see him again.

Before I could say anything to him, my boyfriend indicated that we were all leaving and for me to get in the vehicle (the one I was riding in at the beginning of my dream). I got into the backseat. I remember thinking that he would get in beside me, but instead the vehicle I was in filled up with other unidentified people. I watched my boyfriend get in another vehicle of the same type with other unidentified people and drive away.

Background: My dad was one of my best friends and confidants. Although we lived in different cities, I was in contact with him almost weekly, just to say hi, or whenever I had a problem and needed a sounding board. My dad died suddenly in his car this year—on the day after my birthday. I spoke to him on the telephone the night before he died, and the last thing he said to me was, "I'll call you tomorrow." It's been eight months, but in some illogical, childish way, I'm waiting for that call. Of course, it won't happen.

When I woke up from the dream, I was completely disoriented, and really felt that I had talked to my dad, had hugged him and clung to him. I felt his presence around me. Everything that I experienced in the dream (from start to finish) was with me when I woke up. My boyfriend asked me when I awoke what the dream was, but anxiety left over from the dream prevented me from telling him.

Although the dream happened a week ago, I remember every detail of it. It was the most vivid dream I believe I've ever had (or remembered) in my life.

—Margot, Age 22, Single, USA

Whenever someone we love dies suddenly, friends and family who are left behind feel a special type of loss. Because we are unprepared for the death, we are deprived of the opportunity for closure—a chance to say good-bye, a time to clear up lingering misconceptions or misunderstandings, and a chance for a final hug.

Judging by Margot's description, her dream allowed her to experience, very powerfully, the love she has for her father. Margot's father's love for her is reciprocated. They are together, and he holds Margot for what "seems like a lifetime." It is understood in her dream that a great distance separates them. Margot asks if her father will ever be back, but he tells her no. He has moved on in his life, and will not "be back here again."

In reports of contact with the newly dead, we are often left with the impression that the dead linger awhile among the living after passing on—checking on friends and family, and taking care of special cares or unresolved items. Once they are assured all is okay, they appear gently to move along. If Margot's father was preparing to move forward into the next phase of his life journey (they say it never ends), it appears he visited to assure her of his love, give her comfort and strength, and to say good-bye—for a while.

On either side of this extraordinary dream encounter, Margot's current boyfriend figures prominently. There is an uncomfortable feeling in the car at the beginning of the dream that causes Margot to ask to be let out. After her meeting with her father, Margot rejoins the group, but difficulties communicating resume. Margot wants to tell her boyfriend about her meeting, but before she can speak, he directs her to get into a car. Margot waits for him to join her, but as the dream ends, they are passengers riding in separate vehicles.

Cars in dreams are common metaphors for the self—for the direction we are headed in our lives. Difficulty communicating in dreams is a reflection of difficulty communicating in real life. If Margot's boyfriend occasionally does not listen well to her emotions about her father's passing, or if he appears to avoid the topic (wants to ride in a separate car), Margot may need to recognize that death, for many people, is a delicate and uncomfortable subject. Her father's passing has touched her deeply, and caused her to understand death, intellectually and emotionally, at an early age. Is this the distance that now separates Margot from her boyfriend?

The gift that death bestows upon the living is awareness that our hours in the sun, genuinely, are fleeting. In death's shadow we learn that every day is a good day to smell the roses, to perform a kind act, to contact an old friend, to breathe deep in the ocean of life. By providing contrast, death sharpens our vision of the miracle of life.

It appears that Margot's father did indeed keep his promise to call. At the same time, his visit opened a door that will remain open in Margot's life—a door to a profounder appreciation of life's genuine mysteries.

"The Confirmation"

In my grief following my husband's death, I constantly questioned whether he really loved me. In the dream, I am seated in the center chair of a long row of seats that are lined across a street and blocking traffic in both directions. My husband is busy passing out flyers to all the drivers of the cars we are blocking. When I ask what the flyer says, he hands me one. On the flyer is a list of ten things that he loves about me. I start to cry and when I look up, he is gone and I am no longer in the street.

Is this an answer to my doubts about his love? He died from lung cancer, and I was angry at him for dying instead of giving up his smoking and living on with me and his family.

He also came to me in a dream with a warning that the lock on my front door was broken, and he firmly told me to fix it. When I checked, it really was broken. I am still having a rough time letting go of guilty feelings and anger, even though it has been four years.

–Vanessa, Age 64, Widowed, USA

The early passing of Vanessa's husband reminds us of an old saying: "Death is hardest on those we leave behind."

Vanessa has contributed one of the most passionate displays of love ever recorded in a dream. A man loves his wife so much that to prove it he lines chairs across a busy street, blocks traffic in both directions, and while his wife sits and watches, he passes out flyers declaring the ten things he loves most about her. He may be crazy, but Vanessa knows her husband's heart is in the right place.

It's time for Vanessa to let go. Her husband loved her deeply, and judging by her other dream, he continues to watch out for her. When they meet in the next world, Vanessa can give him grief if he still smokes. Until then, Vanessa should forgive him, and enjoy the warmth that springs from a heart that is loved.

Engagement Ring

Engagement Ring: Symbol of a committed relationship. Feelings about the engagement ring reflect the dreamer's real-life feelings about an engagement or proposal. Unattractive rings or rings that do not fit indicate disappointment in a suitor, or feelings that the dreamer is unprepared to commit. If a dreamer is embarrassed to show her ring publicly, she may feel her engagement or status in a committed relationship is premature. Pleasant dreams about being proposed to by a suitor should not be interpreted as precognitive. Instead, a dreamer's emotional preparedness for marriage is indicated.

Ring: If a ring was received as an heirloom, the ring holds associations with family generally and with the family member who bequeathed the ring specifically. Lost rings symbolize feelings that one is losing contact with the person or memory. If a ring is damaged or a stone is missing, this may reflect disappointment in the relationship, or a separation or death.

♦ **Interpretation tip:** Lost, damaged, or unattractive engagement rings symbolize feelings of unpreparedness for a committed relationship. Are you sure you're ready?

* * *

Dreams about engagement rings cause springs of hope, and fears about commitment, to run freely in our hearts. Our first dreamer, in "Engagement Ring," has recurring dreams about being proposed to by her boyfriend. The rings she receives, however, are sending an important message. Our second dreamer, in "Drop the Rings," is under pressure to make a commitment. Is she ready? Our final entry, "Smash the Ring," shows a woman in transition, who is prepared to defend her newly won territory.

Engagement Ring Dreams

"Engagement Ring"

I have had a recurring dream in which my boyfriend proposes to me. In each dream there is something wrong with the ring. One time I thought it was ugly. Another time it was irritating to wear, causing a red spot on my finger. In all of the dreams I show the ring off and act happy, but inside I am unsure and disappointed by the ring.

My boyfriend and I have been dating on and off for four years. We argue a lot and often wonder if we should be together. What is this dream saying to me?

–Shelly, Age 22, Single, USA

Engagement rings are highly visible, public announcements that we have committed ourselves to a partner—who we trust will reward us with a lifetime of devotion, happiness, and growth.

Shelly's recurring dreams of engagement rings show that she is questioning her commitment to her current boyfriend. Is he "the one" with whom she really wants to spend the rest of her days? Should she keep trying to work things out, or is it time to walk away? The difficulties Shelly lists in the relationship—being on again, off again, and frequent arguments—are legitimate warning signs of incompatibility.

Shelly's dreams should not be interpreted literally as signs that her boyfriend doesn't have money or good taste (the ugly ring dream), or that he would miss getting her ring size right (the ring that causes a sore spot). On the contrary, Shelly's emotions in her dreams reveal its true meaning. The engagement ring is a symbol of the future of her relationship. When she tries it on for size and shares it with her friends, Shelly feels unsure and disappointed.

If Shelly knows inside that she and her partner aren't a match, the best thing she can do is answer the door—and gently step out of her partner's way. If this dance is over, a new one needs to begin.

"Drop the Rings"

Recently, I have been stressing over my relationship with my boyfriend. I love him very much, but we are in college now, and I feel pressure because all of our friends are breaking up. I am worried this will happen to us. Then, I had this dream.

I am at someone else's wedding, and I do not know the bride, but I know the groom. I am very late, so I run to the altar to apologize. When I get there, though, the groom turns into my boyfriend of one and a half years, and he asks me to marry him. The ring is very small and looks green. I agree, and the marriage goes on.

After the marriage, he drops the rings and we must look for them. I find mine and notice that the engraving, "I Love You, Jessica" is backward on the inside of it. The ring is also very ugly. Then we walk away from the wedding, and when I look down, I am holding a very small baby. I seem to understand that this is the baby of my new husband and I think, "Was I pregnant during the wedding?" And I do not know the answer.

I give the baby to my husband, and tell a group of women who have gathered to never have a baby at eighteen. I feel very strange that I gave birth at such a young age. However, when I go see my husband and my new baby, I feel very good inside, and very loved and happy. I'm not sure what this means since I got mixed messages. I felt loved and afraid at the same time.

–Jessica, Age 18, Engaged, USA

No wonder Jessica is confused. She didn't even know whose wedding she was attending, and next thing she knows, she is a new bride with a baby. That would be quite a day for anyone.

Jessica feels stressed about her commitment to her boyfriend because she is in college and all her friends are single. The marriage ceremony in the dream represents her commitment. Being "late to the wedding," however, is a familiar dream metaphor for feelings of being unprepared. Also, the ring Jessica's boyfriend gives her, another symbol of commitment, is "small and green," and Jessica thinks it is "ugly." After her boyfriend drops the rings on the floor (another sign of unpreparedness), Jessica notices the inscription on the inside of her ring is backward. (Can anything else go wrong?)

As if this weren't enough, Jessica is soon holding a newborn. The baby is small, which is a sign that any future plans Jessica and her boyfriend may have in this direction (having a baby) are *undeveloped* at this point in time. (Translation: Kids are still far off in the future.) As if to answer Jessica's own question about making such a big commitment so early in life, she tells a group of girls to "never have a baby at eighteen."

Jessica's dream reflects feelings that she is too young, at present, to commit fully to her boyfriend. The happiness she feels, however, when she visits him at the end of the dream, reflects the true love she feels for him.

This dream appears to be all mixed up, but its message actually is clear: It's time for Jessica to put a pause on her wedding plans. (We notice she signed her name "Engaged.") There's no reason to hurry, and it's too early for Jessica to be worrying about marriage, especially with the responsibilities of college on her mind. Jessica should tell her boyfriend that dating is fine, but that marriage and children will both come later in her life.

"Smash the Ring"

For the past five months I have been seeing an old lover from way back in my high school days. We had been apart for almost fifteen years and one day I just ran into him outside of my work. Sparks flew immediately and we fell in love all over again. The problem is that I am married. I recently have decided to leave my husband of eleven years to pursue this relationship—with the man who I believe is my soul mate. Now for my dream.

For some reason I was not able to find my boyfriend anywhere for almost two weeks. I had no idea where he was or why he would disappear without a trace, and without telling me. So one day he shows up with another woman, and she announced that they had just gotten married. I was so devastated. She showed off a huge diamond ring, which I snatched from her finger and proceeded to stomp on, until it was completely smashed and ruined.

Meanwhile, my boyfriend did not say anything. I asked him: "How could you do this to me?" He just stood there with an ashamed look on his face. Also, the woman he married was my brother-in-law's ex-wife. She and my boyfriend have never even met.

My boyfriend and I have a great relationship. I never have felt this way about anyone before, and he feels the same. I do not know what to make of this dream. Please let me know what you think. I am desperate to find out.

–Paige, Age 30, Separated, USA

Paige is nervous as she leaves her husband of eleven years to pursue a heated romance with an old boyfriend. The engagement ring in her dream symbolizes her hopes for a committed relationship with her new man, but significantly the ring is worn by another woman. Are Paige's hopes for her future misplaced?

Paige's dream reveals that some of her early enthusiasm for her new romance is being replaced with fear. Specifically, what will happen now if her boyfriend, in whom she has invested heavily, fails to perform as promised? Judging by her signature (Paige signs her name "Separated"), Paige has already burned a bridge with her husband. Will she be left alone?

Dreams about betrayal are common during periods of self-doubt and insecurity in relationships, but the difficulty Paige has communicating in her dream is most likely significant. In the dream she searches for her boyfriend for a period of two weeks, and is mystified that he could "disappear without a trace, and without telling me." Is her dream a sign that she already has recognized, on a subconscious level, gaps and partial communication in her relationship? Is her partner withholding important information from her? Does he hold more than one romantic interest?

The anger Paige feels in the face of betrayal is represented by her violent destruction of the engagement ring. Her boyfriend's refusal to defend himself, or to explain his actions, is a second reference to his difficulty expressing emotions. In an emotionally volatile time, the message of this dream is clear: Paige is advised to proceed carefully in her new relationship. Only time will tell whether the cracks she perceives in this knight's shining armor are real, or if they are only reflections of her fears.

Exam

Exam: Dreams about test-taking and exams reflect pressure to "pass a test" or to "graduate to the next level" in our personal or professional careers. The stress we feel in our waking life reminds us of how we felt in high school or college before we took an exam. Dreams about math, algebra, and calculus classes (subjects involving numbers) reflect concerns related to money and finance. Exams that involve two subjects may reflect a need to make a career choice.

Graduation: Dreams about successful graduation are happy dreams that symbolize positive transition to the "next level" of accomplishment in our personal and professional lives. We sense fulfillment and achievement, and receive admiration and respect from our peer group. Failure to graduate indicates feelings that we are falling behind and not advancing to the "next level."

School: Dreams about being in a school may reflect feelings that we are "learning a new subject" as we enter a new phase of our career. Schools are natural settings in teen dreams, and may hold reference to social anxiety and peer pressure, in addition to concerns about performance. Schools also carry references to obedience, to rules and hierarchies we adhere to, and to authorities we are required to respect.

Locker: Because lockers are the location of our personal belongings in school or at a gym, they are associated in dreams with concerns about identity. Not being able to locate one's locker, or difficulty remembering the combination, may symbolize doubts about one's identity or role among friends or classmates.

Principal: Principals are authority figures in dreams, like police and parents. They are most likely to appear in a school context.

♦ **Interpretation tip:** If you dream you are back in high school or college taking a test, identify the challenge in your waking life where you are concerned about your performance.

✳ ✳ ✳

Curiously, back-to-school dreams are not memories of an earlier, carefree period in our lives. Instead, we're always tense and anxious. We can't believe we forgot that last assignment.

In "Graduation Blues," a woman wishes she'd paid more attention in school. She'd have more confidence as she prepares to reach "the next level" in her waking life. In "Behind on My Revisions," a dreamer still worries about completing a final assignment—thirteen years after he already did it. In our final entry, "Missed Requirement," a twenty-nine-year-old man has disappointing dreams about being sent back to high school. Like all back-to-school dreams, it's not about the past: It's about the present.

Exam Dreams

"Graduation Blues"

I have a recurring dream (this has been going on for many, many years now) in which I am at my high school, trying to get to my class. I can not find my class, and I know that if I don't get to that class and make up my work, I am not going to graduate.

When I wake up from my dream my heart is pounding, and I sit up in bed and wonder if I have received my graduation diploma (which I did). Why do I constantly dream this same dream over and over again?

My opinion is that I wish I had tried harder and had not hooked school (missed school without permission) like I did the last two years of school.

I feel that I am way too stupid to go to college; and besides, if I failed at that, people would probably see just how stupid I really am. Perhaps I am just not satisfied with the way my life is turning out—what do you think?

–*Andrea, Age 45, Married, USA*

Back-to-school dreams are common among busy people—from professionals who are stressed about a "mountain" of tasks they know they must complete at their offices, to mothers who worry, occasionally, about how they will possibly coordinate their children's activities, in addition to their own. In each case, the dreamer is feeling the weight of a challenge that looms ahead. The anxiety reminds us of feelings we experienced in high school or college, as we prepared for a final exam: Will we pass the test?

In addition to representing immediate tasks that require completion, back-to-school dreams can also reflect broader issues. Finishing high school and college are both milestones in our lives. We expect that, upon completing them, we will arrive at a new location in our lives: good job, enough money, being happy in our work. If we feel behind in our lives—we have not yet arrived at a status we envisioned for ourselves (marriage, having children, career success)—we may feel like we are kids again, waiting to pass the exam, so we can graduate to the next level. Will we ever achieve our expectations of success?

Andrea's recurring dreams concern the subject of graduation. Rather than reflecting stress from her past, however, Andrea's dreams suggest doubts about her ability in her current life—to "graduate" to the next station that she envisions for herself. Andrea's real-life concerns may include a better job, a desired social status, or—it is hinted—a level of education that she feels is equal to her ability.

Andrea's dreams are calls to action. They are reminders of goals she has set for herself, and of the normal doubts and fears that accompany any new project or challenge. If Andrea enrolls in the college class she has been considering, she will soon be doubly rewarded. Her anxiety dreams will stop (she will be achieving her goals), and she will learn that, with maturity, she is a better student than she gives herself credit for.

"Behind on My Revisions"

I have a dream whose exact content I often can not remember, yet I wake up with the feeling that I am getting behind with my revisions and the examinations are only just around the corner. This leads to momentary panic. It can take several seconds for me to realize I have not taken an exam in over thirteen years and there are no tests to pass.

The dream is disturbing because it seems to be recurring since I took my finals at university. Is this my inner self trying to tell me to stop procrastinating and get on with changing my life, since I feel I have not achieved much since leaving university? Or is it a leftover trauma from the time of my finals, when my final-year project overran, almost into the time when I had to take my final papers? Is it possible to stop this dream in the future? I have been looking for the answer to this dream for over thirteen years.

–James, Age 37, Single, United Kingdom

James's dream is not a leftover trauma from the days, thirteen years ago, of his final papers and examinations. On the contrary, his dreams reflect stress over current issues—that remind him of the tension and self-doubt that he experienced when he was a student at university.

James acknowledges that he has doubts and insecurities regarding the progress of his career. His dreams about failing to graduate, accordingly, reflect fears that he will not achieve his expectations. The dreams also reflect angst about a continuing period of stagnation and procrastination in his life. James knows that he needs to get on with changing his life, but he has been unable to take the first steps.

If James feels he is in a rut, his dream is an encouragement to recognize the goals that he has for himself, and to initiate concrete steps in his daily life to advance himself forward. Most likely, James will find a talk with a career counselor, to learn what opportunities are available to him, both practical and reassuring. The journey of a thousand miles begins with a single step, and James's recurring dream is a clear sign that he wants to get started.

"Missed Requirement"

I have a recurring dream that I have to go back to school to fulfill some requirement I missed previously. I'm twenty-nine. And it is usually high school that I have to go back to, although sometimes it's university. There are usually other friends who have to go back, too, but not people I consider really good friends. It's usually a pretty disappointing dream and I wake up feeling set back or discontented.

–Christian, Age 29, Single, Canada

Christian's dream is a good illustration of the frustration and disappointment that characterizes back-to-school dreams. Does Christian feel that he is falling behind on his career goals, stuck in a frustrating job, or unhappy with his romantic progress? If the dreams arrive in concert with stressful periods at work, Christian may be worried about his ability to "complete an assignment" or "pass the test" in the eyes of his coworkers. The message of test-taking dreams is always the same: It's time to rise to the occasion, and to begin working on our goals. The sooner we do, the better we will feel.

Ex-Lover

Ex-lover: Surprise! Ex-lovers often appear in dreams just when our relationship with a new lover escalates in commitment (engagement, wedding date, children). Accordingly, dreams about being romantically involved with an ex frequently represent fears about commitment with a current lover, rather than genuine attraction to the ex. Similarly, if you dream your spouse or lover is reunited with an ex, ask if you have been feeling insecure lately, or inadequate, in your relationship.

Ex-lovers may represent a lingering sexual or emotional attraction, especially if the relationship ended abruptly, without closure. Do you still wonder if it could have worked out differently? Do you miss qualities that your ex possessed? Ex-lovers who continue to pursue former partners in real life may show up negatively in dreams, as haunting or stalking characters.

♦ **Interpretation tip:** If an ex-lover appears in your dreams, ask if you achieved emotional closure with this partner. Is it time to make contact, or is it time to move on?

✳ ✳ ✳

Will our ex-lovers ever go away? "First Love" is a powerful insight into the true motivation that underlies most fantasies of ex-lovers. Similarly, "Engaged" provides eloquent testimony to the power of unspoken romance. (If they don't talk back, what's not to like?) Our next entry, "The Return Fantasy," highlights the difference between the ones we rejected and the ones who rejected us. Our final dream, "Walk Away," shows a man in transition, who decides that his feet, indeed, are strong enough to carry him forward.

Ex-lover Dreams

"First Love"

I married the man I adore and we have recently found out that we are to become first-time parents. For the last two months, however, I have been having dreams of a man that I knew all through my school years. He was my first boyfriend, kindergarten through the eighth grade, but we have not dated in at least nine years and I have not seen or heard of him in at least five years. I can honestly say I do not think about him at all.

My feelings were never on an intimate level with this guy. We remained friends all through school, but to say that we were attracted to one another once we got older is a stretch. I have moved away and not even thought of home or any of my old friends in several years. This guy was not my high school sweetheart, nor did he have any other large importance in my early adult life. Why am I dreaming of him all of a sudden? Now, in my dreams we are not sexually intimate, but we are closely connected. We will kiss and hold hands and hug, but I have not had a sex dream about him. Can you please help? I am very distraught about this whole thing. Why now after all these years is he in my dreams?

–Alondra, Age 23, Married, USA

Alondra's dreams about her first boyfriend—a person whom she has not thought of in over five years, much less considered as a viable romantic partner—began at the same time she learned she was pregnant with her first child. Like other men and women facing significant escalations of romantic commitment, Alondra is nervous about the commitment that childbearing represents, and her mind is working overtime: "Is my husband the right partner? Are we really going to make it until death do us part?"

Alondra is dreaming about this other man because as a young girl (kindergarten through eighth grade) she almost certainly fantasized about—and even role-played—being married and having children with him, like most children do.

Because Alondra has a realistic sense of this man's location in her life—she has not had any adult relationship with him—her dreams are harmless, yet also illuminating. Now that she is confronted with the reality (there's no turning back from parenting) that this childhood fantasy really won't ever materialize—she is clearly mourning its passing.

Alondra is distraught over her dreams, but she has no reason to hide from or resist the feelings expressed in them. (In fact she can rest assured that her husband has experienced his own share of commitment jitters.) On the contrary, Alondra's dreams are simply letting her know that she is making a significant transition in her life—from young woman to mother. As we all know, she has a lot to look forward to.

"Engaged"

I keep on dreaming about this guy who was a friend in high school. Although he didn't know it, I was completely in love with him, and to this day I am very fond of him. I have not seen him in about seven years because I went away to college and lost contact with him. We wrote to each other for about a year after I left.

I keep on having dreams where we are spending time together as boyfriend and girlfriend. I have had this dream three times in the past week or so. Within the last month I have also dreamed about us having a child together.

I am getting married in September. Am I getting the wedding jitters, or do these dreams have a meaning???

–Shannon, Age 25, Engaged, USA

It's a bit disconcerting, isn't it? Shannon is engaged to a man she loves very much—and now her mind starts playing tricks on her. Instead of Shannon's future husband starring in her dreams—him carrying her across a threshold into their new life together—it's someone from her past whom, granted, she always had a thing for, but she never really connected with. And Shannon is dreaming about having children. Could the timing of her dreams be any worse—or more significant?

To allay fears that she may be marrying the wrong man, it is important that Shannon recognize how little she actually knows her dream man. They were good friends in high school—when she had a secret crush on him—and when Shannon corresponded by mail during her first year of college. But since then, Shannon hasn't seen or spoken to this man in seven years. More important than the time that has elapsed, however, is the time when Shannon's dream began—right before her wedding. If this old love is really such a dream man, how come Shannon wasn't dreaming about him all along?

In light of her upcoming nuptials, it is natural for Shannon to be flipping through the Rolodex in her mind, as it were, of past loves she has known. Nevertheless, there is also genuine danger in Shannon allowing herself to overfantasize a past love—or in Shannon's case (even worse), a past crush. Shannon runs the risk of idealizing a relationship that actually never existed. If she keeps this fantasy alive in her mind, then she will invariably begin to compare her real relationship (with her fiancé) to it. This comparison is unfair to both Shannon and her fiancé. She will be disappointed when the relationship doesn't measure up to her fantasy, and she will also be frustrated that her husband isn't like her dream man.

Naturally, Shannon is wondering if her dreams are a sign from her subconscious to make contact with this person. If she thinks it will ease her worried mind, there certainly is no harm in calling him up. If, on the other hand, Shannon recognizes that she is just nervous about getting married and that she really loves her fiancé, then it may be best to let this dream rest and begin concentrating on the real world.

"The Return Fantasy"

I have recurring dreams about a man I was once very much in love with. Manuel broke my heart and moved away. Since then, I have had very "real" dreams about him trying to come back to me, but in each instance, something keeps us apart. Upon awakening, I have a sense of sweetness, love, and joy that is unlike anything I have ever experienced. I am currently happily married to a very wonderful man who satisfies me in every way. So why does Manuel keep coming back to me in my sleep?

—*Valerie, Age 31, Married, USA*

The lovers who break our hearts are different. We keep on wondering why, and we keep on leaving the door open—no matter what reality tells us. Why do we do this? Usually it has to do with our own ego. The key factor in the dynamic is that they left us—and not the other way around. They didn't want us. But we still want (need?) the confirmation of our desirability and attractiveness—so we let the return fantasy linger.

Valerie's dreams nevertheless show a realistic assessment of her situation. In her dreams, something always keeps her apart from her ex. This "something" is the real world.

Valerie deserves to be congratulated on building such a great relationship with her husband. This is a genuine accomplishment. As for her return fantasy, Valerie needs to let it go. She's outgrown it.

"Walk Away"

About six months ago I ended a relationship (it was a bad breakup). Last night I dreamt I was riding on a bus with her. Her ex-husband was driving. I never met the man but was absolutely sure it was her ex. The bus stopped and I got off for a while. When I got back on I walked down the aisle and noticed that everyone on the bus had an expression of great loss or sadness (I kept thinking "wreck" when I was looking at them). I did not want to be around them.

The bus started moving and I walked to the front. The lady I had broken up with was stretched out across one of the seats that sat sideways, with her hands tightly covering her face and bawling out loud. She was saying something but I could not make it out—("I can't do this anymore"?). I stepped down into the exit and the driver turned to me and said, "She's at it again! Had enough of her yet?" My first response was to defend her, but instead I asked him to let me off.

He drove for a while; we came to the bottom of a hill and then went straight for a couple of blocks, and made a right turn. Went one block and made a left, where he stopped and let me off from the middle lane of a three-lane, one-way street. I was on the curb and turned to walk to the central bus plaza (where the bus would have ended up if I had stayed on). But after a couple of steps I thought, "I am about halfway from my home here." I then turned around and walked. My last thought before waking up was wondering if my shoes would last until I got home. I woke up feeling pretty good.

–Nicholas, Age 46, Single, USA

Sometimes it feels pretty good to "get off the bus"—especially when the bus is a symbol of a bad relationship. In the aftermath of a failed relationship, it is apparent that Nicholas has also gained some empathy for the bus driver—his lover's ex-husband.

It is always difficult to walk away from someone with whom, at one time, we felt so much potential. Nicholas's dream, however, indicates he has grown tired of many of his ex's qualities. In the dream she appears emotionally out of control (an "emotional wreck"), and everyone who surrounds her on the bus has "an expression of great loss or sadness." Is it Nicholas's opinion that his ex brings sadness to everyone she touches?

The appearance of his ex's former husband—who is driving the bus—suggests Nicholas's feeling that he is "walking in his footsteps." In their attempts to build a relationship with this woman, it is likely that both men experienced similar difficulties. Accordingly, Nicholas holds a sympathetic view of the bus driver's predicament. In the dream he does not bother to defend his ex to him, and also agrees with his advice to "get off the bus"—the same decision the bus driver made several years ago.

Nicholas's dream indicates that his ex-girlfriend has her share of emotional problems. Nicholas, however, appears to have realized that he is not obligated to stay involved in an unhealthy relationship. As for his resolve to stick to his decision—represented by the ability of his shoes to carry him home—it is evident that Nicholas believes he has "plenty of soul" for the trip. He awakens with an emotional confirmation that he made the right decision. (Emotional health feels good, doesn't it?)

Eyesight

Eyesight: Dreams about having difficulty seeing are common metaphors for an inability to see clearly in waking life. If we dream that a friend, business partner, or relative is blind or can not see clearly (he or she has lost her eyes, glasses, or contact lenses), we may be perceiving a blind spot, weakness, or area of naïveté in this person. Exaggerated eyes or glasses (on another) may indicate that someone can see you clearly, or perceive your true motivations. Oversized glasses or contact lenses may symbolize an attempt to absorb a large amount of information, especially at work. Something in our eye indicates a development that is annoying—that we are experiencing difficulty managing, or which is causing us embarrassment. Closed eyes symbolize unconsciousness, lack of awareness, or not wanting to see. Inability to maintain eye contact indicates avoidance of intimacy. Loss or injury to the eye suggests impaired ability to see, due to emotional stress or trauma.

◆ **Interpretation tip:** What issue are you avoiding? Can't you see it? Note the location (work, childhood home, automobile) and people in the dream (coworker, sibling, romantic partner) for clues to the issue or relationship in question.

* * *

Difficulty seeing in a dream reflects difficulty seeing in real life. In "Eyes Fall Out," a young woman, clearly, is having a bad makeup day. Is the real reason her eyes fall out, however, because she needs to "take a look at herself"? "My Cousin Is Blind" shows how the blindness of others often acts as a symbol for naïveté in dreams. Are we surprised that our dreamer is older, and therefore thinks she is wiser, than her younger cousin? Our final dream, "A Clear View," shows the importance of vision generally in dreams. Our dreamer's ability to see clearly in her waking life is reflected in her dream.

Eyesight Dreams

"Eyes Fall Out"

In my dream I don't know where I am, but I have the feeling my parents are nearby. I'm trying to do something to my eyes (probably remove my makeup), but it's very difficult, so I use a solution. The makeup comes off: mascara and false lashes I had worn a long time ago, and which I thought I had removed. (I've never worn false lashes but I've been intending to buy some for some time now.)

But with my makeup the top of my eyes and a part of my lids also come off. Apparently these are detachable and the doctor usually does this when examining your eyes. It feels a little bit strange, but it doesn't hurt at all.

I look in the mirror to try to put back the pieces. My eyes look strange. I still have the lids and lashes but they're very thin and you can tell there's a piece missing from both my eye and lid. In order to put the pieces back together I have to take out the rest of my eyes— which also come out easily—like they're supposed to. I can still see, even though I have no eyes left (they're in my hand).

I keep trying to put back all the pieces, but I can't. The pieces are very slippery and I can't put them back in place. So I ask my dad what to do. He tells me that the doctor did the same thing to him when he had his eye operation. (My dad did have a few eye operations, but a long time ago, before I was born.) Again, I have no idea where I am, so finding a doctor to put my eyes together seems impossible. So I continue to try and fix them but I can't.

By now I'm starting to get frustrated, and because the pieces are very fragile, a piece gets crushed between my fingers. Still, that doesn't worry me too much, and I continue my useless struggle.

I have a lot of dreams in which I get frustrated about something that doesn't work or I can't do. Also my eyesight isn't perfect. I wear glasses (well, more contacts lately), but I can manage without them. They're only for long distances.

I have a vague suspicion this dream is about my friend with whom I had a fight that day. The situation with him is complicated, but to cut it short: we met in a chat room, we talked for two months, we met in person, it didn't work, I was *very* upset, my best friend got in the middle, I ended the friendship with her afterward, and I'm still talking with him (a lot). Anyway, I'm not over him or what happened (this was four months ago) and I wonder why he's still talking to me if he didn't want to be my boyfriend. (He didn't reject me, but he didn't make any moves in that direction—even though while chatting he was all for a relationship.) Thank you very much for your time.

–Erica, Age 19, Single, England

Erica's dream is a combination of three familiar dream metaphors. As the dream begins, she is removing her makeup in a mirror—a sign that her dream reflects concerns about appearance. Significantly, Erica is also removing a pair of false eyelashes that she thought, in the dream, she had removed a long time ago. Finally, after Erica takes out her eyeballs to repair the damage done by removing her makeup, she experiences difficulty replacing her eyes—a direct allusion to difficulty seeing.

The fight Erica had with the man she fancies (whom she has sacrificed a best friend for) most likely is the cause of this dream. When he chose not to begin a romantic relationship after they met in person, it's natural that Erica would wonder what the problem was. Before they met (while she was chatting on-line) he was "all for a relationship." Was it something, then, about her appearance that caused him to cool his pursuit?

The false eyelashes are a second reference to appearance. In the wake of this unspoken rejection, Erica most likely has thought about ways of enhancing her appearance. Curiously, though, in Erica's dream she also thought she had removed these eyelashes "a long time ago." Is it possible the false eyelashes allude to her on-line disguise that she thought she had removed when she met her friend in person several months ago?

The difficulty Erica experiences replacing her eyeballs indicates difficulty seeing. Aside from the obvious metaphor—that she doesn't understand her on-line friend's motivation—is she also confused by some of her own actions of late? Specifically, in pursuit of this on-line romance, Erica tells us she has lost contact with one of her best friends. As her relationship with this man continues to be disappointing, is it possible that Erica feels she has lost her direction?

Has Erica considered swallowing her pride, and reestablishing contact with her best friend? As for her cyber-pal, it may be time to let him drift gently back to the world of chat rooms only. Erica's dream indicates that it's time to get her values and priorities clearly in focus.

"My Cousin Is Blind"

Recently I dreamt that my little cousin, Julia, married her longtime boyfriend. However, in the dream she was losing her eyesight and was told by a doctor that she would be completely blind by her wedding day.

I was really upset by this—especially over the fact that she wouldn't see her wedding dress. However, both Julia and Ben were totally unfazed by this traumatic news.

Two weeks after I had the dream, Julia told me that she and Ben had got engaged (which is great news) but I'm still really haunted by my dream!

I'm very close to Julia, and have been her "responsible elder" throughout school and our younger years. Could the dream signify a reluctance to accept that she's all grown-up?

–*Daniela, Age 29, Married, Australia*

Daniela's insight into her dream shows twenty/twenty vision. She still thinks her little cousin is too young to get married. (Daniela is reluctant to accept the fact that she's "all grown-up.") Her dream reflects this concern by showing her heading into her wedding day "blind." And does her little cousin care? Not one bit! (Love is blind, doesn't Daniela remember?)

Daniela writes that Julia's engagement is great news, but her dream suggests that she still has reservations. It is true that being older, she indeed may "see better" some of the difficulties and potential problems that Julia today can not. And now that Julia has cast her vote, a period of Daniela's relationship with her is drawing to a close. Does she worry how Julia will fare—without her "big sister" there to guide her?

Daniela has been Julia's "responsible elder" most of her life. Now that Julia is stepping bravely, if a bit naively, into her future, it is time to support her, and keep her reservations to herself. All "parents," at some point, have to let go. And then they have to be content to watch their handiwork progress from a distance.

"A Clear View"

I dream I wake up and go to my back door. It smells fresh and wonderful outside. I look at my neighbor's yard and the shrubbery is completely cut down. I can see his house and everything completely. That dream ends and I'm walking on a sandy beach. It also smells wonderful. I feel calm and at peace. I see a conch shell. I pick it up and turn it over. I can see into it like a movie camera. I see my ex-husband. He is doing things I never imagined him doing: drinking heavily, taking drugs, and having sex with lots of other women. It's like I'm seeing someone I never knew at all.

I come from a Christian background, and I divorced one and a half years ago because my husband was using drugs, was abusive, and was running around on me. I found out about all this suddenly. I gave him a choice, and he chose other women and drugs. I have two children—one is handicapped. I recently dated a neighbor briefly. We met because our yards join and his shrubs had overgrown into my yard. We spent a day trimming them so my son could swing without them hitting him in the face. They are still overgrown, but trimmed. My neighbor is a fine Christian. He told me he felt I still had unforgiveness in my heart against my ex. I really don't think so. He may be moving because of a job transfer, so we have not pursued our friendship. I don't know what the part of my dream about my neighbor means. I think the part about my ex is that I don't think I ever knew him.

–*Karen, Age 30, Divorced, USA*

When Karen looks out her back door and views her neighbor's house, the air smells fresh and wonderful. She also notices his yard. In the dream, the shrubs she trimmed recently with her neighbor are entirely cut back. This allows her to "see his house and everything completely." The metaphor employed by Karen's dream relates to vision. She is able to "see" this fine man—represented by his house and yard—plainly. Nothing is hidden or obscured from view.

As if to compare and contrast these two men in her mind, Karen next finds herself walking along a sandy beach. Just as a conch shell in real life allows us to "eavesdrop" on a distant ocean, Karen's dream conch opens a window that allows her to view her ex-husband's past (and present) activities: drinking, drugs, and women.

Beaches in dreams are symbolic locations of resolution, because they are areas where conscious (land) and unconscious (water) forces meet. Her neighbor has suggested that Karen still holds feelings of unforgiveness in her heart, but Karen's dream suggests otherwise. From this location of resolution, Karen is able to view her ex plainly, with a sense of peace and perspective.

Christian wisdom teaches us to hate sin, but to always forgive the sinner. After a disappointing first marriage, it is clear that Karen feels relieved to be free of her former husband, and that she can "see clearly" the values she needs in a future partner.

Faceless

Faceless: Faceless people in dreams indicate that the identity of a person is unknown in waking life, or is camouflaged to protect the dreamer from making a painful recognition at the conscious level.

Faceless lovers are common in dreams that reflect anticipation of romance or marriage with a partner who is unknown to the dreamer. If a dreamer is already romantically involved, faceless lover dreams suggest romantic dissatisfaction—the dreamer is searching for "someone else"—whom he or she has not yet met.

Chased by a faceless person suggests that the fear or emotion you are "running from" is not specifically identified. Recurring dreams of chase by faceless persons may represent memories of repressed and avoided traumas. Can you identify the perpetrator of the trauma by clues located in the dream (gender, location of the dream, clothing worn, your age in the dream)?

Please also see: "Chase."

♦ **Interpretation tip:** If the dream is disturbing, ask if you are avoiding recognizing difficult feelings about a friend, family member, loved one—or yourself.

* * *

What can be more puzzling, or frustrating, than a dream about a faceless lover? "My True Love" shows a young woman with a longing for romance who wonders if her dream lover will ever reveal himself. "Faceless Man" is submitted by a dreamer who wants to know: Why does his girlfriend keep dreaming about a faceless stranger? Our final dream, "Shadow on the Wall," instructs us that some things in life are meant to be unknown—until we choose to fill in the blanks.

Faceless Dreams

"My True Love"

My dream starts with me walking behind what I guess is my true love. He holds my hand and leads me past some trees to a clearing. I can't see his face. I'm walking a step or two behind him, but I can never get a clear view of his face.

When we come to the clearing, it's next to a lake or body of water. We go to sit down on a blanket he laid out for us when I start to have an out-of-body experience. I'm now looking at both of us as we stare out across the water, watching the moon. I can see myself but still can only see the back of his head. Then we sit to watch the sun rise. This is a recurring dream.

Background: I am single, but am dating someone very special to me. The info you need to know is that I love romance. I would really like the fairy-tale ending, but of course that's not likely to happen.

–Zoe, Age 22, Single, USA

Who is this mystery man, and when will he and Zoe meet in real life?

Zoe's dream is an excellent example of the frustration that faceless lover dreams can cause. Because Zoe is a romantic, it is natural that she dreams, from time to time, of her ideal mate. Her dreams are enjoyable, and they are recurring, but there is always one nagging frustration. No matter how hard Zoe tries, she can never plainly see her lover's face. She always follows behind him as they walk, or he turns his head when she positions herself for a better view.

Zoe writes that she is currently involved with someone special, but her dreams suggest that her heart is still undecided. The meaning of Zoe's mysterious dream is that she has not yet met her romantic ideal. Rather than mislead her by making up a face, her dream instead is instructing Zoe that this person, genuinely, is unknown.

When Zoe does meet her true love, she may know him by this sign: Her faceless lover dreams will vanish like a sunset, and will trouble her no more.

"Faceless Man"

I have a wonderful relationship with my girlfriend, who is a very mature twenty-one-year-old. We are the best of friends and love each other very much. The only problem is that she keeps easing away from commitment.

Sometimes I think she just wants to take her time, but other times I feel like it's something more. She told me recently that a faceless man keeps reappearing in her dreams. I wonder if there may be some relationship between these two things.

—Steven, Age 19, Single, USA

Steven is a nineteen-year-old man dating a "very mature" twenty-one-year-old woman. His girlfriend keeps easing away from a committed relationship, however, and tells him she keeps dreaming about a "faceless man." Steven wants to know: Is the faceless man a sign to move on? Is his girlfriend trying to "drop a hint"?

Faceless people appear in our dreams in two contexts: when we are avoiding painful awarenesses (including memories) in our lives, or when we are uncertain about the future. Because Steven's girlfriend is not chased or attacked in her dreams—clues that would alert us that disturbing feelings are involved—her dreams about a faceless man, like Zoe's, instead suggest uncertainty about the future. In response to Steven's pressure to agree to a committed relationship, her dreams about a faceless man do indeed hold symbolic import: Steven's girlfriend is not ready to commit.

"Shadow on the Wall"

My boyfriend and I recently broke up because he moved two thousand miles away. We both feel that things could work out for us in the future, but we also agree that some time apart would help us to know what it is like to be alone for a while (for growing purposes).

Last night before I went to sleep I asked for an answer in regard to the future of our relationship. I also asked to see who I would be with in times to come. I dreamt that my boyfriend and I were making love in an unfamiliar room. We were talking about how good it felt to be together again.

While we were making love I noticed his cat in the corner. It jumped up on a bookshelf and cast an enormous shadow on the wall. The strangest thing about the shadow was that it had blank spaces where the cat's eyes would be. That was the end of the dream. What in the world does this mean?

–Kaylee, Age 18, Single, USA

Before going to bed, Kaylee incubated a question that she hoped would be answered in a dream. Kaylee wants to know: Whom will she be with in times to come? Will she still be with her boyfriend, from whom she is currently separated? Or will there be another lover in her life? With a head full of hope resting on a pillow, Kaylee sleeps with confidence that her dreams will allow her to see the future.

In a dream remarkable for its reference to the unknown, Kaylee finds herself pleasantly reunited with her current boyfriend. The happiness they share, and their intimacy, are both positive reflections on their relationship. The enormous shadow cast by the cat, however, is a classic dream symbol representing the unknown. (Dream analyst Carl Jung wrote volumes about the shadow as a symbol of unknown aspects of the self.) Significantly, Kaylee's attention in the dream is focused on the identity of the shadow, represented by the cat's eyes. Can Kaylee see her future? Can she see the face of her future romantic partner? The dream gives a disappointing, and at the same time empowering, answer: no.

What is the meaning of Kaylee's mysterious dream? The future is undecided. Only Kaylee has the power to choose her partner—whose eyes will replace this shadow.

Falling

Falling: Falling in a dream symbolizes lack of emotional support in our waking lives, and uncertainty about the future. Falling dreams are common during periods of emotional irresolution and uncertainty: separations, divorces, difficulties at school, abrupt job loss or transition, personal hardship, or the death of a spouse or partner. Fears of landing (hitting the ground) represent uncertainty about the future (we don't know "where we are going to land") and fears about survival. Dreamers may fall endlessly, onto sharp objects, into water, or "through the earth." In all cases, the ground (support) has been "pulled out" from underneath them.

Most dreamers awaken from falling dreams just before they hit the ground. This is the origin of the popular myth that "if you hit the ground, you will die in real life." Dream reports of hitting the ground, however—of bouncing off it, falling through it, or of dying upon impact (the dreamer witnesses his or her own death, and the dream continues)—are common. The myth is false.

Hypnagogic hallucinations: Falling dreams that occur immediately upon falling asleep are known as hypnagogic jerks, and are not assigned special psychological significance. This is an involuntary response to the relaxation of the balancing mechanism in the inner ear that occurs naturally with sleep onset.

◆ **Interpretation tip:** If you dream about falling, ask yourself what event recently caused you to "lose your sense of support." Are you worried about the future?

✳ ✳ ✳

Falling dreams alert us to the fact that we have entered a period of emotional free fall or material insecurity. In "Fall into Water," a woman's recurring dreams about falling have begun to give her the creeps. Is there an easier solution to her dreams other than avoiding the swimming pool all summer? In "Cliff-Hanger," a responsible woman is worried about managing her growing responsibilities. Will she learn to reduce her obligations, to get her feet back on the ground?

Falling Dreams

"Fall into Water"

I do not always have the same dream but it is always the same theme. I dream I am falling into oceans or deep bodies of water.

I always know before I fall that I am going to fall. In my dreams I replay the moment right before I fall over and over again, so that I can avoid falling, but I always fall. I am usually in a car, although I have sometimes just appeared in the middle of deep water. As a result of these dreams I am developing a deep fear of water. I can't even enjoy the beach and I seldom go into pools, although I am fascinated by sea animals.

I have been having these dreams since I can remember (as a child), but in the past few years they have taken their toll on me. I think it could be many possibilities. One, a past-life experience. Two, fear of failing or an unconscious feeling of current failure. Or perhaps it is my own way of letting myself know I'm having or approaching a mood low.

I do not have any mood disorders, or any that have been diagnosed. Please help. I would like to enjoy the beach again, and be able to go swimming or driving near water.

–*Ruth, Age 27, Separated, USA*

Ruth informs us when she signs her dream report that she is separated from her husband. This fact lets us know there is more than enough uncertainty in Ruth's life to explain her falling dreams—without Ruth having to worry about a past-life experience!

Separation in a marriage is an incomplete status. Ruth isn't happily married, nor does she possess the closure of divorce. What is the result? Ruth's personal life is on hold, and she doesn't know where she stands. The lack of physical and emotional support that Ruth feels in her waking life, and her uncertainty about the future, are experienced as a "free fall" in her dreams.

Water is conspicuously present in all of Ruth's dreams. Because water is a consistent symbol for emotions, Ruth's dream about being stuck in a car, as she sinks into the water, is a compelling metaphor that shows a woman surrounded by overwhelming emotions as she tries to reach a destination in her life. Because she is thinking about her dreams literally, instead of metaphorically, Ruth has developed a significant phobia about water, and now doesn't even like to swim in a pool or drive near a beach.

Ruth has noticed a correlation between the frequency of these dreams and periods of instability in her waking life (occasionally in childhood, and now more recently, during this period of separation). Ruth's dreams are clear warnings that she is overwhelmed emotionally. If she isn't already visiting a relationship counselor, her dreams are encouraging her to take the first step, and make an appointment. The more control Ruth asserts over her future, the sooner her dreams about falling will vanish. When they do, it will be time for a relaxing, and well-deserved, swim at the beach.

"Cliff-Hanger"

Background information: I started a new job about seven months ago. I'm happy in the department and things are going well. I've been married for a year next month. The main source of stress in my life is credit card debt.

I have had dreams in the past that I am falling, usually off a roller coaster or an elevator. However, my most recent falling dream has me hanging off the side of a mountain. I'm holding on for dear life and crying while I seem to be waiting for someone to help me. At the same time, I'm looking down and wondering if I am going to die from the fall.

–Danielle, Age 27, Newly Married, USA

As a newly married woman, we know Danielle has had an exciting year. (Weddings are always "roller coaster" rides of emotion.) In her professional life, she also has begun a new position—happily with a company she likes.

Roller coasters are common symbols in dreams that reflect abrupt fluctuations in our emotional lives. (First we're up, then we're down.) Elevators also symbolize emotional ups and downs, but often in the context of our business careers. Because Danielle's dream life is full of roller coasters, elevators, and tall mountains, we know she has had plenty of "highs and lows" recently. The fact that she is falling off these vehicles, or hanging from the side of a mountain, lets us know that she has been worried about "hanging on" during an occasionally wild ride.

Danielle's latest falling dream significantly includes a change of location. As her life begins to settle down, Danielle's fears of falling no longer include a roller coaster (her relationship) or an elevator (her career). Now her biggest concern appears to be a "mountain" of debt. In her dream she is hanging on to the side of a mountain, but she is crying, and wishing that someone would rescue her from her plight. Her fear of death as she looks down at the ground below represents her fears for her survival. Will she ever be able to pay down her debt, and achieve financial security?

Danielle has "held on" and successfully resolved her relationship and career issues. If she shows the same tenacity paying off her debt that she has demonstrated elsewhere in her life, she and her husband will be back on solid ground in no time.

Fire

Fire: Fire in dreams is often a symbol of transition, because it destroys objects and changes them from one state to another. Fire also functions as a consistent symbol of warning and urgency. If a parent dreams her child is caught in a fire, for example, she may be concerned about a new period of growth she is witnessing (transition) that is causing her alarm and which requires urgent attention. Fire can also be a symbol of passion and creation, as in "a smoldering fire" or burning desire. In the context of a home, fire can be a symbol of familial warmth, as in a fireplace. Dreams about fire should not be interpreted as precognitive.

Please also see "House": "Defending My Home."

Fire truck: Symbol of crisis, emergency, and desire for assistance. A threat exists that the dreamer needs help with. Can you identify the urgent situation?

◆ **Interpretation tip:** Note the location of the fire for clues to its meaning. If your dream is accompanied by feelings of urgency, ask what situation in your waking life wants your immediate attention.

* * *

When something burns in a dream, it's a clear sign that we need to pay attention. "Car on Fire" shows a woman who has a destination she wants to reach. The situation is urgent! "Smoldering Desire" reveals a woman whose passion is emerging. Can she capture a burning vision on her sketchpad, to assist her memory of it, before she is forced to hide it away?

Fire Dreams

"Car on Fire"

Last night I dreamt that I was stuck in my car and it was on fire. I was in the backseat and was holding my baby, although I have no children in real life. The fire was almost completely engulfing the car except for me and the baby.

I turned away from the fire and could feel my back burning, but my primary concern was the baby. I couldn't open the doors, but just as we were about to burn up, I remember that the back window was built to be kicked out if necessary. So, I kicked out the back window and got the baby out of the car, but I woke up (sweating) before I could get out.

I have no idea what it all means, but here's what's been going on with me: I was just a bridesmaid (again) this last weekend and I have had the blues the last couple of days about my twenty-seventh birthday this week. I don't usually obsess about these kinds of things and it really bothers me that I have let it get me down. I am single and *all* of my friends are getting married. I made the decision yesterday to go for my MBA.

—Esther, Age 27, Single, USA

Judging by Esther's dream, we have to ask if things aren't "getting warm" over in her part of town? All her girlfriends are getting married, and it appears that their nuptials are putting Esther in "the hot seat."

The fire in Esther's dreams is a metaphor for the pressure Esther feels to catch up with her friends, all of whom are getting married, while she is still single. To make matters worse, her twenty-seventh birthday is approaching this week, which is a reminder that the clock is still ticking—and that Esther isn't getting any younger. After being a bridesmaid (again) at one of her friends' weddings, the pressure's so strong that Esther is treating this situation like a four-alarm fire.

The baby in Esther's dream symbolizes her hopes for a future family, and her desire to nurture herself and her career. The car symbolizes the direction she is headed in her life. Significantly, Esther's car is missing its driver. Her location, stuck in the backseat, also suggests a position of powerlessness. Is she waiting for someone to come along and show her the way?

Just as the flames get unbearable, Esther suddenly realizes that she does, indeed, have an exit plan. If Esther is not getting married in the next few years, it appears she has decided to make the most of her time, by pursuing a Master's degree in Business Administration (MBA).

Esther's dream shows the "heat" she feels to catch up with her friends and join the newly married set, but her escape from the burning car—with baby in tow—shows that her dreams for the future are alive and well.

"Smoldering Desire"

I dreamed about myself when I am older, around middle age. In my dream I am married. My husband is no longer desirable to me. I see him naked. He has an erection that becomes a long pole.

In the next scene I am with a woman and we decide to become lovers. In robes we sneak to the basement of my house. On the floor there is an old shag carpet. There are closets. No pictures on the walls or any furniture.

Then I see her nude, and I am topless. Then suddenly she is burning. Slowly, like embers. There is some smoke, but mostly I see her burning like a piece of paper burns. Starting with her head going down her shoulders.

And she just stands there, motionless, almost posing. It is so beautiful I run to pick up a drawing tablet and a pencil lying on the floor and begin to draw her. I draw and draw as she slowly smolders.

Then, my husband comes downstairs and I drop the drawing tablet, put on my shirt, and pretend nothing has happened. I wake up.

–Helen, Age 20, Single, USA

Helen's dream about sexual exploration is significant for many reasons. First, it shows that she is curious about having a romantic relationship with a woman. Second, it shows us that her attraction, in addition to being sexual, is also aesthetic. When Helen goes downstairs with this dream woman, presumably to have sex, the dream woman slowly begins to burn. Her beauty is so great Helen immediately wants to draw her—an artist capturing a literally "burning" vision. It is clear from Helen's dream that she has a sophisticated appreciation of feminine beauty.

Fire in dreams is a common symbol for transformation. (When something burns, it changes into something else.) Fire is also a symbol of passion. Is it possible, then, that Helen's dream is reflecting changing thoughts, and smoldering passions, in her feelings toward women? Is it also possible that the woman in transition (the woman she sketches) is really a reflection of herself?

Just as Helen begins to feel comfortable with her clothes off (feelings exposed), good old "social norms" (dressed in the costume of her husband) comes down the stairs, and the mood is spoiled. Marriage, in this case, represents traditional choices in relationships. This vision of the future, at least at this point in time, leaves Helen bored.

While Helen's dream reflects curiosity about same-sex relationships, it does not mean she is lesbian, or even bisexual. Rather, it simply reflects a natural desire to explore her sexuality. This is a fire Helen should continue to keep a playful and sophisticated eye on—and allow to burn.

Flying

Flying: Metaphor of personal power in dreams. Dreams about flying freely—without difficulties staying aloft or the presence of obstacles—are indicators of self-confidence and high self-esteem. We feel we can reach any destination easily, and that we are "on top of the world." Dreams about obstacles—trees and power lines are common—reflect real-life obstacles to empowerment and doubts about our ability to reach a destination. Dreams about escape from an attacker by flying are common, and demonstrate resourcefulness in avoiding conflicts or challenges. Fears about crash landings reflect uncertainty about the future: We don't know where we are going to land! Flying dreams are more common in children than adults.

Power lines: Being caught in power lines or being unable to rise above them indicates a struggle for empowerment on the path to reaching one's destination.

◆ **Interpretation tip:** If your flight is a struggle, work to identify the obstacles that stand in the way of your goals.

* ⁂ *

Flying dreams come in all shapes and sizes. In "Power Lines" we see a dreamer who is struggling to stay aloft. Is it a coincidence that she also can't rise above power lines—a recurring symbol in her dreams? In "Flying High," a dreamer's positive outlook and elevated social status both appear to be giving him a lift. There's nothing he can't do. By contrast, "Fear of Falling" shows a dreamer whose only crime is having learned how to fly. Now that she is soaring once again in her life, can she teach herself how to land? Our final dream, "Wings of Love," is a lesson in how to fly. Given the right circumstances, we can all learn how.

Flying Dreams

"Power Lines"

Ever since I was about seven years old I have had the same dream. I am flying in the air, but I always have trouble staying up. I never touch the ground but can barely keep my arms flapping to keep up and stable. Sometimes I hit power lines or dodge them, but usually when I am flying it is to help or to get away from someone. I am twenty-five years old now and I have had them maybe once or twice a week since the age of seven. Please help—books are of no help!

–Mercedes, Age 25, Single, USA

Many readers will envy the frequency of Mercedes' flying dreams. Imagine—free of gravity! Able to soar through the skies at will. But why do we always have to flap our "wings"?

Actually, not all flying dreams are the same. Some are exhilarating and are accompanied by senses of power and freedom—we fly easily and are thrilled by the view below us—while others, like Mercedes', reflect difficulty staying aloft—and often occur when we are escaping danger.

Power lines are a recurring symbol in flying dreams. Dreamers frequently write of "trying to fly above the power lines" or of bumping into them. The metaphor is apparent: How we are flying in our dreams—whether we are soaring easily or struggling to stay aloft—is an indicator of our personal sense of power.

Because flying dreams recur so frequently for Mercedes, it will be easy for her to create the association in her mind that whenever she is flying she *must* be dreaming. This association will then allow Mercedes to explore her dreams consciously—also known as lucid dreaming.

Mercedes' dreams suggest that her life, currently, is a "struggle to stay aloft." Once she recognizes that she is dreaming, Mercedes can ask the dream what the power lines that she keeps bumping into represent. Whatever it is, it is a situation Mercedes needs to overcome.

"Flying High"

I am a fifty-three-year-old man who is the envy of all of his friends and family. Even though I have seven brothers and sisters, I am the only one to "suffer" this phenomenon.

The two types of dreams that I have most often are about vampires and flying, with the flying dreams occurring at least three times a week. It seems as though I am trying to be a show-off, as the dreams usually have me flying above people for them to see me.

I know that there is something associated with power lines in flying dreams, but they have never been a problem for me, as I simply soar above them. I even do well when there is rain present.

I have rescued many people many times in my dreams, but mostly it just seems to be me showing off by flying around, and above people. I have never taken the stance of Superman (arms out in front of me). I fly with my arms down at my sides, or by flapping them.

The only interpretation of these dreams that I have ever had (unprofessional) has been that most people say it's because I'm so happy all of the time.

I thought the dreams would end in '98 after I was pronounced a "terminal" patient, but they did not. I can have these dreams even taking a one- or two-hour nap in the daytime. And this will be hard for you to believe, but I have gotten up to use the rest room in the night, and gone back to sleep and started having the same dream again.

I have recently had some new dreams where I was healing people of everything from broken legs to blindness. Also I have had three or four in the last month where I was going back in time to when I was a child, and I was fixing all of the things that I knew would go wrong in the future.

But one thing is for sure—when I sleep, I will always dream. I'd like to say more, but now it's time for a nap. . . .

–Dr. Walter, Age 53, Divorced, USA

In addition to being the envy of his friends, Walter is the envy of dreamers everywhere—who wish they, too, could enjoy such frequent "flights of fancy."

Walter's signature informs us that he is a physician. Has he identified the correlation, yet, between his professional life and his dreams? Doctors hold an "elevated" status in any society. Walter's dreams reflect this lofty position by showing him flying above friends and others. The frequent rescues that he performs are direct references to his professional work. As a doctor, saving lives is Walter's business.

The theme of power continues in his most recent dreams. Lately he has become something of a miracle worker; healing broken legs, giving sight to the blind, even altering the past to effect a better future. These are all powerful acts, curiously performed within the context of flying easily and unhindered above the earth.

We are fortunate in our lives when we are able to do what we love. In Walter's case, it appears that his career, chosen long ago, continues to pay him social and emotional dividends. Despite his recent terminal diagnosis, it is apparent that he still feels like he is "on top of the world." We applaud his soaring spirit.

"Fear of Falling"

I have had the craziest dream now for several years. At some point in my dream, I realize that I can fly. I have always known how to fly. I am just remembering it again now. I begin to soar and fly all over the earth, high above fields and mountains and plains. I have a wonderful feeling of joy and liberation. I begin laughing happily.

Then suddenly I can hear my own laugh, and I realize that I am really evil and a witch. This distresses me so much that I lose my ability to fly. As the dream ends, I am falling, falling, falling, and I am so sad. Then I wake up.

–*Fiona, Age 38, Separated, United Kingdom*

Flying dreams are everyone's favorite. For a magical moment in our lives, we are liberated from the burdens of gravity—and from the weight of our earthbound cares. "Free, free, free!" we exult, as we glide above the Earth. Has any brief moment ever been so intoxicating?

If we fly too high, however, a wave of doubt can suddenly pass through us. Is there something wrong with this picture, we ask, something that doesn't add up? Do we really have the power to fly? And what about the curious art of landing? Do we know how to do it?

Fiona's flying dreams show a wonderful flight of fancy that is interrupted by a moment of self-doubt. Significantly, in her dream it is a peculiar sensation of guilt that paralyzes her in midflight and sends her falling back to Earth. Fiona informs us when she signs her dream report that, like many others with falling dreams, Fiona is currently separated from her husband. If her separation has brought Fiona a newfound sense of liberation, represented by flying in her dream, is it also possible that occasionally she is plagued by lingering feelings of doubt and guilt, represented in her dream by her awareness that she is "evil" and a "witch"?

Fiona's dream suggests that she is "soaring to new heights" in her personal life and professional career. If she occasionally feels a need to restrain her enthusiasm, Fiona should take her dream's warning in stride. If, on the other hand, Fiona's dream reflects a simple fear of empowerment, then Fiona should be wary of voices that say she does not deserve such a magnificent flight. The views from the heights can be dizzying, but they are only visible to those who have taught themselves to fly.

"Wings of Love"

Last night I dreamed I was going to my gym for an early morning workout. On my way, it occurred to me that I could fly, so I lifted my arms and began to make slow, long, flapping strokes, each lifting me higher into the sky. Even though I knew I could fly, I was afraid that if I went too far I would fall; so I always returned to the safety of the ground quickly.

I was so excited to do this that I wanted to teach others how to fly. Saying "Trust me, I won't let you fall," I'd take each person's hand into mine and together we'd flap our free arms, rising into the sky. Some became very afraid; and even though they stopped flapping, I kept my word and didn't let them fall.

Arriving at the gym, I received a phone call that I'd been given a job offer with great pay. I became very happy; and even though I was to return the call right away, I chose to fly. Rising with the sun breaking over the horizon, I could only think of teaching others.

–Russell, Age 35, In Love, USA

As we read Russell's dream, our minds search for the clue that will inform us what spectacular event has occurred in Russell's life that could make him feel so positively elated—like he is "floating on air" right now. Is it a new job? Did he get the leading role in a play? Finally, the clue comes—when he signs his dream report. Congratulations to Russell on being in love. (Do we know of any other force that can make gravity take a holiday?)

Few dreams can rival the sense of confidence and euphoria experienced in a flying dream, especially when we are able to control our flight and soar more or less at will. Not surprisingly, these dreams are associated with feelings of "high" self-esteem: success, control, confidence, and "being on top of it all." (Flying dreams are so much fun that Freud believed they represented sex. Modern dream researchers disagree.)

The heart does take wing when we are in love, and Russell's dream reveals all the necessary conditions that enable this joyous event to occur. Paramount is an environment of trust and safety. Accordingly, it is significant that Russell first tells his students, "Trust me. I won't let you fall." When he adds commitment and follow-through to the recipe, as he demonstrates in his dream, even the most timid hearts learn to take flight.

So many of us who attempt this magical journey of the heart fall and are hurt; some never dare to fly again. The wisdom that Russell's dream imparts to us is twofold: Learning to fly takes practice and courage; and under the right conditions, we can all learn how. This is a message whose urgency, indeed, rises above more earthbound concerns. May Russell's love be a beacon of light and abundance to others who dare to fly.

Hair

Hair: Symbol of personal style and self-presentation in dreams. Cut hair (especially a bad haircut) symbolizes creativity curtailed and pressures to conform, often in a work-related context. Red hair is a common representation of anger or passion. Dyed hair can indicate either creativity or conformity. Long hair is a symbol of creativity, and on women can be a symbol of seduction. Dreams of gray hair, hair falling out, and baldness reflect concerns related to age, deteriorating health, and passing beauty. Long beards and white hair are symbols of wisdom. Letting one's hair grow suggests increased creativity and a willingness to try a new approach—a "change in style."

Dreams about gray hair, hair falling out, and baldness are also common during anniversaries that remind us of our age. Did you recently celebrate your thirtieth, fortieth, or fiftieth birthday?

◆ **Interpretation tip:** Who or what made you change your symbolic hairstyle?

* * *

Hair is a curious symbol in dreams. Aside from its association with beauty (men and women who are concerned about appearance and aging often have hair-falling-out dreams—similar to teeth-falling-out dreams), hair is a powerful symbol of self-expression. In real life, how we choose to wear our hair—long, short, afro, braided, up, down, colored, bleached, curled, highlighted, permed, shaved—allows us to express ourselves personally and socially, and, in some eras more than others, politically.

In "Cut My Hair," the strong feelings that most of us attach to our hair are revealed. Is our dreamer really worried about a bad haircut—or is there another explanation? "Dye My Hair" shows a dreamer who can't seem to change her look. In our final dream, "Lose My Hair," a woman fears she is gradually going bald. Is her life really going "down the drain"?

Hair Dreams

"Cut My Hair"

I am a recently turned twenty-eight-year-old woman. Some background info on my present life: I hate my job, but it pays well. I am under contract negotiations and may end up striking. I am taking a trip by myself soon to Scotland and Ireland, and presently I have no relationship.

I have very long hair and last night I dreamt I went to a beauty shop. As an observer, I saw a woman accidentally get her hair buzzed off by an inexperienced stylist, and she ran out yelling. As a participant, I didn't see this happen. I sat down next, and told the girl to just trim the ends. I couldn't see the mirror. When she was finished, my hair was cut above my shoulders.

I was so angry and upset. I woke myself up screaming and crying (I talk in my sleep). When I fell back to sleep I continued the dream, making threats of legal action and just yelling and crying. Then I woke up again, still very upset.

—Bridget, Age 28, Single, United Kingdom

Given the background Bridget provides, it's not hard to guess the link between her dreams and her recent job stress. Work is frustrating, with threats of legal action looming. In Bridget's dream, her visit to the hairstylist was frustrating, and threats of legal action again were made. Do we see the connection?

Bridget tells us that she hates her job except for the pay, and that she may be going on strike in the very near future—due to a labor dispute. Accordingly, Bridget's dream is a strong message encouraging her to reevaluate the benefits of her job, in lieu of other, more creatively rewarding positions. Significantly, Bridget's position as an observer in the dream shows that she knows she is going to get a bad haircut (she watches another woman have her hair buzzed off, who leaves running and yelling), but she goes ahead with it anyway. Is her dream a warning that she needs to get serious about finding new work? After all, Bridget doesn't want her "crimp" to become a "perm."

"Dye My Hair"

I had a dream that I was trying to dye my hair auburn. I did everything correctly, but when I was done, my hair was still its usual color—brown. This upset me so much I started to cry. Still crying, I stood up and looked out the window and I saw every single female outside with hair the exact shade of auburn I had unsuccessfully tried to dye my hair. Then I turned around and looked in the mirror. My hair had somehow changed to auburn, but I didn't have a face. I had no eyes, mouth, or nose.

Can you help me understand this dream?

—Priscilla, Age 13, Single, USA

Priscilla's dream about dyeing her hair reflects her desire to fit in with the crowd. Curiously, in her efforts to blend in, it is clear that Priscilla also recognizes a price she must pay: She will lose her identity.

Priscilla's attempt to dye her hair represents her desire, to some extent, to take on a new persona. While it's not a big deal to dye our hair (it's right up there with getting a new haircut), Priscilla's dream is a clear warning against putting too much investment into a new hair color, and by extension, into her external appearances. When Priscilla succeeds in making her hair color auburn—just like "every single female outside the window"—she also succeeds in losing her individuality—represented by her missing eyes, nose, mouth.

What's the message of this dream? Priscilla should enjoy her new look—but she shouldn't forget her "roots."

"Lose My Hair"

I'm currently in the process of moving from England, where I have worked for five years, and returning home to Ireland, as my mother is ill. I have never had this dream before, and I found it quite disturbing.

In my dream my hair was falling out in massive clumps—and vanishing down the plughole in a shower. I was going bald! Can you please help explain this dream?

–Ella, Age 27, Single, United Kingdom

At a young age, Ella is worried about growing older. Her dream about becoming bald is a common representation of fears of aging, related to dreams about locating gray hairs on our body. The reason Ella dreamed it, however, may catch her by surprise.

In the background information that Ella provides, Ella mentions a significant event that's almost certainly the cause of her never-before-experienced dream. Ella's mother is ill. As Ella prepares for her move back to Ireland, the realities of her mother's declining health are weighing on her mind. Curiously, instead of seeing her mother with gray hair, or with clumps of hair gathering in the drain as Ella bathes her, Ella instead sees herself.

The answer to this dream riddle is that, in our parents, we often see our truest reflection. As Ella witnesses her mother's deteriorating health, Ella is gaining a foretaste of her own inevitable decline—following in her mother's footsteps. Owing to the same logic, Freud said the death of our parents is the single most traumatic event any of us will ever experience. The reason is because when we watch our parents die, any illusions about our own immortality (at least in this world) are dashed. If we are honest souls, our parents' deaths force us to recognize our own eventual passing. And death, said Freud, is one of our deepest fears.

Ella's dream, accordingly, reflects a gentle brush with mortality. The Grim Reaper has knocked at Ella's family's door, and Ella's dream reflects her awareness that one day, the Reaper will also come for her.

Healing

Healing: Dreams about healing reflect feelings of renewal after difficult emotional periods in a dreamer's life. Common healing themes include "recovering from surgery," or being diagnosed with a medical condition, for which one then undergoes treatment and recovers. Medical instruments, X rays, surgery, and the removal of infected organs are common themes.

After the procedure is performed, the dreamer may be wearing a cast, be sitting in a wheelchair, or located in a medical environment with others who also are rehabilitating. Dreams about healing are positive dreams. The dreamer is recovering after a difficult emotional period (divorce, romantic separation, loss of a loved one).

◆ **Interpretation tip:** If you dream about recovering from a wound or surgery, ask what emotional trauma you are healing from.

* * *

Few dreams hold as much symbolic import as dreams about healing. A corner has been turned, a new day is risen from the ashes. In "Therapist Is Operating on Me," a dreamer's experience in therapy is explored through the metaphor of surgery. Our dreamer wants to know: Is it supposed to hurt this much? In "Garden of Renewal," another dreamer finds hope, and strength, at the end of a long and weary road. Her dream is a message of hope to all souls on the path to spiritual renewal.

Healing Dreams

"Therapist Is Operating on Me"

I am lying in my bed and my therapist (a woman whom I trust completely) is operating on me. She cuts me open from my sternum down to just below my belly button. She takes out my *whole* insides.

I sit up and am completely empty. I get up and I am bleeding, so she instructs me to lie down. When I lie down I am lying next to a dark woman who is asleep. She has also been cut open, but my therapist has taken her insides and put them inside me.

Later, I am lying on the bed telling my husband about the operation and crying because the wound hurts. I look down at the cut and see that although it is holding together, there are no stitches. I am worried about this but my husband reassures me that my therapist knows what she is doing and everything will be okay. The wound hurts a lot.

Note: I have taken a break from counseling and haven't seen my therapist for about a month.

–*Victoria, Age 35, Married, Canada*

We all know that therapists help us to "see inside ourselves." Fortunately, because the therapeutic process concerns thoughts, feelings, and memories (instead of kidneys, livers, and intestines) therapists don't need to cut us open every time we go for a visit! But as Victoria's dream clearly shows, just because therapists don't use knives, this doesn't mean that the healing process is without pain.

Victoria's dream shows her therapist removing her insides and replacing them with the insides of another, darker woman who lies sleeping beside Victoria. One interpretation of Victoria's dream, popular in Jungian analytic psychology, would be that the darker woman represents Victoria's "shadow"—those aspects of her personality that, over time, she has tried to avoid recognizing and has actually worked to keep hidden from herself. The reason the woman lies sleeping beside Victoria is because these feelings, though they are very close to her, still are unconscious.

The goal of therapy, stated plainly, is to enable us to understand ourselves as realistically and honestly as possible, and to encourage us to make healthy and self-affirming decisions based upon this knowledge. Accordingly, therapy asks us to embrace avoided material and bring it into the light of day for two reasons. First, if we make a habit of avoiding reality, we wind up with an impaired vision of the world. This, in turn, affects our ability to respond to the world realistically and effectively. The second reason avoiding feelings (any feeling) is unhealthy is because it means we're not listening to ourselves. The first rule of self-esteem is that we always want to listen to, and validate, our feelings.

Significantly, Victoria's dream does not identify, specifically, any issues that she has been working on in therapy. Instead, the dream appears concerned with the therapeutic process itself. In light of her recent decision to take a break, is it fair to ask if Victoria is reevaluating the benefits of treatment? In essence, is the pain of treatment today worth the promised gain in quality of life tomorrow? Similarly, despite Victoria's conscious voicing of trust in her therapist, in her dream Victoria wonders aloud about her therapist's method. It is Victoria's husband who reassures Victoria that her therapist knows what she is doing.

A different interpretation of Victoria's dream would be that she feels her therapist is misdiagnosing her. In the dream the therapist is trying to put someone else's "dark insides" inside of Victoria. This suggests that Victoria feels the therapist is trying to make Victoria into something (a person with dark intentions and motivations) that Victoria does not believe is fair or accurate. Does Victoria feel that her therapist sees and understands her clearly?

If Victoria does have doubts about her therapist, she is encouraged to speak openly with friends and acquaintances who have been through therapy, and to take notes and compare experiences. Pain is part of the therapeutic process, but so also is increased self-esteem and self-confidence. Additionally, therapists have different styles and techniques. Victoria doesn't want to shoot the messenger who is the bearer of hard news—but she is entitled to several opinions.

"Garden of Renewal"

At the time of my dream, my children were ages five and nine. My husband was working four jobs (his choice), and I was going back to nursing school. I was basically planning to be able to support myself, because I was very unhappy with him. I was pregnant when we were married, and it was an abusive situation. I wanted to stay home with my children, but felt I needed to be able to work.

In the dream, I was heavily burdened, internally, and bulging with weight. I was dragging myself along a road on a very hot day, barely able to walk. I felt awful inside, and in despair.

I came to a rock wall that surrounded a beautiful garden. I could see trees and hear birds, and feel cool air all around the garden. I crawled until I found the gate. Inside I could see beautiful shrubs, flowers, and trees—and lush green grass, like carpeting. I slowly made my way (I was drawn there) to the corner of the garden where a large, wonderfully green tree, like a sturdy oak, stood. I collapsed in front of the tree, and then my body opened up and lots of garbage, pus, and waste matter poured out, steaming in the air.

I felt a great release, and lifted my head to look at the tree, which seemed to be the source of my peace. As I raised my head, my body healed, and I became a butterfly, soaring over the garden with a sense of freedom and wonder. The tree seemed to be nodding in approval and I flitted from flower to flower, being nourished and filled with beauty and joy.

After this dream, I was able to feel confident and independent. I had a sense of release from guilt and "garbage." I finished school, and three years later I asked for a divorce. I felt forgiven and new.

I "laid down my burdens" at that tree. I became a new creation. I believe that God was that tree, and I was able to allow Him to release me from my fears and guilt that had been growing in me for years. The garden represented new life, as well as the butterfly. It had such peace, harmony, beauty, and lushness—as I had never seen before. I have never forgotten that dream, and hold on to it as a symbol of change, strength, hope, and peace.

–Elizabeth, Age 49, Remarried, USA

It's not often that we have dreams as powerful and transforming as Elizabeth's, but when they do come, they can give us strength and confidence to overcome tremendous adversity. The inner guidance we receive can sustain our vision for a lifetime.

At a difficult time in Elizabeth's life, when she was burdened with many responsibilities—and a heavy heart—her dream encouraged her to witness a future that, with hard work and dedication, she understood lay within her grasp. In her dream the path to transformation was outlined. Elizabeth had to release her guilt (forgive herself) for decisions made in her past, and allow herself to become a new person—symbolized in the dream by metamorphosis into a butterfly. Her dream's choice to represent her renewal through the symbol of a butterfly is especially apt. Butterflies are caterpillars that successfully emerge from cocoons of transformation.

Elizabeth's dream was a healing event in itself, but it is clear from her report that her dream was only a beginning, and not an end. The tree of life that she experienced as God in the garden instructed Elizabeth that renewal was possible, but it was Elizabeth's strong will that created her current happiness. After three years of steady growth (in a cocoon?) from the time that she had this dream, Elizabeth was able to free herself from an unfulfilling relationship, and she was able to provide for her children. Today she is the butterfly that yesterday she once dreamed of becoming.

For every reader who finds him- or herself in a similar location of despair, Elizabeth's dream is a powerful reminder that change is always possible. When hope, hard work, forgiveness, and spiritual grace converge—miracles can, and do, happen.

House

House: Houses in dreams are frequent metaphors for the self, with upper levels reflecting higher mental processes—such as thinking, consciousness, and spirituality—and lower levels (cellars and basements) indicating subconscious feelings and awarenesses. Specific rooms hold associations with various aspects of the self: the bedroom (sexuality and privacy), the kitchen or dining rooms (food and appetites), the living room (lifestyle). Roofs of homes are locations of perspective—the ability to see a great distance—and also may indicate the transition between the living and the spirit world. Houses in ill repair can be metaphors for health concerns of the physical body or emotions (feeling "run-down"). New homes and houses under construction represent transitions in our lives, and projects we are working to complete, respectively. Large houses with many rooms can be metaphors for extended family lines. Missing walls may symbolize absent or inadequate boundaries in family relationships, and lack of privacy.

The discovery of unknown rooms in a house, typically a pleasant dream, reflects the discovery of hidden or forgotten aspects of the self, often after a period of sacrifice of personal goals. For example, a woman who rediscovers a passion for art or business after her children have left the nest may dream about finding new, empty rooms in her house that she is excited to decorate.

Hotels are common symbols of impermanence in dreams, because of their association with travel. Hotels frequently represent relationships in transition, or infrequent contact among friends or family members. Hotels also hold allusions to illicit romantic liaisons, which are often consummated within their confines.

Castles in dreams hold associations with wealth and gran-

deur, and mythic wisdom. They are frequent locations in dreams for issues concerning the higher self and spiritual growth. Please see "Stairs":
"In the Basement."

◆ **Interpretation tip:** If you dream about living in a new house, ask
what transition in your spiritual and emotional life is being represented.
If you dream about an old home that you used to live in, are you still
managing emotional issues related to that time period?

✳ ✳ ✳

The houses included in this chapter reflect the different emotional
states of our dreamers. In "Basement Obstacles," a young woman is surprised to encounter so much junk in her basement. Is it time for a spring
cleaning? In "Defending My Home," a dreamer is worried about his
longevity—and about his ability to survive an attack. Our next dream,
"An Extra Room," reveals the excitement of discovering new rooms in a
home. Our final entry, "Secret Room," shows a dreamer on a private
quest for solace. Some places are best visited alone.

House Dreams

"Basement Obstacles"

There is this guy that I like and he popped up in one of my dreams. I
was in what was supposed to be my house. Oddly, the bottom half of
the house was transparent. I was standing inside and he was outside,
looking through the transparent part of the house and motioning for
me to meet him at the front door.

As I was running to the front door, I had to push various things out
of my way. Another oddity was that where the living room should
have been there was a room with a cement floor, much like an
unfinished basement, including stacks of boxes and other junk.
Again, I had to push aside things, as I was essentially wading through
the boxes, trying to reach the front door. By the time I got to the front
door, I saw him driving off in a Jeep. What does this mean?

–Safina, Age 21, Single, USA

Houses in dreams are consistent symbols of the self, with upper levels representing conscious and spiritual aspects of the personality,

and with basements and cellars alluding to subconscious feelings and awarenesses. Significantly, Safina's home in the dream is transparent. The man she likes is able to see into her home, and encourages her to meet him at the front door. Unfortunately for Safina, she must wade through boxes of junk as she crosses a living room that suddenly resembles an unfinished basement. When she reaches the front door, her friend, who we assume has grown impatient, has already left.

The obstacles Safina encounters in her dream may be specific to her relationship with this man, or they may comment more generally on her emotional preparedness for a romantic relationship. The unfinished basement and boxes of junk are strong symbols that suggest unresolved emotions—perhaps from a previous relationship? The transparency of Safina's house may allude to the transparency of Safina's attraction to this man, but it also may reflect feelings of exposure. Was Safina unable to clean up her act in time to make emotional contact with this man? The metaphor expressed by Safina's dream is clear: Safina needs to "clean her house" (get her emotional world in order) before she can become romantically available for a new man in her life.

"Defending My Home"

I've been married seventeen years and have had my job (I'm a mailman) for fifteen years. The night before, I dreamt that I had a fight with my wife about her job. She's anxious about it (she's a school bus driver) and has an ongoing issue about wanting to be home before and after school, to be with our teenage boys. I'm worried about the financial pressures this may bring, if she decides to stop working. In fact, I tend to worry about finances a lot.

I was out in the middle of a prairie with nothing visible except for my house, which I am admiring from the outside. It's a sizable log cabin, beautifully made with perfect logs, with the cracks filled in with mud. Suddenly I become aware that several people are approaching with the intent of destroying my house. I go inside to defend the house. I can't remember the details of the inside of the house or the methods that I use to defend it, but throughout the dream I am confident that I can repulse the attack and be victorious even though I am outnumbered by several to one. (My impression is that there were perhaps two dozen or more people attacking my house.)

In the process of defending my house it becomes necessary to move up to the attic. Again I don't remember the processes involved. I just remember being up there and still being confident that I will come out of this victorious. While I'm up there I notice the details of the attic. Although rustic, I notice that the attic is well constructed, as I had previously noticed that the outside of the cabin was well made and attractive. The ceiling is just the raw logs of the roof, but again they are perfect and well sealed. The floor of the attic is made of finished slats, which are also very regular and fit together nicely. But as I am sitting up there I look down and notice that the attackers have completely torn down the walls of the lower level, so that only the supporting beams are holding up the attic.

These are all intact at this point; however, a couple of the men begin to set fire to them, and yell up at me that when they get me, they are going to rape me before they kill me. At this point I wake up.

I believe my dream stems from my anxieties about whether my physical body has the stamina to finish out my postal career. In particular I feel troubled and guilty about the fact that I've put on an extra ten pounds over the past year or so, which I can not seem to lose no matter how I try. I also have arthritis in one knee and tendonitis in my left hand. I'm particularly concerned about the tendonitis because I play the piano as a side job.

My interpretation of my dream is that I feel like my body is under attack from numerous sources. At this point things are stable (solid supporting beams) although deteriorating (large holes in the walls) and most of the time I feel confident that I will finish my career just fine. I feel like my mind (the attic) is intact. But I have fears that a transition is coming that will destroy my ability to earn a living (setting fire to the supporting beams) after which I will lose control (be raped). The dream was likely brought on by the discussion with my wife, which brought these anxieties to the forefront.

–Dylan, Age 54, Married, USA

If Dylan's wife only knew what she put him through! Perhaps they can agree, in the future, to discuss finances in the morning?

Dylan correctly identifies the argument he had with his wife the previous night as the cause of his dream. When his wife expressed her desire to be home with their two boys, Dylan became worried about the financial risk that the reduced income could cause. It is clear that Dylan found the discussion both alarming ("Fire!") and provocative ("Attack!"). The angry mob that attacks his home may represent Dylan's fears about having to deal with bill collectors and bankers. After all the miles Dylan has walked to earn his home (through wind and rain and snow . . .), losing it now, certainly, would feel like a violation (rape) of himself.

Dylan's fears extend to include concerns about his physical health and stamina. As a mailman and part-time pianist, Dylan frets about illnesses that could impair his ability to perform either job. While Dylan is confident about the condition of the attic (his mind), he has begun to notice deterioration in the lower sections of the house, typically related to the body in dreams. The main supports are solid, but Dylan has begun to observe some holes in the walls (his weight gain, arthritis, and tendonitis).

Happily, Dylan's "attic" is in great shape. In fact, if Dylan and his wife put their "attics" together, they will surely discover a way to achieve both their goals.

"An Extra Room"

In my dream I am in my apartment. I walk into a room that seems familiar yet unfamiliar at the same time. It is like an extra room in the back, that I did not know was there, or that I was in very seldom or had forgotten. The room is pleasant, although rather empty.

In the room there is an empty chest of drawers and a large empty cabinet. Then I notice that the room leads out onto a balcony. I step onto the balcony but a man notices that I am dressed only in my nightgown, so I quickly go back into the room. In reality my apartment has no balcony.

This theme of finding extra rooms has occurred many times over the last few years. Sometimes the room will have a piano in it— sometimes two pianos. The room is always pleasant and nearly empty.

I have been through a lot of changes in my life in the last ten years. I moved out of the house where I grew up, and the house was sold. I learned I had heart disease—and overcame it. My mother also became ill, and died in 1996. Last fall I started a new job as a legal secretary, after fourteen years at another law firm.

I am literally in a new life. I feel as if I am finding myself all over again. I believe that we do this more than once in life. When my mother was ill I pushed all of my own feelings and desires down deep within myself, so that I could be there for her. I am now just starting to rediscover them. My life is relatively good, but I want something more, and I do not know what.

As far as pianos go, I took lessons as a child, which was my own idea. When I reached junior high school, I dropped piano and took up flute—which came easier to me, and which I really liked. I took up piano again in high school because I thought I wanted to be a professional musician. Again, it was hard for me and I dropped it when I started college. Today, I still play the flute (no more piano) as an amateur, and perform publicly two to three times a year.

–Renee, Age 48, Single, USA

Houses in dreams are common metaphors for the self. Dreams about finding new rooms, accordingly, are associated with periods of self-discovery.

A new room in a house typically represents an aspect of ourselves that we have neglected for a while (we forgot it was there) or it indicates an area of growth that we would like to expand into. The dreams are most common among people who, like Renee, have had to sacrifice a hobby, desire, or passion in their life for a period of time (often to care for their family) who then rediscover these lost areas of interest. Significantly, Renee's recent dream also includes a theme of emotional exposure. As she walks through the new room and discovers a balcony (a room with a view to her future?), a man observes her dressed only in a nightgown. Is Renee exposing previously "covered" aspects of her personality? Is she growing emotionally prepared for romance in her life?

After a difficult period of caring for her mother, Renee has embarked upon a period of searching and self-discovery. The pianos she finds are associated with childhood lessons, but also, and much more importantly, with an earlier, very serious, creative goal: becoming a professional musician. The symbolic value of the pianos (an artistic pursuit) confirms the "new room" theme as a metaphor for rediscovering "lost" talents and passions.

Renee's dreams are encouraging her to rediscover the importance of creative expression in her life. In the midst of change, the search for a new medium—that will enable her to expand her self-understanding and re-create herself—has begun.

"Secret Room"

I've been having a recurring dream for many years now that I can't figure out. It starts out with a few people following me into this old abandoned house in the middle of the woods. I'm telling them to follow me to this particular room in the house that can be somewhat difficult to get to. We end up crawling through narrow crawl spaces, squeezing through very skinny hallways, and even braving a cement ledge around half the house (which can end up miles high), just to get to this room. When I reach it, I realize that no one has been able to complete the journey except me.

I look around at this tattered, dark, empty room with no light (yet light exists because I can see), and realize that I am utterly alone—for miles. I know there is no one in the forest surrounding me, let alone the house. In real life, I would have been terrified, but for some strange reason I am completely content. In fact, I have never felt this much at peace except in this room in a dream.

I'm not depressed, or upset, and haven't been. I can't figure out what this dream means. The only thing I can think is that it might relate to my spiritual quest in life. I've taken a liberal stance toward religion and am "freelancing" it. In other words, I pick what I need and apply it to my faith and relationship with God. I'm wondering if this could possibly be related to my conversations with people about spirituality, and trying to get them to understand me. Hope you can help.

–Sydney, Age 31, Single, USA

In an effort to show her friends a private, secret room, Sydney leads them to a deserted house in the middle of the woods, and soon begins a fantastic climb. Sydney squeezes through narrow hallways, slides through skinny crawl spaces, and even winds up outside the house on a ledge that, when she looks down, she realizes is several miles above the ground. This is no ordinary room, and it is no ordinary journey!

Climbing in dreams is a familiar metaphor for attempts to reach a goal or destination in our lives. The narrower the path, and the higher it leads into the sky, the more likely it is that our dream concerns lofty aspirations. Will we reach fabulous new heights in our career? Will our spiritual quest lead us to new levels of empowerment and wisdom?

Feelings are always the truest indicator of a dream's meaning. Once

Sydney reaches her secret room, she realizes she is utterly alone, yet a tranquil feeling of peace and contentment fills her nevertheless. The feeling is so powerful that Sydney writes, "I have never felt this much at peace except in this room in a dream." The fact that the room exists in an abandoned house suggests that Sydney would like to visit these feelings more frequently.

Sydney associates this dream with her personal growth and understanding of God. Her dream shows us that she finds this journey toward spiritual atonement (at-one-ment) challenging, private, exciting, and rewarding. As for her friends, who were unable to join Sydney in her private room, is it possible they discovered their own secret rooms along the way?

Jail

Jail: Dreams about jails, prisons, and courtrooms reflect feelings of guilt and being judged. Has someone accused you of acting improperly or irresponsibly? Is your behavior or suitability as a parent being evaluated, either socially or by the legal system? Dreams about jails and courtrooms are common during separation, divorce, and custody hearings. Dreams about jail can also indicate feelings of restricted freedom or self-expression. Has someone got you trapped? Being caged in a cell while others are set free reflects feelings of abandonment.

◆ **Interpretation tip:** If you dream about being sentenced in a court of law, ask where in your life you feel judged by family, friends, or peers. Feelings of guilt are often present prior to committing an act. Are you contemplating a "crime," and are you nervous that you will be discovered?

* * *

Jail is never a happy place, as the dreams that follow make plain. "Fear of Prison" takes us inside the mind of a former "criminal". As he plots to revisit the scene of a crime, it's not the job he fears—it's getting caught. "Sentenced to Death" shows an execution that is about to be performed in public. Has someone committed a social crime? Our final entry, "The Barges of Captivity," show a woman imprisoned by an indifferent keeper. If his watch is really so informal, why hasn't she escaped already?

Jail Dreams

"Fear of Prison"

I have a recurring dream that has me killing someone (sometimes a family member, sometimes a stranger). But that's not the scary part, because the dream doesn't dwell on how or why I've done it.

I spend the rest of the dream afraid of being caught (certain I will be) and locked away in prison forever. Locked away from everything and everyone I love. There is also an underlying feeling of embarrassment, from having disappointed people close to me (my mom, my brothers, my wife). But it's the fear of isolation that's most intense. It's incredibly frightening.

As for my background: I had an affair in the past, and it almost ruined my marriage. My wife and I were able to salvage our relationship, however, and move on. I have a contract with my wife not to contact this lady ever again . . . but I recently did (about the time the dreams started again). I had this dream many times during our previous affair.

–Drew, Age 38, Married, USA

The murder that Drew commits in his dream is a romantic betrayal of his wife that he fears will end their relationship, and banish him forever from his family. Significantly, Drew's dream is less occupied with the act of murder than it is with his fear of being caught.

Drew's dream represents feelings of guilt in advance, for a crime that Drew feels dangerously close to committing. Despite a contract with his wife to never again speak to the woman with whom he previously had an affair, Drew recently initiated contact with her, and now feels himself on a slippery slope to betrayal. In his dreams Drew is embarrassed and ashamed, and is evaluating the consequences of a second betrayal. This time Drew's wife will not be so understanding, and Drew's separation from his family, represented by jail, will be a sentence that is imposed.

It is always significant to note when a series of recurring dreams began. Drew's dreams commenced immediately following his contact with his former mistress. Can Drew hear the warning that is knocking on his door?

At a critical moment in his life, Drew's dream is a welcome reminder of the pain that betrayals cause, and of the steep penalties one pays for violating a family's trust. As is always the case, even if Drew's affair were never discovered, Drew must still live with the inner awareness of betrayal, and with the weight of concealing his true self from a loved one. Paradoxically, in an effort to achieve intimacy, Drew will only succeed in isolating himself from those he loves most. It's an obvious equation: The affair is not worth it!

"Sentenced to Death"

I have recently been going through a separation from my husband of fourteen years. It is a second marriage for both of us. I moved out a month ago and bought a house with my sister.

Last night I dreamt that I was at some sort of lodge in the wilderness. My husband was there and he was accused of doing something that meant he would have to be hung by rope till death. I don't think what he did was very bad, not like murder or rape.

As his wife, I was required to be hung as well. I thought that was very unfair due to the fact we were separating. I remember him clinging to me as we walked toward the rope in the living room of this beautiful lodge. People we knew (not in real life) were sitting around waiting very casually. My husband was crying as they pulled him away from me to take him to the rope.

I started talking to my sister on the phone. When they told me it was my turn I started to cry and told her good-bye and that I loved her. As they pulled me away from the phone I heard a choking sound. My husband had survived the rope.

They untied him and said that, as he had survived, I would not be put to death either. I was very relieved. I woke up then, thinking I had to write this down.

–Naomi, Age 51, Separated, Canada

Naomi's separation from her husband of fourteen years feels like a "death sentence." The fact that her husband does not die in the dream informs us that his "death" (and Naomi's) is only symbolic. A time in their lives is "passing on"; a new period is beginning.

Naomi's dream places her in a luxurious lodge, with a group of friends (in the dream) standing idly by, watching. The social context of the dream informs us that Naomi is concerned about social appearances—as she traverses a difficult emotional period. Although her husband committed the crime (did he initiate the separation?), Naomi is also included in the sentence (because they were married), and is aware that she, too, will die. Is Naomi feeling the eyes of society judging her? Has Naomi committed a social crime—the stigma of a second failed marriage?

Naomi's relationship with her husband still appears to be amicable. In the dream Naomi is sympathetic to him (Naomi doesn't think what he did "was very bad"), and she offers him support as he is led to his death. It is clear from her dream that Naomi's bond with her husband is strong. If Naomi hasn't already done so, now is the time to visit a marriage counselor, on her own at first, if she prefers. As Naomi works to gain perspective and clarity about her relationship, a trained third eye will be a terrific help.

"The Barges of Captivity"

This dream takes place over a very long time—years. I am one of a group of captives all dressed in plain white gowns. I don't know why, but I know that our captors really are, in some way, superior. They don't treat us badly, just indifferently, as though we were animals. They move us frequently, often by water on a barge. There is always water nearby throughout the dream. As the years go by my feelings toward my captors (whom I rarely see) go from fear to rage to resignation and hopelessness. (Interestingly, I distinctly remember the gowns we wear becoming older and dirtier as the dream progresses.)

Suddenly, I have escaped and I am running away from the water through a town that becomes the town I grew up in. I race past an old woman crouched in the gutter and I stop to look at her. I realize she is me and that my life has been wasted. Then I wake up. My dreams are often this detailed, and very often include water images, but I never had this one before. The colors are very vivid. The time of day is always evening or dusk. I had this dream about a month ago, and I can't stop thinking about it. I'd appreciate hearing any thoughts you might have.

—Cassie, Age 33, Long-term Relationship, USA

Cassie's dream reflects her feelings of being in a romantic relationship—with a power imbalance that definitely is not in her favor.

If Cassie thinks back upon her dream, she most likely will recall that her captors, as a rule, were men, while her fellow captives—dressed in white gowns—were women. Cassie writes that her captors are not cruel, but that they are indifferent. Can Cassie think of a situation in her real life where she feels similarly trapped? Might it be her long-term relationship with her boyfriend?

To understand this dream it is important to recognize that the white gowns that Cassie and her fellow captives wear symbolize wedding gowns. By extension, her fellow captives collectively symbolize the plight of many women in their thirties who would like to start families, but who are "held captive" due to the absence of a committed partner. Finally, the superiority of her captors most likely is an allusion to the fact that men are not subject, as much as women are, to the steadily droning toll of Nature's bio-clock. Men can father children well into their sixties. Is this the superiority Cassie perceives in the dream?

The choice of the dream to represent Cassie on a barge in water is significant. Water in dreams symbolizes emotions. Barges, meanwhile, are vessels designed to carry a heavy load. (Does Cassie feel "weighed down" by her emotions?) Barges, also, have no power source of their own. In this way, Cassie's dream indicates a passivity in her response to her relationship. Is Cassie "waiting" for her long-term boyfriend to decide her future?

Cassie observes that the white gown she is wearing is "becoming older and dirtier as the dream progresses," a dream metaphor that she is moving past her prime wedding years. Over the course of several years (the same amount of time that she has dated her boyfriend?), her emotions "go from fear to rage to resignation and hopelessness."

Cassie escapes from the barges of captivity only to find an old woman crouched in the gutter of the hometown in which she grew up. To her horror, Cassie recognizes her face as her own, and realizes she has wasted her life. This scene represents Cassie's fear of leaving her current relationship. The time of day in the dream, evening or dusk, is yet another dream allusion to time running out.

Cassie's dream is a strong metaphor for feelings of powerlessness, and as such is an urgent call to action. Cassie's boyfriend is either aloof to her desires at this point in time, or he is enjoying the power imbalance that Cassie, by not taking more active control of her future, is allowing to exist. The solution is simple: If the heart-to-heart doesn't work, it's time for Cassie to get off the barge—and stretch her legs.

Lost

Lost: Common metaphor for feelings of doubt, insecurity, and confusion about one's direction in waking life. Note the location of the dream. Being lost in an office or business context indicates uncertainty about your career path. Being lost in a romantic context (can't find your partner in a crowded location) suggests difficulties communicating, or physical obstacles to intimacy. Being lost in a travel context—airport, train, or subway station—suggests a period of transition, and uncertainty about the future. Dreams about losing objects associated with identity—purses, wallets, car keys—are common in the wake of job transitions, separations, divorces, and the death of a spouse. (We feel we have "lost" our identity.) Dreams about being lost are also common in the elderly, who worry about the consequences of failing memory, and during periods of depression.

Wallet and purse: Because they hold our identification papers (driver's license, Social Security cards, student IDs) and our money (cash, checkbooks, bank and credit cards), wallets and purses in dreams are highly associated with personal identity and feelings of empowerment. Dreams about losing one's purse or wallet are common following significant changes in one's life status—for example, from being married to being separated or divorced, or after "losing" a job or enduring a forced transition in one's career. Because purses hold women's beauty supplies, in dreams they have associations with feelings of self-confidence, self-presentation, and seduction. The inability to find a purse in conjunction with concerns about appearance (can't find makeup) indicate feelings of being unprepared for a social presentation. Because purses are private locations that can be opened and closed and that contain valuables, including products related to feminine hygiene, associations with female genitalia, and with the womb, may also be present.

Passport: Dreams about arriving at an airport without a passport indicate feelings of unpreparedness for a career or romantic goal. Lost passport dreams may also indicate feelings that a dreamer is "losing" his or her identity—through extended stay in a foreign country—or through being absorbed into a foreign culture, for example, by marriage. Lost passport dreams are common reflections of literal anxieties during actual travel to foreign countries.

◆ **Interpretation tip:** If you are lost in a dream, ask where you feel uncertain of your future course in waking life.

✳ ✳ ✳

Being lost in a dream reflects feelings that we have "lost our direction" in waking life. In "Lose My Car," a woman in transition has momentarily misplaced her car. Can she get back behind the wheel of her life? In "Sense of Direction," a college student has a recurring dream about being lost in a subdivision. Has she lost her way? In "Wrong Direction," a woman dreams she's headed in the wrong direction. Is it time to try a new highway?

Lost Dreams

"Lose My Car"

I had a dream that I went to a shopping mall, parked my car, left everything in it, and went into a store. I decided to buy something but my purse was in the car, so I went back to the parking lot to find my car and I couldn't find it. It was nighttime and very dark, few lights in the parking lot, lots of people milling about, but I just couldn't find my car. I was trying to think of who I could call to help me but I didn't want to be wrong and then find it and have them laugh at me.

I am currently going through the breakup of a relationship and my ex is one of the people I was thinking of calling to help me, but he is a very critical person and recently told me I can't survive without him—so that made me even more determined to look harder for my car in the dark parking lot.

When I awoke, the dream was so real and vivid. And I had a very anxious feeling (and still do after over an hour of being awake).

—Amber, Age 35, Single, USA

A car is how we get from one place to another. Accordingly, how a car performs in a dream—or doesn't—reflects feelings of personal effectiveness. If, as in Amber's dream, we suddenly realize we can't find our car, the dream is a metaphor for feelings of uncertainty about the future. We don't know how we are going to get from one place to another.

Purses and wallets in dreams are tied to our sense of identity. Inside both are several items we regularly use to prove our identity to the world, and to assert our power: driver's licenses, Social Security cards, credit cards, cash, and checkbooks. If we lose a purse or wallet, we are temporarily disempowered, and identity-less, until we either find it or replace its contents.

Amber's dream reflects her change in status (loss of identity) since separating from her ex, and represents her uncertainty as she sets out to tackle the world on her own (can't find the car). Her ex's recent challenge that Amber can't survive without him appears to have raised doubts in her mind. Can Amber arrive at a successful new location in her life—without the help of her ex?

Amber's determination in the dream to solve her problem herself is a vote of self-confidence for her future. Amber may feel temporarily disoriented as she adjusts to her new status, but her dream suggests she soon will be watching this relationship from her rearview mirror.

"Sense of Direction"

I'm lost in a neighborhood/subdivision that I don't know. I'm trying to look for a building, but I'm not sure which one. For some reason I'm dressed up and wearing high heels, plus I have my bicycle with me. I pass by this family that is arguing with each other rather heatedly, and as I go around the corner another neighbor (a man in his mid-fifties) apologizes for the arguing and goes around the corner to shoot them. But that part is not important to me, it seems. Just the fact that I'm trying to find something: either a certain house, or trying to find my way out of the subdivision.

Every time I have this dream (about once or twice a month for the past year or so) the houses are the same, I follow the same route, and no matter how hard I try, I can't turn around and follow where I'm coming from.

A little info on myself: I'm twenty years old and have been considering moving out on my own (I live with three roommates and I want it to be either me alone, or me and someone else). I also want to go back to college but I don't know what I want to do. I don't know if this has anything to do with that, but that's what's been going on lately in the past year or so.

Also, I don't know if this has any relevance, but I am five feet eleven inches tall, and I don't even own a pair of heels. I'm constantly in beat-up clothes, and I don't own anything nice really. My bike is my mode of transportation at the moment.

—*Anastasia, Age 20, Single, USA*

Anastasia is all dressed up—with nowhere to go! Given the background she has provided, it's easy to guess that being lost in the subdivision represents her current housing dilemma. Anastasia wants to get out of her present living arrangement, but she still hasn't found a place, or decided whether she wants to live alone or with just one roommate. (Is it any wonder she is riding around in circles?) Anastasia also hasn't made a decision yet about returning to college. Does she feel she needs more "direction" in her life?

The shooting in Anastasia's dream does not appear to hold much significance. The arguing that occurs, however, may be an echo of her current living arrangement (three roommates). Is this a situation she wishes she could leave behind (shoot)?

Bicycles in dreams often function as sexual metaphors (because of the motion). In Anastasia's case, because she rides a bike in real life, her bicycle appears to be a literal representation of her current mode of transportation. High heels also suggest sexuality in dreams, because often women feel sexy when they wear them. High heels are also associated with being older, and with getting dressed up for a social occasion.

Anastasia's dreams suggest that she is ready—heels and all—for her rendezvous with the future. Her indecision about college and housing, however, is most likely holding her back. Anastasia should take her recurring dream about being lost as a call to action. It's time to make a date with a college guidance counselor, to begin narrowing down career choices that appeal to her most. Anastasia may also have started to outgrow student housing, but a roommate whom she respects and gets along with could be a good companion. If Anastasia accomplishes these simple steps, she will immediately regain her sense of direction.

"Wrong Direction"

I have had a recurring dream for years now. I always misplace my car, of all things. Not my keys and not my purse—my entire car! I forget where it is and other times I dream it's stolen. I also dream that I am driving and am lost and going in the wrong direction all the time.

I started dreaming this more intensely the last few years after my husband and I separated and then got back together, separated, got back together—you catch the drift.

–Rachel, Age 41, Married, USA

Cars in dreams are familiar metaphors for ourselves. If we are lost and "headed in the wrong direction," it means we're feeling confused about our way in life.

Given the background Rachel provides—she and her husband are separating, getting back together, then separating again—it's easy to see why she is confused about her course. Until this situation is resolved in her waking life, her dreams will continue to reflect this uncertainty.

Rachel distinguishes between losing her car and losing her keys or purse. Keys and purses in dreams are tied to feelings of identity. Accordingly, this dream doesn't show confusion about who Rachel is—just where she is going.

The message of this dream is clear. The sooner Rachel gets a road map for her life firmly in hand, the sooner these dreams will stop. A visit to a marriage counselor will help: This will put Rachel back behind the wheel—and headed in the right direction.

Monster

Monster: Common symbol in children's and teens' nightmares that represents any fear that the dreamer believes threatens his or her safety. Monsters may threaten, chase, or attack a dreamer, and often are associated with fears concerning school or family issues.

Because monsters represent unidentified fears, successful therapies include exercises that help the dreamer identify his or her concerns specifically. Was the dreamer being chased at school (problem at school), at home (family issue), or on the set of a movie (scary film)? Did a cousin, sibling, or grandparent recently die, and is the child or teen now concerned about losing his or her parents? Scary movies and television programs are easily incorporated into the story lines of children's dreams. Parents, accordingly, must exercise appropriate guidance concerning children's viewing choices.

In mythology, monsters are an archetypal theme. The hero must vanquish a monster before he can marry the beautiful princess and achieve psychological completion. In adults, recurring dreams of attack by monsters or shadows alert us to fears and traumas that remain unidentified. To achieve psychological completion and wholeness, the monster must be identified and vanquished.

Night terror: Unlike nightmares (which occur during REM sleep and which represent fears and anxieties), night terrors are partial arousals from deep sleep that usually occur within three hours from bedtime. During a night terror, a child arouses from deep sleep (as in sleep walking) but is unable to fully awaken. The partial arousal causes a half-sleep, half-awake state that causes the child to become disoriented, and subsequently to panic, scream, or run violently through a home.

Parents should be reassured that night terrors are a physical symptom, and do not hold psychological meaning. Children typically do not remember night terrors, and should be encouraged to return to sleep immediately, without attempts to fully awaken them. Night terrors usually affect children ages five to eleven. If your child suffers from night terrors, try using a strong night-light to reduce the disorientation that occurs during arousals. This will allow your child to return to sleep calmly after a partial awakening from deep sleep.

◆ **Interpretation tip:** Children live in a world full of powerful "big people," who often exhibit outbursts of anger and sudden, unpredictable behaviors. Is this the connection to monsters?

* ※ *

Each of the dreams that follow illustrates a different aspect of the monster dream spectrum. In "Shrinking Monster," a child's fears chase him repeatedly down the hall of his house. Until one day . . . he decides to greet them. In "My Shadow," another young man carries on a terrifying conversation with his shadow. Reflecting on his dream, the boy is puzzled: Why couldn't he recognize the shadow as part of himself? Our final entry is a classic example of the fear that "Night Terrors" often cause—in parents.

Monster Dreams

"Shrinking Monster"

I used to have this dream almost every week, where I would walk out of my bedroom. As I walked past the bathroom, the door would open and this monster would come out and chase after me. The dream would end as I jumped down the stairs.

This dream went on and on until one night, instead of running, I stopped and said hello to this monster. He said hi back to me. That is how the dream ended and I never had any of those dreams again.

—Tony, Age 14, Single, USA

Tony's dream is an excellent illustration of how we can learn to conquer our nightmares—by facing the fears they always represent.

In younger people's dreams, monsters are symbols for a wide variety of fears. As kids in a "big persons'" world, monsters often represent adults we know (or have seen) who frighten us. Adults, like monsters, are bigger and stronger than we are, and sometimes can act mean, get angry, or yell at us—for no apparent reason.

Based on Tony's dream, we don't know what in particular he used to be afraid of. It may have been fears we all face growing up: doubts about our abilities, being nervous at school or with friends, or problems with parents or family.

Once Tony decided to face his fears (he got tired of jumping down the stairs) the monster never came back. What's the message of this dream? Monsters, like fears, grow bigger when we put them in a closet. This is why it's important, when we have scary dreams, to look closely at them, to understand what our fears are. As adults, we can all take a tip from Tony's dream. When we look a monster straight in the eye, the monster immediately begins to shrink, and usually leaves for good.

"My Shadow"

I dreamt that I was walking home one day from school when suddenly my shadow began talking to me in a crazed voice, saying, "I will follow you and kill you in your sleep."

You know how your dreams sometimes skip around, so you don't know something that you actually know in real life? Well, that's how I felt. I felt like I didn't know who or what my shadow was.

The day before I had that dream, I was thinking about my shadow coming alive. Does this have anything to do with my dream?

—*Damien, Age 12, Single, USA*

Carl Jung wrote that the shadow side of our personality is the part that holds on to all our fears: thoughts and feelings that we don't like to recognize about ourselves—or others. Is Damien able to identify his shadow? Maybe he isn't always as happy as he would like. Maybe things aren't always so great at school, or at home with his parents, or with some of his friends. While it is healthy to put a good face on things, sometimes we can get scared about whether everything will work out. This is when our shadow starts whispering in our ear: "Maybe all our worst fears will come true."

When working with children's nightmares, parents are advised to encourage their children to use creative ways to identify and relieve the fears expressed by the dream. If a child is chased by a monster, a helpful therapeutic exercise is to have the child draw the monster, or act out the dream using stuffed animals. Parents will gain valuable insight into their child's fears by asking where the monster is located. Is it at school? (A bully or strict teacher, or fears of social interaction?) Is it at home? (Arguments between parents, fears of separation or divorce?) If the fear always concerns a particular theme, such as death, parents should look for experiences of death that have touched their child's life, such as the death or illness of a family member, relative, or a childhood friend.

Nightmares in children are so common that they are considered to be normal, and parents are advised against overreacting to them. The key variable to watch is whether or not your child's daytime performance and mood appears to be affected. If it is, it is time to explore your child's fears, and perhaps enlist the help of a child psychologist, who can help make an evaluation. If the dreams are forgotten by breakfast, it is best to let sleeping monsters lie.

"Night Terrors"

My six-year-old daughter has night terrors, and this has been going on for about two years now. She usually has them within thirty to forty-five minutes of falling asleep, and then after the first episode she continues to sleep through the night. She will sometimes go for months without having them, and then suddenly start having one every night. When she is having one, she seems to be in a state of panic. We immediately go to her, stay with her and speak to her softly, until it is over and she is back to sleep.

Is there anything that we should be doing differently? When I mentioned the night terrors to her pediatrician he did not show concern and only said that they are hereditary (I, too, had them as a child). What advice can you give me on what to do while she is having one and ways to prevent or minimize them? Thank you.

–*Carol, Age 38, Married, USA*

Night terrors are one of the most disturbing sleep disorders that parents can witness in a child. As Carol's pediatrician's mild lack of concern suggests, however, they actually are far more distressing for a parent to watch than they are for the child to experience.

Night terrors are a subset of a broader class of sleeping disorders called "confusional arousals," related to disorders of sleepwalking and sleep-talking. During a confusional arousal, the mind gets stuck, as it were, between sleeping and waking. The arousals almost always occur during the first third of the night, during arousals from deep (nondreaming) sleep.

Arousals from deep sleep are difficult even for adults, but sleep in young children, as any parent knows, is profoundly deep. Occasionally, the mechanism that controls sleep stages in young children (ages five to eleven) is not fully developed. The result is that a child can partially arouse—hence the "awake" characteristics of the behavior we witness—yet at the same time remain deeply asleep. The disorientation caused by this merging of states often causes a child to panic, and subsequently to yell, scream, or run wild-eyed from his or her bed (eyes wide open). Despite the manifest trauma of the event, night terrors, by definition, are not psychological events. Nor are they recalled by children upon full awakening.

Because night terrors are disorders of the physical sleep stage mechanism, parents are advised to keep children with terrors on regular sleep and nap schedules. Every effort should be made to create a climate of regularity for the child, so that his or her still-forming rhythms of sleep and waking can develop and solidify. Anecdotal reports suggest that loud noises or other stimuli—such as pulling covers over a child or tucking her in—can precipitate a confusional arousal. The theory is that the partial arousal that occurs during such an adjustment may develop into a confusional arousal—with all its disorientation, screaming, and panic.

Once an arousal has subsided, parents are advised to allow their children to immediately return to sleep. Many parents—frightened by the peculiarity of their child's behavior, and also mistaking an arousal for a nightmare—seek to console their child after the initial panic abates. The consoling process—which involves talking softly and giving the child soothing rubs—often will bring the child to full awakening, which then can preclude a speedy return to sleep. Parents are instructed to enter a child's room when they hear an event to prevent injury should the child get up and run, but they are recommended to leave the room and allow the child to return to sleep as quickly as possible after the incident is over.

Unlike nightmares, which are a reflection of psychological anxiety, confusional arousals are considered a relatively normal stage in a child's sleep development. Carol's daughter, at age six, is in her prime night terrors years. If Carol follows the guidelines recommended by sleep specialists, and if she places a night-light in her daughter's room to minimize confusion and disorientation during arousals from deep sleep, she will notice a marked decrease in the frequency of these events. As her daughter's sleep patterns mature, her arousals will quickly be outgrown.

Naked

Naked: Symbol of exposure and emotional vulnerability. Being naked in a dream typically reflects feelings that others can "see through" our social disguise or presentation, into our "true self." Nudity in a dream also may reflect feelings of being unprepared in a business or social context, or fears of being exposed or caught for a crime or impropriety. Naked dreams are common in the wake of a social blunder or faux pas, and can represent feelings of embarrassment or shame, or a sense that one's behavior is being closely examined. If no one else notices our nudity, the dream indicates we may be feeling oversensitive. (No one else "sees" our discomfort.)

Naked dreams are rarely sexual, unless sex is explicitly included. Comfortable dreams about nudity with a lover suggest emotional exposure and authenticity in a relationship. Being naked or partially attired in front of a potential partner may indicate that we have "revealed" our sexual interest in them. Dreams about removing clothes unsuccessfully (there is always another shirt underneath) indicate fears about emotional intimacy. Dreams about uncomfortable nakedness or partial nudity may also reflect feelings of unwanted sexual attention. Swimming naked in a pool suggests an honest immersion in one's emotions.

♦ **Interpretation tip:** If you dream you are naked in public, ask when your emotions were recently exposed in waking life. Did you embarrass yourself in front of friends, family, or at the office?

* ✳ *

Naked dreams always make us feel somewhat uncomfortable. What private part of our life, we wonder, recently became exposed? In "My Birthday Suit," a dreamer who used to be partially clothed in her recurring dreams is now naked. Is there a reason for her sudden change in appearance? In "Naked Feelings," a dreamer is embarrassed to find herself partially exposed, and in bed with a crush, in one of her college lecture halls. Is her affection on display, or is she just in a hurry?

Naked Dreams

"My Birthday Suit"

I have had my share of "naked" dreams over the years, but in this latest dream I was confronted by a person in my dream who asked me why I was in the office in my underwear. Before, my nakedness was invisible to everyone but me. Recently a new boss took over, and he has informed me that my position is being "restructured" and "eliminated."

—Tatyana, Age 47, Single, USA

The addition of a new boss to Tatyana's workplace has added a twist to her dreams. Whereas previously her nakedness went unnoticed (a common theme in exposure dreams, indicating that others do not perceive our shortcomings as readily as we do), recently her coworkers have begun to "see" her undress. What accounts for this change?

In the past, Tatyana's naked dreams most likely reflected a normal sense of vulnerability that she felt, from time to time, on the job. Did anybody notice that she took all of Friday afternoon off? Could they tell that she bluffed her way through the accounting meeting?

Today, however, the mood at work is much more serious. All positions and personnel are under increased scrutiny, and Tatyana was recently informed that her position is being restructured and eliminated. Is it any wonder that she feels a thousand eyes are upon her?

What's the message of this dream? Now more than ever, Tatyana wants to make herself visible on the job as key personnel. Preferably she will be fully attired in her best business suit—and not her birthday suit!

"Naked Feelings"

I am a twenty-one-year-old single female and I attend university. I liked and had been flirting with a twenty-five-year-old student named

Sam for the past year. I have never told Sam that I am interested in him because he is in a long-term relationship. After all this time, I have come to realize that nothing will ever happen between Sam and me. But for some reason, I have many dreams about him, although less and less as time goes on.

Here's the dream: I enter a classroom where many students are attending a lecture. In the back of the classroom there is a bed where John (a guy who once asked me out) lies partially naked. He invites me to come into this bed, where I also become partially naked, meaning my shirt is on but not fully buttoned and my pants are off but I'm still wearing underwear. There is a white duvet that covers the bottom part of our bodies. I am unsure if the bed is an actual bed or just desks put together, but I know that it feels like a bed and there are pillows.

John is soon replaced by Sam, who then stays in the bed with me for the remainder of the dream. Sam is nearly naked, too, but he does not seem to be self-conscious about it, even though I am. Sam caresses my shoulder and my hair and puts his arm around me at one point but nothing too physical happens. At one point he caresses my back to find my underwear but does not find it, even though it is there. I do not feel happy about being in this bed with Sam because I feel guilty that I am not attending the class. I am also worried that people will notice us. At the same time, I do not feel horrible about being in this bed, but I do feel a little trapped to stay under the covers because I'm not wearing any pants. I also feel that I should be in this bed with Sam, that it is where I am supposed to be, that we are together.

The class is still going on but no one is paying attention to Sam and me; they are engrossed in the lecture. Later, as the class ends or breaks, different people come up to the bed and I pretend that I am not in it and that Sam is not there and I talk to those people as if everything is normal. I am holding on to the white cover in order to cover my bottom half. Most people talk to me as if everything were normal—failing to see Sam and me partially naked in a bed. Sam doesn't care. He's just lying in the bed at this point. He has the cover on but he's not trying to fool people. John notices that Sam and I are in the bed together.

Then the dream takes a twist when my archenemy from high school, Krista, enters the room and tells me that I am, too, embarrassed about the situation because my face is flushed and that if I don't want people to notice, I shouldn't be so embarrassed. Finally she says that I should just come out with it because it's so obvious. Then Sam tells me the same thing, that I should just let the class know what's going on. He then points out that it is so obvious because he can't even find my underwear.

—Sara, Age 21, Single, Canada

Now that Sara has decided that things aren't going to work out between her and Sam—is she embarrassed for having fallen for him so publicly? Can all her friends "see through" the cool exterior she is projecting?

In her dream, Sara's attraction for Sam could not be on more public display. Sara and Sam are both partially undressed, lying in a bed that is symbolically located in a college classroom full of their classmates.

As the lecture ends, Sara is embarrassed by her exposure, and tries to cover herself with a sheet and pretend that she is not in a bed with Sam. Most of her classmates go along with her version of the story (do not notice her nudity), but significantly, two people do. John is a man who previously tried to date Sara. When Sara rejected John's advances, did he become aware that Sara was interested in someone else? The second person who notices Sara's exposure is Krista, Sara's arch-rival from high school. Krista is a woman who, we can be sure, would relish the opportunity to expose any weaknesses she could in our dreamer.

In the wake of deciding that her crush on Sam will not be realized, Sara is feeling hurt and vulnerable. Her dream of being naked in public reflects feelings of vulnerability, and her suspicion that everyone who knows her must be able to "see" how attracted she really was to him. As she copes with her disappointment, Sara's dream offers a poignant insight into her awkward emotions. Most of Sara's friends don't notice her "naked feelings." In this way, her dream is encouraging Sara to relax about how others perceive her. Her feelings are not so "transparent."

Paralyzed

Paralyzed: Dreams about paralysis occur during partial arousals from REM sleep, when the body fails to respond to commands for movement issued by the semi-awake dreamer. The resulting physical state is confusing. A dreamer believes he or she has awoken, but feels trapped in an unresponsive body. Borders between dreaming and reality also become indistinct, as dreamers drift between REM and waking.

Dreamers who panic upon feeling their body's paralysis often dream there is an intruder or an evil presence in their bedroom that is holding them down or pressing heavily upon them. During this confused state, dreams about intruders, attackers, supernatural possession, out-of-body experiences, and abduction by aliens all are common. The paralysis of the body that occurs during REM sleep, however, is protective: Its function is to prevent us from physically acting out our dreams. Accordingly, dreamers need to be assured that they are not experiencing repressed memories, or visitations from evil spirits.

Intruder dreams: Dreams about intruders experienced in the context of paralysis represent fears about vulnerability that are caused by the sensation of immobility during REM. The dreams may also reflect literal fears of intruders, especially among people who fear for their safety due to a bad neighborhood, or a previous robbery attempt. Symbolically, dreams about intruders without accompanying paralysis may represent someone who is too close in your personal life, who is violating your boundaries.

Can't move: Dreams about being unable to run away from an attacker or of being unable to hit an opponent indicate feelings of powerlessness in waking life. Dreamers engaged in attempts to escape or to do battle find their limbs are heavy—

like they are "stuck in cement," "fighting underwater," or "moving in slow motion." The dreams suggest that a new strategy is required to manage a problem. Conversely, the ability to hit an opponent strongly or defeat an attacker indicates feelings of strength compared to an adversary.

◆ **Interpretation tip:** If you experience paralysis in conjunction with an intruder dream, try to remember that you are dreaming, and that you are not in danger. Resist the urge to panic (there is no attacker), and instead try to relax and explore the dreamscape consciously. Your body is tired, and does not want to wake up yet. No one has ever stayed paralyzed!

* * *

The disorientation experienced during episodes of REM paralysis can be terrifying. REM paralysis prevents our movement, limits our breathing, and stifles our ability to call for help. Drifting in and out of REM, a dreamer can experience terrifying visions of attack and manipulation.

In "Evil Presence," a dreamer wonders what dark force is making visits to haunt his sleep. Has a repressed trauma been awakened? "Intruder" reveals a dreamer who fears she is having a supernatural experience. Have the recently deceased come back to haunt her? Our final dreamer has an even more "far-out" explanation for her dreams. Is she being "Abducted by Aliens"?

Paralysis Dreams

"Evil Presence"

I have had this bizarre dream three to four times per night for the last two nights. In the dream I am asleep in my bed when someone or something evil enters the room with malicious intent. I am still asleep in the dream and am attempting to awaken to protect myself. I sense in the dream that if I do not awaken before the intruder gets me that I will die. I am unable to scream myself awake and finally awaken because I am actually physically whimpering (my mouth wouldn't work to scream).

The actual dream itself is not that disturbing to me, but the frequency of it is. I haven't been able to sleep. I am not frightened about sleeping, but this dream occurs approximately every ninety

minutes. I have experienced sleep deprivation off and on for the last
four years mostly due to school and my career, and have only
occasionally experienced sleep paralysis dreams.

I am not worried about intruders, nor do I feel myself in danger in
any way that I am aware of. These dreams have all occurred when I've
been sleeping on my back.

Does the frequency indicate that I am repressing an unresolved
issue? I have had many major changes over the last two years, but
none that I would call oppressive.

–Phillip, Age 32, Single, USA

Intruder dreams are some of the most frightening nighttime experiences
we have. The common theme, in all of them, is a terrifying sense of vulnerability. Phillip has asked the key question that all people who have these
dreams want to know. What is their psychological significance? Are we re-
calling a repressed memory from long ago? Is an evil spirit haunting us?
Were we abused as a child? And just who is "this man" (the attacker almost
always is male) who attacks or chases us?

All of Phillip's questions are legitimate, but before he complicates his life
with a past that does not exist ("unresolved issues"), it is important to understand the physiology of REM sleep. First, it is no coincidence that
Phillip's attacks occur in ninety-minute intervals. The human sleep cycle
also is ninety minutes long, with REM sleep appearing faithfully at the end
of each cycle. Second, the paralysis that characterizes Phillip's attacks is
also a defining characteristic of REM sleep. Every warm-blooded creature
on Earth (the entire warm-blooded animal kingdom) experiences an absence of muscle tone—known as "muscular atonia"—during REM. If we
partially arouse from REM sleep, this absence of muscle tone is experienced as paralysis.

In a famous experiment performed in 1963 by the French scientist
Michel Jouvet, it was demonstrated that the brain actually sends commands for movement during REM sleep, to move in accordance with our
perceived needs in the dreamscape. The signals are prevented from being
passed on to the body, however, by a mechanism at the top of the spinal
cord, in the brain stem. This paralysis allows us to dream, for the most part,
in peace. When we occasionally become aware of this paralysis during a
dream, we experience sensations of weight, heaviness, and feelings that we
can't move.

As a rule, dreams about intruders are not memories of experiences of being attacked. Rather, they are a universal response experienced by men and women alike to the vulnerability we feel when we realize our "REM paralysis." Phillip astutely observes that his dreams are associated with periods of sleep deprivation, and with sleeping on his back. Sleep deprivation, indeed, is a known culprit in sleep paralysis events. If our bodies are REM-deprived, they often refuse to release us from REM until we make up the lost sleep. Many sufferers of intruder dreams recommend sleeping on their sides.

The message of this dream fortunately is simple: It's time for Phillip to roll over and catch up on his sleep, undisturbed by ghosts, goblins, or threats from his past.

"Intruder"

Background information: I have been married two times. My ex is deceased.

In my dream there is usually a male figure, always in black and dull white, who enters my bedroom. He either sits down on the side of the bed or gets in bed behind me. Then he pushes so hard on my back or stomach that I cannot breathe. (I do not know who this is—all I can pick up on is that he is male.)

It is like he is taking all of the air out of my body. I wake up confused and the dream seems so real that it is scary. (Also, this only happens when my husband has already left for work or is outside of the house. It does not happen when he is home.) I have had this dream on several different occasions. This morning the thing entered the room from a door behind me, and let me know he was the same person.

Please help me understand this. Is this my ex coming back for me? I do not like him.

—*Wendy, Age 62, Remarried, USA*

Wendy has noticed that she only has intruder dreams when she is sleeping in her bed alone. This observation has fueled a dark fear: Is it possible her ex-husband, who is deceased, is haunting her? Is this why he only visits when her husband is away?

Wendy's dreams reflect several common features of sleep paralysis. The pressure she senses on her chest and stomach (Wendy dreams the intruder pushes her) is caused by the lack of responsiveness Wendy feels in her chest when she tries to gasp a breath of air. Because her body is still in REM sleep, her waking, breathing muscles are not yet active. As a result, when she tries to expand her chest, she feels like she can't get any air at all. It is similarly significant that Wendy only suffers these experiences when sleeping alone. Because sleep paralysis is caused by partial arousals during REM sleep, this suggests that Wendy sleeps with one ear open (is more prone to arousal) when her husband is out of the room.

In the Middle Ages, experiences of sleep paralysis routinely were attributed to "incubus"—possession by evil spirits, who wrestled at night with a dreamer's soul. Like her ancestors before her, Wendy also wonders if she is being visited by an evil spirit. In this case, the evil spirit is her deceased ex-husband.

As Wendy knows by now, there never really is an intruder in her room, and she is also still able to breathe during these dreams (though she cannot activate her exterior chest muscles). The solution to her dreams of sleep paralysis, accordingly, is understanding. Next time this intruder comes to visit, Wendy should remind herself it's just the same old dream, and see if she can't move an arm or leg to help break the spell of paralysis. If Wendy counts to thirty, and tries wiggling her toes and fingers, she will be fully awake in no time.

"Abducted by Aliens"

I have had several dreams throughout my life that I wake up from and have a feeling of "they're here." I don't ever see who "they" are, but in my dream I know it is aliens. I usually see bright lights outside the window and I am paralyzed. I can only move my eyes. It's a horribly scary feeling. And then I wake up.

My family teases me that I am really being abducted. But of course I don't want to believe that. I don't recall if any changes are going on in my life at this time. It seems I just have these dreams from time to time, usually when I'm at home with my parents, where I grew up.

–Ivy, Age 45, Married, USA

Ivy's recurring dream is a very good example of things that go "boo!" in the night, that actually have a simple explanation. Modern science has informed us that the paralysis of REM sleep is benign and functional (it prevents us from acting out our dreams). We also know that the demons and visions of intruders that we encounter during sleep paralysis episodes are simple representations of our fears brought to life. Paralysis makes us feel exceptionally vulnerable.

The reason Ivy can move her eyes during these attacks is because her eyes are the only part of her body that aren't paralyzed during REM sleep. (That's why they call it REM: Rapid Eye Movement sleep.) The reason the visits occur more frequently at her parents' house than in her own home is the "strange bed" phenomenon. Most people report more arousals, and more restless sleep, when they sleep away from home in a "strange" or unusual location. Finally, the lights Ivy sees may also be the source of her arousal. Did a car's passing headlights cause the partial arousal, and become incorporated into her dream story line?

Historically, sleep paralysis was always believed to be a temporary possession—by "incubus," evil spirits, the deceased, or by witches. (It was never a friendly ghost.) Today we can add UFOs and aliens to the list of our possessors, but the real culprit is actually much closer to home: some tired nerve cells, sitting at the top of the spinal cord—who are trying to get some extra zzzs—and who don't want us to wake up. (Just a few more minutes!)

Rat

Rat: Symbol of betrayal and persistent annoyance. Like most animals in dreams, rats typically represent people we know in waking life. In a romantic context, a rat may refer to a person whose intentions, we feel, are underhanded or dishonest. In a business context, rats are symbols of distrust and betrayal, as in a coworker who is willing to please the boss at another's expense, or someone who would betray a business to a competitor. Attacking rats may symbolize disturbing feelings that are "gnawing" at the dreamer—that are consistently present. Rats in a cellar represent avoided feelings that need to be identified. Rats in our beds may be symbols of romantic infidelity.

Dreams about being bitten by a rat reflect feelings of having been poisoned or contaminated in a business or romantic relationship. Rats also hold associations with poverty, disease, and filth. If a person lives in a location where rats are frequently pests, the dreams may represent a literal fear of rats, or of being disturbed by rats during sleep.

◆ **Interpretation tip:** Who's the rat in your life? Pay attention to the location of the dream (school, office, home) for clues to the rat's identity.

* * *

Rats in dreams, like rats in real life, are never great company. Our first dream explores the identities that rats often assume. Can we successfully "Pin the Tail on the Rat" in this amusing cast of characters? Our second dream, "Rats in My Home," demonstrates rats as symbols of persistent annoyance. Our dreamer wants to know: Is it possible to trade in her dream rats for something a bit less obtrusive? Our final entry, "Rat at the Office," explores the symbolism of an aggressive rat at work. Our dreamer tries to be nice, but the rat won't leave her alone.

Rat Dreams

"Pin the Tail on the Rat"

Two things from last night's dream seem to be on my mind. They have been bothering me all day.

I first remember dreaming about this rat. It was pretty big and had two long buck teeth/fangs. It was first sitting on the couch across from my bed. It hopped down to the floor and made its way to my bed, where my boyfriend and I were sleeping. (I knew it was a rat but it almost looked like a kangaroo the way it moved.)

I can't remember if my boyfriend invited this rat up on the bed or if he just didn't do anything to prevent him from coming up. But I was scared of the rat and was encouraging David (my boyfriend) to prevent the rat from coming up. David was scared himself and got up from the bed.

At this point the rat jumped up and onto me, up to my face, where it stuck its rat claws into my face. It didn't really hurt but I am still grossed out by it. (I wasn't able to get up from the bed because I was sleeping on the side by the window.) Then the subject changed. . . .

I then remember opening the door of my apartment to find this new guy from our building standing behind it. I was topless and stuck my head out to tell him I wasn't dressed, but for some reason my breasts were exposed to him. I tried covering them while he told me that he was only stopping by to give me something. He was about to leave when for some reason he came into my apartment. He seemed to have known my boyfriend, because they shook hands and this guy called David by his first name.

I don't know if it matters but the new guy in my dream is someone who just moved into my building. I have met this new guy a few times in my lobby and found myself interested in and attracted to him. A few days ago, I asked the doorman to have him call me. He never did. I guess I got the wrong impression when he flirted with me and even went as far as to call me cute. I know that the doorman reached him because I asked him the next day.

My boyfriend and I have been together for almost three years, but lately I am wondering if our relationship will ever make it to the next step. I would never think of cheating on him—and never have. David assures me that everything will fall into place for us (moving in together, getting engaged, etc.). But I feel like I've heard it for so long that for the first time, I decided to explore other possibilities (the new guy). Lo and behold, he didn't call me back.

–Andrea, Age 30, Single, USA

Andrea is disappointed that the new guy in her apartment building, with whom she recently had a flirtatious moment, never called her on the telephone. (That rat!) In the dream she is also disappointed that her boyfriend does not protect her from the "rat" coming into her bed. (He's a rat, too, for not defending her.) Finally, the rat that lands on her face suggests that Andrea may feel like a rat herself. Her recent need for attention has caused her to flirt with another man, unsuccessfully, behind the back of her boyfriend of three years.

Andrea tells us that she is frustrated with the progress of her relationship with her boyfriend, and that, as a result, she recently decided to explore "other possibilities" (the new guy). In a comic twist in her dream, her sexual interest in the new guy is revealed when he suddenly appears knocking at her apartment door. Andrea is topless behind the door, but her breasts are exposed nevertheless. Significantly, Andrea's boyfriend David remains oblivious to any undercurrent of attraction. (Will he ever defend his territory?)

Andrea is puzzled by the symbolic meaning of the handshake between the men in her dream. In a telling moment she writes of the new guy: "He seemed to have known my boyfriend, because they shook hands and this guy called David by his first name." The new guy appears to know about David, and respects his territory. (Did the doorman tell him?) With this new perspective, can we also understand the primary image of the dream? The rat on her face symbolizes Andrea's embarrassment of having revealed her sexual interest in the new man, when he has learned that she already has a boyfriend.

In our game of "Pin the Tail on the Rat," Andrea gets a tail, for flirting behind her boyfriend's back, and so does her boyfriend, whose complacency has made Andrea feel insecure. The only member of this cast of characters who doesn't get a tail is "the new guy." So far, he has behaved like a gentleman.

"Rats in My Home"

I typically have a hard time remembering my dreams, but over the last several weeks I have had dreams that have included rats. In last night's dream, I was in a big house (I think) with many people. I don't know or remember who the people were. There were rats running around everywhere. I was trying to climb onto the furniture to avoid the rats. I found them to be very scary.

Toward the end of the dream, I was standing on a couch. There were several men there. I finally felt comfortable enough to sit on the couch (with my feet up). One of the men was holding me. I suggested that the rats be replaced with mice because at least the mice would be too timid to show themselves in public. I thought things would be much better if mice were there, as long as we didn't have to see them.

I am married and have a one-year-old child. I have a feeling that the rats represent various family members. I generally have a good relationship with my family (blood as well as in-laws). Everybody gets along well and we all look out for one another. However, there are certain family members who have a tendency to drop by unannounced and stay at our house for long periods of time once they are here. My feelings about this seem to fit in with my apparent preference for the more unassuming mice.

–Brittany, Age 28, Married, USA

In this dream, Brittany did not mind acknowledging the existence of the rats, but she did wish that they might be more timid (like mice), and not show themselves in public. Once she makes the connection between the rats and her family members, the meaning of her dream suddenly becomes clear. Brittany accepts the presence of "certain family members," but she would still prefer to "see less of them."

Now that Brittany is a new mom, it's no wonder all the relatives are dropping by: They want to see the newest addition to the family. While her family's intentions most likely are good, has Brittany considered asking her husband to let the "rats" know that occasionally she gets tired, and it's best if they announce their visits and keep them brief? Brittany's hands are full—literally and figuratively—and new moms, especially, need their peace and quiet.

"Rat at the Office"

I had two separate dreams last night about rats. I can't remember the first one, but it did wake me up. In the second dream I was at work and had to use the men's bathroom, which turned out to be a single-stall bathroom. My coworker, who is also a friend, stood outside to stop people from coming in.

As I was using the bathroom a rat started to nibble on my feet. I opened the door to let him out and he managed to get back in. At this point he was very aggressive. He was jumping up at me and trying to take bites. I just remember the tail and hard fur rubbing up against me. I couldn't get my pants up to go running out and my screaming didn't cause my coworker to come in. All I kept thinking about was the fact that I couldn't get bitten and hadn't gotten bitten yet.

When I finished and was able to get out, the rat jumped on me and was holding on to me. I had to pry him off my chest and he finally did bite my fingers. I then had to pry him off my fingers and throw him against a wall and start running toward my office. As I woke up the last thing I remember is that the rat was running after me.

Rats don't scare me. I even had one as a pet in my wilder, teenage years. I haven't come across any since then, but a rat wouldn't be something that normally would send me running. I am twenty-nine years old and have just broken off a four-year relationship with somebody I work with/for. I have also been involved with somebody else and that relationship is moving forward.

–Rebecca, Age 29, Divorced, USA

Rebecca is trying to move forward in her romantic life, but it's apparent that she can't shake a rat from her past.

The office context of this dream lets us know that Rebecca is struggling with emotions related to her work environment. Because she has just broken off a four-year relationship with a coworker, and because rats in dreams typically represent people we know who have betrayed us or treated us poorly, and because the rat in this dream is masculine, we have every reason to suspect her dream concerns her recent romantic breakup.

Toilets in dreams are familiar metaphors that express our need to "release private emotions." The fact that Rebecca is using the men's stall to "release" her feelings (with the support of her coworker) suggests she is trying to put her relationship with her male boss/coworker behind her. The rat that at first is only annoying (she opens the door to let him out) soon becomes aggressive. Are the tail and hard fur pressing up against her sexual metaphors? Is her former lover jealous and aggressive, as Rebecca finds her way with someone new?

The bite symbolizes an emotional injury, and fears of contamination or infection. As Rebecca works to move forward in her life, her dream is a reminder that she is still wrestling with difficult feelings concerning her ex. These feelings need to be identified and resolved before Rebecca can pass this relationship "out of her system."

Roller Coaster

Roller Coaster: Roller coasters symbolize periods of emotional instability in our lives: the abrupt highs and lows of a volatile romantic relationship, for example, or of a sudden family crisis. Like other vehicle dreams, roller coaster rides symbolize an attempt to reach a destination. Roller coaster dreams are common in the months preceding a wedding, when a bride or groom may be experiencing "roller coaster rides" of emotions as he or she prepares for the big day. Falling from a roller coaster indicates fears that a destination will not be reached. The location of many roller coaster dreams—in an amusement park—suggests activities that we may have embarked upon "for amusement"—for example, a romantic pursuit that is not entirely serious. Roller coasters that travel over water symbolize an emotional ride.

◆ **Interpretation tip:** Are you "hanging on" through a series of emotional "ups and downs"? It's time to get your feet back on the ground.

* * *

Despite their associations with pleasure and amusement in waking life, roller coaster rides in dreams are almost always terrifying. Our first entry, "In the Dark," explores roller coasters as symbols for emotional upheaval. During a period of transition, our dreamer faces an uncertain future. Will she arrive at her hoped-for destination? Our second dream, "Losing My Way," shows a woman who fears she may become lost—after a wild ride.

Roller Coaster Dreams

"In the Dark"

I have this recurring dream in which I'm on a roller coaster at night, traveling to a vacation destination. It's usually some part of California (mainly San Diego). Here's the really confusing part. It's always at night, and the roller coaster is traveling over an ocean black as night. Sometimes I get to my destination, but sometimes I get detoured and wind up in a really awful place.

Most of the time I'm traveling with my family (my mom, dad, and younger brother). Anyway, if I make it to my "San Diego" destination, my family and whatever friends who were on the roller coaster arrive with me. If I don't make it and wind up in a god-awful place, I'm always alone. I seem to fight to stay alive in these places, but rarely do I ever get out.

Background: I'm a twenty-six-year-old female, living with my boyfriend, and I have no children. I moved in with my current boyfriend about a year ago, right after a six-and-a-half-year relationship with another guy. I have high anxiety, and have panic attacks every so often. (They seem to increase when things at home aren't good.) I find myself questioning my current status with my live-in every day. It's not even that he's too terrible (not that he can't be terrible!), but I think about my ex a lot. He's also in my dreams— usually the roller-coaster, black-ocean-at-night, going-to-San-Diego dream. What's up with San Diego? Well, to me it's one of the most beautiful places I've ever been to. (I've traveled the United States since I graduated from high school in '93). I am very close with my family. Anyway, I plan on moving to San Diego eventually—hopefully within the next year or so. Right now it seems further and further away, living with my boyfriend. I guess I'm in limbo between staying with him, or achieving my dream and living in San Diego.

–Maria, Age 26, Long-term Relationship, USA

Maria is riding an emotional roller coaster. She writes, "I find myself questioning my status with my live-in every day." She also doubts that she will ever achieve her dream—to live in San Diego—if she stays with him. What's worse, the anxiety this dilemma is causing is creeping into her waking hours. Maria is having occasional panic attacks, which she notices are more frequent when "things aren't good at home."

Maria's dream is representing her current emotional state—"I'm in limbo"—with a powerful dream metaphor. Water in dreams is always associated with emotions. The fact that Maria is traveling above an ocean in a roller coaster at night suggests that, emotionally, she is experiencing "ups and downs," and that she is "in the dark" about her future. In her mind's eye, Maria foresees two possible destinations. Either she will arrive safely in San Diego (note that her family arrives with her in these dreams), or she will wind up in a "god-awful place," alone and fighting to stay alive.

It is significant that Maria's current boyfriend does not appear in her dreams of the future—a sign that Maria does not envision herself with him. By contrast, the appearance of her former boyfriend and her family in the "going-to-San-Diego" dreams indicates a comfort she felt with him, and that she still feels with her family.

The timeline Maria outlines suggests she may have moved in with her current boyfriend too quickly. Maria's dreams and her waking panic attacks should be giving her food for thought. Her current relationship is a "ride" she wants to get off.

"Losing My Way"

I am on a giant roller coaster with my fiancé and my mom and dad and we're zipping along as it starts to rain. Soon there is a massive wave from a broken dam and everything is flooding beneath us. We're okay for a while because we're up so high, but the ground is getting soft and the roller coaster begins to fall into the water.

I find my fiancé, but not my parents; just my mother's purse. We swim and eventually find land, then walk to what seems to be my grandparents' house. The house doesn't look like theirs, but like a house that I very vaguely remember from a long time ago. I want to find a way to the roof so I can look from there for my parents in the water. A German shepherd dog walks up to me and *asks* me what's the matter. I say I can't find my parents and the dog sniffs the purse to get the scent and then goes off to look for them.

My family had a German shepherd when I was growing up, plus I'm getting married soon, so I can see all the references to family. What I don't understand is the water, the ride, or the house.

—Amy, Age 30, Engaged, USA

A
s in Maria's dreams, the roller coaster in Amy's dream symbolizes the emotional "ups and downs" that precede a wedding. The conspicuous appearance of water (which also appears in Maria's dreams) again alerts us to an emotional time in Amy's life.

Amy's dream represents an outpouring of fear (a massive wave from a broken dam) that she will become separated from her parents once she becomes married. After the giant roller coaster falls into the water (after the wedding), Amy finds herself alone with her fiancé, and is unable to locate her parents. Significantly, as she swims, Amy holds on to her mother's purse. Because purses in dreams are highly associated with identity, the dream suggests that Amy will be looking toward her mother as a role model during the early period of her marriage. The final clue that the dream concerns fears of separation occurs when Amy climbs to the roof of a house (also associated with family) to search for her parents, but still cannot find them. The appearance of the German shepherd from Amy's childhood suggests that Amy's current fears of separation remind her of similar fears from childhood.

Amy's dream is an excellent illustration of the multiplicity of fears and uncertainties that surround large transitions and commitments in our lives—in Amy's case, marriage—that give rise to feelings that we are on a wild ride, and that we need to hold on tight. As she and her fiancé "swim" toward their new identity as a married couple, Amy will seek the guidance and support that her mother can provide.

Sex

Sex: Sex in dreams is a common metaphor for attraction to, and desires to be close with, qualities that our dream partner represents. Accordingly, sexual dreams should not be immediately interpreted as literal expressions of physical desire. Pleasurable sex with a boss or coworker may represent an attraction to power or good working chemistry, respectively. Enjoyable sex with a friend may indicate the closeness of the relationship, or attraction to qualities in our friend that we find appealing.

Sex with a significantly older person, to whom a dreamer is not romantically attracted in waking life, typically reflects desires for increased security or guidance on behalf of the dreamer. Sex with a significantly younger person may be an association to innocence, naïveté, or to a dreamer's early sexual experiences. Dreams about rape or sex with a person whom we dislike in waking life may reflect feelings of violated boundaries, or of being forced to "get along" in a difficult situation.

Sex with celebrities reflects feelings that our social status is moving up in the world. (Celebs think we are attractive.) Difficulties consummating a sexual act may indicate frustration in a business or romantic relationship—one is unable to agree to terms or achieve emotional closure. Mutated, scarred, and wounded genitals reflect feelings of sexual inadequacy, past sexual trauma, and concerns about the sexual health of a relationship (including fears of disease), respectively. Frequent interruptions by authority figures during sex may symbolize a dreamer's guilt regarding the sexual act, or an absence of privacy. Dreams about same-sex relationships by heterosexuals are common and can reflect feelings of getting in touch with one's masculine or feminine self—or simple curiosity.

Sex in dreams also represents literal desires. Frustrating

dreams—inability to complete the act, a partner disappears, being interrupted by one's parents (teen dreams)—may reflect feelings of sexual frustration in waking life. Dreams about rape may reflect literal fears of sexual assault, especially in women. Dreams about sex with partners outside your primary relationship often reflect feelings of sexual dissatisfaction at home. Dreams about a partner having sex with another person typically reflect feelings of insecurity. (Please see "Betrayal.") Sex with a stranger indicates sexual curiosity generally. Did a stranger catch your eye?

◆ **Interpretation tip:** If you don't find your dream partner romantically attractive, ask yourself what qualities this partner symbolically represents.

✳ ✳ ✳

The dreams included in this chapter either reflect attractions to qualities that various dream partners represent, or they are expressions of literal attraction delivered in a variety of disguises. Our first dream, "Sex with My Father," shows a woman in transition, who is looking for a healthy role model in her life. "Sexual Voyeur" reveals a man who is shocked by the metaphor used in his dream. Is he really a pervert? "My Best Friend" raises a poignant question: Will our dreamer let her romantic feelings out of the closet? "Satisfaction" is next, and is an amusing tale about sexual release in the dreamscape. Our final entry, "Sex with the Devil," is a tale about temptation. In the Bible, the penalty for eating forbidden fruit is isolation. Can our dreamer resist temptation?

Sex Dreams

"Sex with My Father"

Background information: My family and I are best friends. My dad and I are very close. I consider him to be my very best friend. Nobody in my family has ever abused me in any way. I am single now and am a virgin.

I recently had a dream about having sex with some man (I very rarely have sex dreams). When I looked up at him, he was my father. It was a little weird but it felt more like I was having sex with a friend, not my father. It has really been disturbing me. It makes me sick to think that I had a dream like this. What does this mean?

–Isabella, Age 20, Single, Canada

Isabella has had the classic psychoanalytic dream that we all fear. (Is it true what Freud said, about desiring our parents?) Upon awakening, she feels sick and disturbed, but significantly, in the dream, Isabella feels emotions of friendship and warmth.

Isabella states she was never abused in her past, and that her relationship with her father is excellent. What is the likely meaning then, of her not-uncommon dream? Instead of being a literal reflection of sexual desire for her father, the dream indicates qualities that Isabella will find attractive in a man, as she chooses a future partner.

Judging from her dream report, Isabella's father is a healthy role model for a future mate. If she succeeds in locating a man like him, she will have found a partner who will never abuse her, who will treat her with respect, and who will be her best friend. Isabella's dream shows her using this positive relationship with her father as a road map for the future.

"Sexual Voyeur"

This dream has disturbed me for a couple of days now. It is pretty embarrassing because of the content and the actions involved.

I am in a third-story apartment with a ten-year-old girl and her mother, neither of whom are related to me, but I know them somehow. They are playing together on the floor and I am watching television.

I get up from the sofa and look out the window. In the parking lot are two thirteen-year-old girls in the backseat of a dark blue convertible. They are innocent-looking and both are wearing sundresses. As I am looking at them, one straddles the other and they begin kissing. They seem to be experimenting but they also seem comfortable in their actions. I can't believe my eyes.

I want to tell someone about it, but I'm afraid that the mother, who I know would find it interesting, would think it a bad influence and leave with her daughter. So I turn back to the window. At this point, the mother leaves the apartment and the ten-year-old girl comes over to the window with me. She sees the girls in the car and asks me what they are doing. I tell her they are kissing and that they must really like each other.

She agrees, and is now nude in front of me and asks how much I like her. In the dream, I'm not horrified by this (although I am now) and quickly find myself being sexually aroused, although there is never any intercourse. I woke up when her hand touched my genitals.

I am sorry if this is inappropriate for your analysis, but I am really troubled by this. I have *never* found a child sexually attractive and can't imagine why I would dream such a thing.

I'll give you some brief background info about myself: I am thirty-one years old, male, not married. My girlfriend moved an hour and a half away last summer. We don't talk very often and, in fact, I haven't seen her in over a month, although we have talked during that time.

One of my best friends told me about five years ago that my girlfriend was a lesbian, but changed her mind, and now has recently changed her mind back. I can loosely associate some meaning in the dream with these two people, but I don't know what real meaning there is. I do remember in the dream I was happy with the girls' willingness and fearlessness about doing this.

Please tell me I'm not really a pervert. (I know I'm not, but I am not comfortable with this dream.)

–Mark, Age 31, Long-term Relationship, USA

Given the background Mark provides, it is normal that his dreams contain themes of sexual exploration. Mark suspects that his girlfriend may be bisexual, and during a lull in his relationship with her, he believes she may be reexploring same-sex relations. Mark's dreams are disturbing, however, because they frame this exploration in the context of Mark having a sexual encounter with a child.

Like sexual dreams about partners who are significantly older than the dreamer, sex with people who are much younger typically indicates attraction to qualities that the dream partners represent, rather than specific literal attractions. The young girls represented in Mark's dream, accordingly, do not represent a literal attraction to young girls. Instead, the age functions as an association with an earlier period of sexual innocence and experimentation. The two girls whom he watches in the car from his window (clearly a voyeur's position) are experimenting with their sexuality. Is this a representation of the experimentation that surely weighs on Mark's mind, as he suspects his girlfriend is with another woman? The location of the sexual encounter, in a car, is a second clue that the experiment is taking place at a distance from him. It is significant that in the dream Mark finds the experimentation intriguing, and does not make a value judgment about it.

The age of the girls, by association, also harkens back to memories of a more innocent period of sexual exploration in each of our lives. For example, games of playing doctor and of playing husband and wife with friends of the same sex at these ages are normal. It is so normal for children to experiment with their sexuality in same-sex relationships, that to not experiment, genuinely, is abnormal.

Mark's dream shows that rather than being threatened by his girlfriend's sexual exploration, he finds it erotic and empowering. (He is impressed with the young girl's fearlessness.) If this is true, then perhaps it is time for Mark to break the ice and begin to speak openly about sexual choices and orientations with her. Mark's girlfriend will appreciate the support and the fact that he is not judgmental.

"My Best Friend"

Last week I had a dream that I was at my best friend's house. We were lounging around and drinking wine like we always do.

All of a sudden we're in her bedroom and she is seducing me. I was totally into it and loved everything about the sex that we had. She knew exactly how to pleasure me.

Then out of the blue I'm driving home and I just keep thinking to myself, "I don't remember driving there," over and over again.

As I enter my neighborhood I see a very bad car accident. When I get home I get a phone call from my sister that my mom was the person in the accident and she's dead. Then I wake up.

What do you think? I've been dating a guy for about three months now, and I also have had a very stressed-out relationship with my mom lately, in case that helps.

–Amanda, Age 22, Single, USA

Would Amanda's mother "just die" if she knew Amanda was attracted to women? That appears to be the message Amanda's dream is telling us. . . . Or is there a deeper meaning?

Amanda doesn't tell us whether she has ever had sex with another woman, or if she has even contemplated or joked about it among friends.

Judging by her dream, though, the thought has crossed her mind subconsciously. After she has sex with her friend, Amanda is suddenly in a car, returning quickly to her home. Significantly, Amanda is unable to remember the drive over to her friend's house. What is the meaning of this curious dream metaphor? The dream is telling us that Amanda's flight of fancy (her dream of sex with her friend) was not a conscious thought process.

Sex in dreams is occasionally a metaphor for good chemistry among friends and coworkers, but it can also be a transparent reflection of desire. As we seek to distinguish the nature of Amanda's attraction, it is significant to observe that Amanda took special pleasure from her friend's ability, because she is a woman, to know exactly how to pleasure her. As sex dreams go, this one is highly sensual. It is clear that Amanda enjoyed the experience—including the seduction by her friend—fully.

At the end of her dream, Amanda witnesses a serious car accident in her neighborhood, and soon learns that her mother is dead. Death in dreams is a consistent symbol for change and separation, and the meaning of her mother's passing, accordingly, becomes clear when we consider the context of the dream. Amanda's flight of fancy—her willingness to consider a lifestyle that her mother will not approve of—is a significant challenge to her mother's authority. As Amanda asserts her independence and continues to make decisions about her sexuality and lifestyle, her mother's reign as an arbiter of morals and values is coming to an end. In her mother's place, Amanda is now rapidly ascending to the throne of deciding what's best for herself—including her sexual self-expression. What's the meaning? Mother's little girl is leaving the nest (like all healthy children do) and is ready to explore the world on her own.

"Satisfaction"

In my dreams, I can not only usually tell that I am dreaming, but I have control over what I do in one category only: sex. Once I am sure it's not real, I have sex with all sorts of people: old, young, strangers, friends, family, famous people, men, women . . . I always have an orgasm and it happens about twice a week—for about six years I'd say.

I have a boyfriend who lives in a different state and I see him about once a month. I'm not really a sleep-around girl. Clearly I like to be promiscuous in my dreams, but why do I just pick anybody? Sometimes in the dreams I can't find privacy and the other person won't have sex with me, or we don't really have sex.

Of course I have plenty of dreams where no sex is involved at all. It's quite odd. My friends think I'm nuts; what do you think?

–Amber, Age 25, Single, USA

Amber is the envy of dreamers everywhere! Twice a week she is able to guide her dreams into sexual fantasies with dreamers of her choice: men, women, strangers, and celebrities. There's no risk of sexually transmitted diseases or unwanted pregnancies, no costs, no hang-ups, no need for courtship, pillow talk, or afterplay. And she's sexually satisfied—two orgasms per week!

Amber is curious why she chooses to have sex so frequently in her dreams, and wonders why she is so indiscriminate. Amber's dream lovers are neither spectacular nor specific. On the contrary, they are expedient. The answer to Amber's first question is easy: Amber chooses to act out sexual fantasies in her lucid dreams because she is sexually frustrated in her waking life. Her boyfriend lives in another state, and Amber only gets to see him once per month. Amber's indiscriminateness in the dreamscape also signals a type of sexual desperation—which most likely is born from her experience in lucid dreams. Amber tells us it is impossible to perfectly control the course of her lucid dreams. Sometimes her dream lovers refuse her, or other obstacles to consummating the act appear. In a catch-as-catch-can world, Amber is in a hurry to reach her orgasm, and any person, or thing, who appears in a dream is fair game to help her arrive at it.

But to concentrate too much on the other people in her dreams is to miss their true meaning. In Amber's dreams it's all about Amber—and everyone else is merely a prop on her stage. Amber's concentration on sexual satisfaction is a good illustration of many lucid dreamers' early experiences with gaining consciousness in the dreamscape. In time, Amber's horizon will expand to include more receptive activities in her dreams (seeking insight into problems and challenges in her life, meditation, the creation of art), which Amber ultimately will find more rewarding than merely acting out her fantasies.

"Sex with the Devil"

I had this dream that my husband wanted to divorce me because I had had sex with the Devil. And I was very upset because at the time I hadn't had sex with the Devil yet, but the Devil had convinced my husband that I had, so he would divorce me and the Devil could have me all to himself.

I tried to talk my husband out of it, but he wouldn't listen to me. Then I started running away from the Devil, but he kept chasing me. There were stairs everywhere, and the scenery was really dark red. My mom was there, and a whole lot of people that I don't really know (but I did in my dream), and none of them would help me. They all just said that I would get what was coming to me.

Then the Devil got me, and we did have sex, and I got pregnant, and gave birth to my two cats.

My relationship with my husband is very happy and secure, and I certainly wouldn't be doing anything to cause damage to this relationship. There is this guy at work who is always flirting with me, but I am always telling him no because I am married. My husband would freak if he knew about him, as my husband has caught me cheating on him before. (This was way before we were married, but he is still a little overprotective about it.)

The thing about the cats, though, is strange. It is the first time that I have ever dreamed it. My husband and I are trying to have a baby— could that be it?

–Chloe, Age 33, Married, USA

Devils in dreams are associated with guilt and temptation. Is there an area of Chloe's life where she has been tempted lately by thoughts and desires she feels guilty about?

Stairs in dreams are familiar symbols for sexual activity. (It's the motion we make climbing them, and also the angle at which we climb, which resembles an erect penis.) The deep red color of the dream is another clue that passionate feelings are involved. (Think of "red" roses and of blood "running hot.") To complete this scenario of temptation and guilt, even Chloe's family deserts her in this dream. If Chloe did have an affair, would her family feel it was all her fault?

The Devil in hot pursuit of Chloe is her coworker from her office, who Chloe informs us is often flirting with her, and whom Chloe always refuses. Because she strayed before from her relationship with her husband, Chloe is keenly aware of the injury a new betrayal would cause. Chloe's dream represents the consequences she faces if she were to surrender herself to temptation (give in to "the Devil"), and consummate the affair offered by her coworker.

In a surprise ending, Chloe has sex with the Devil, and subsequently gives birth to her two cats. Cats in dreams are common symbols for babies, because we cradle them in our arms (like a baby), and because we feed, care for, and protect them—usually raising them from kittens to adult cats. Is the mystery of the two cats, in the context of this dream, so difficult to solve? If Chloe were to have an affair now, at a time when she and her husband are actively trying to conceive, Chloe might never know the true identity of the father. Hence—a baby with a mixed identity, or in dreamspeak: two cats!

Snake

Snake: Snakes hold a variety of meanings in dreams, depending on the context in which they appear.

Danger: Fears of being bitten by a snake (or snakes) reflect fears of emotional injury in waking life. Who do you fear may strike suddenly, like a snake in the grass? If a snake bites you, consider the location of the bite. Being bitten in the chest (heart) suggests an emotional injury. Bites on the legs reflect difficulties advancing, and obstacles on the path to achieving goals. Wrestling a snake may indicate a dreamer who is struggling with a poisonous addiction, such as drugs or alcohol, or strong emotional feelings. Killing a snake in self-defense indicates confidence that one will surmount a challenge.

Phallic symbol: Snakes occasionally function as phallic symbols because of their shape. The destruction of a snake may symbolize fears of sexual intimacy, or repression of sexual drives.

Psychological growth and healing: In yogic practices the serpent energy (Kundalini) lies coiled at the base of the spine, rising through energy centers in the body (chakras) in concert with spiritual growth and development. Snakes in this context are considered positive symbols that are harbingers of opportunities for psychological growth and wisdom.

In Ancient Greece, dreams about snakes were happily received as omens of physical and psychological health. Specifically, if someone was ill, a dream about a snake indicated that the healing process had already begun. This ancient link between snakes and the healing arts is visible today in the symbol of the medical profession, the caduceus, where the vital force (a snake) is pictured climbing a winged staff of wisdom. Caring for a snake in a dream indicates a positive relationship with creative energy.

Temptation, evil, and lying: Snakes are associated with deception, betrayal, and temptation because of their biblical heritage. A snake encouraged Eve to eat fruit from the Tree of Life in the Garden of Eden, which subsequently provoked the fall of man, also alternatively interpreted as the birth of consciousness. Because of their forked tongues, snakes are associated with liars. Snakes "hissing in the grass" may reflect awareness of gossip.

Transformation: Because they shed their skin, snakes are associated with change, metamorphosis, and the life force. Ancient peoples believed that snakes did not die (they shed their skin), and thus held the key to eternal life. Pregnant snakes are associated with fertility, maternal wisdom, and opportunities for growth in a dreamer's life. Large snakes can symbolize wisdom.

♦ **Interpretation tip:** If you dream about snakes, ask what recent event has caused you to be fearful that you may be hurt (bitten) in some fashion? Is an opportunity for spiritual growth present?

* * *

Snakes are always powerful symbols in dreams, no matter what context they appear in. Our first dream, "My Mother Is a Snake," shows an adult dreamer who is still haunted by childhood memories of living with a "poisonous" personality. "Chased by Snakes" reveals a dreamer who knowingly committed a terrible deed. Will the snakes ever go away? Our final dream, "Garden of Eden," shows a woman pursued by a snake in a garden. Is it a surprise that, in her waking life, she is also courted by temptation?

Snake Dreams

"My Mother Is a Snake"

I am a thirty-eight-year-old mother of two. I am in remission (three years) from breast cancer. My mother also has breast cancer, and is now dying from a recurrence and is in hospice. I suffered terrible physical and emotional abuse at her hands but, in the face of her death, have managed to be kind and caring to her in spite of the fact that she is still abusive. I have told her many times that she is forgiven. She continues to be abusive while constantly seeking reassurance that I forgive her. I don't think about her or my father much unless I am forced to. Frankly, I am busy having a happy life.

While I was in cancer treatment, my parents refused to have contact with me because I would not apologize for something I had done to make my mother angry.

My recurring dream takes many forms. I usually have this dream after I have encountered my mother, even through a phone call. I am in a dark house—usually the house where we lived while I was ten through seventeen—and my mother is terribly angry. There is loud shouting and something terrible is being said, but I don't know exactly what the words are. I try to move from room to room but can't escape. She follows, accusing me and yelling at me. Sometimes I go outside and hide.

Sometimes my mother will turn into a snake and that is very frightening. I end up turning on my mother and physically beating her up. (If she is a snake, I kill her with a shovel.) I can feel how heavy my limbs are as I try to hit her and it takes a lot of effort. I land blows but they feel soft and ineffectual. I can't stop myself. Usually I am hitting her in the face. This is shocking since I am not a violent person and, frankly, can't tolerate violence. In the dream, I feel sick and degraded about the whole thing. I don't feel triumphant or strong. I awaken and feel that it all really happened, and usually it takes me a long time to reorient myself.

–Alyssa, Age 38, Married, USA

Difficult memories from childhood are being reawakened in Alyssa's dreams—apparently with the slightest of ease. A phone call from her mother during the day can bring back, at night, memories of abuse committed over twenty years ago.

Alyssa's dreams are literal reenactments of the torment once inflicted on her. As her mother chases Alyssa from room to room in a childhood home, she will not allow Alyssa to escape her wrath. Alyssa's mother's metamorphosis into a snake is symbolically potent. Like a snake, her mother speaks with a cruel, forked tongue, and because Alyssa never knows when her mother will strike, she is forced to be guarded in her presence. The venom that spills from her mother's mouth is poisonous. It is a testimony to Alyssa's strength that she has developed immunity to her mother's spirit-killing bite.

Soon Alyssa is provoked to fight. Though Alyssa emerges triumphant in her battles—having landed the most blows—Alyssa observes that her victory, nevertheless, feels like defeat. The difference between herself and her mother is that Alyssa understands that only a sick person could derive pleasure from the torment of another.

Alyssa's dream reveals that the process of forgiveness is still in progress. When Alyssa's mother is no longer able to provoke her into spirit-draining fights, the battle will be won, and Alyssa will be the victor.

"Chased by Snakes"

In my dreams, snakes are either chasing me, or biting at me. A friend said snakes in dreams can represent evil (doing), transition, or betrayal.

I am ashamed, because a few days after these dreams began I betrayed a very close friend who had been better than family to me. She employed me, fed me, and at times even bought me clothes when things were hard for me. I cost her every dime she had, and told lies to people to cover up what I had done.

There are still snakes. What does it mean?

–Hailey, Age 40, Married, USA

It is not hard to see the link between the act Hailey committed and the symbolic meanings of treachery and deceit. Because she betrayed a friend, Hailey feels like a "snake in the grass." Because she told lies, she was "speaking with a forked tongue." In this light, the snakes in her dreams, chasing and biting her, are clear signs of a heavily burdened conscience. Hailey has deceived another human being, but significantly, her dreams show she is unable to deceive herself. The fact that her dreams began before the betrayal occurred shows that, subconsciously, Hailey already was wrestling with the anticipated consequences of her deceit.

The Ancient Greeks believed that snakes in dreams were positive symbols indicating opportunities for spiritual and psychological transformation. According to the Greeks, Hailey's dream is a signal that a life-defining, transitional moment is upon her. Hailey is ashamed because of actions committed in her past, but an opportunity for redemption waits in her future. Will Hailey rise to the occasion, admit her mistake, make amends for damage that was caused, and reclaim the moral high ground for herself? Or will she let this life-changing opportunity pass her by?

The snakes want to know.

"Garden of Eden"

I am riding with my aunt in a car and we stop when we find this beautiful rain forest. I have an overwhelming feeling of how beautiful this place is. It is very bright and full of plants and birds. It feels very peaceful.

We continue to walk and soon pass under the branches of a tree. We spot a boa constrictor in the tree. We don't feel afraid—just curious about the snake. We are still feeling very angelic about this place. I then feel the sack lunch I have in my hand begin to move. I drop the sack and a black-and-red-striped snake comes out. I immediately feel very afraid—like this snake is going to bite me.

I begin to walk away and the small snake follows me slowly. It is always with its head up, like a cobra, staring at me. I find myself behind some rock with the snake on the other side, ready to strike. Behind me is a medium-sized pond. It is full of fish and dolphins. It is dark around the pond due to the canopy of very large trees, but I can tell that above and around the canopy is sunshine, so it is not scary at all. Again, it is very peaceful and beautiful.

As I am staring at the snake, I hear a splash of water in the pond. I turn and look and it is a friend from high school who died of breast cancer. She is swimming with the dolphins. She gets out of the water and she is naked and begins to dry off. When I turn to look back at the snake, my friend hits it on the head with a shovel and kills it. I am relieved but still confused about what just happened. Then I wake up, very confused and emotional.

I am struggling with my home life now. I am not sure about my marriage and whether I truly love my husband. I have met another man and cannot get him out of my mind. He wants to see me away from my family. Just him and me. I really want to, but I know in my heart I should not.

–Melanie, Age 42, Married, USA

The snake in Melanie's dream represents her temptation to have an affair with the man she recently met. During a time of difficulty in her marriage, this man has been encouraging Melanie to begin a secret sexual liaison. She is tempted, but knows in her heart she should not. It is also clear from her dream that Melanie fears this new relationship (the snake) may wind up "striking her"—a dream metaphor for causing her emotional injury.

Snakes in Western cultures are associated with treachery and deceit because of their association with the snake in the biblical tale of the Garden of Eden. It is not a coincidence that Melanie's dream about temptation occurs in a setting that she herself describes as angelic. The rain forest she wanders into is bright and full of plants and birds and sunshine, and has a pond with fish and dolphins swimming in it. As she enters the garden, a snake hanging in a tree (Tree of Life?) completes the reference to the Garden of Eden.

Similarly, the appearance of Melanie's friend, who died of breast cancer in real life and who emerges from a pond in the dream that contains dolphins and goldfish, is yet another reference to spiritual values. Melanie's friend acts swiftly in the dream to kill the snake with a shovel. Given the context of the dream, the message sent by her friend is clear. Melanie is relieved in the dream when the snake that is pursuing her is killed. She will be similarly relieved when she "puts an end" to this romantic temptation.

Stairs

Stairs: Symbol of progress in personal or professional goals. Ascending stairs quickly (jumping several steps at once) may reflect easy progress toward one's goals—or a concern that one is "skipping steps." Climbing very high on stairs so that a dreamer worries about his or her safety or losing balance suggests career goals that appear unattainable. Falling off stairs represents fears that a goal will not be reached. Climbing down stairs can reflect feelings of descending economic or social position. Climbing down stairs into a cellar or basement represents access to subconscious feelings and awarenesses.

Steps of stairs refer specifically to steps that need to be completed, on the path to success. Stairs with missing steps indicate obstacles. Stairs that are in ill repair reflect doubts about one's ability to reach a goal, or feelings that one's strategy is inadequate and needs to be revised. Endless stairs reflect feelings that the journey to the next goal is long, and may not be worth the trip. Cutoff stairs indicate plans—as in an "ascent" to marriage—that are no longer present or that have been withdrawn. Freud observed, correctly, that stairs often have sexual connotations. It's the "repetitive motion," and the angle of ascent, which resembles an erect penis.

◆ **Interpretation tip:** Are you climbing the stairs to success? Try to identify the steps you need to take to reach the top.

✳ ✳ ✳

Whether we are headed up or down, stairs in dreams can be fraught with foreboding. In "The Stairs of Success," a woman is climbing to new heights in her career. Can anything stop her ascent? In "Descending a Stairwell," a dreamer goes down into her subconscious mind to recover a painful childhood memory. Will she remember the way out? Our final dream,

"In the Basement," shows a mother who must take several steps to reconnect with her feelings in order to allow a period of healing to begin.

Stair Dreams

"The Stairs of Success"

Background information: I am originally from Africa, and I have been residing in the USA for over eighteen years. I am in a controller's position for a big company. I do a lot of volunteer work at my church and I am always reaching for new goals. I just bought my first home without the help of anyone.

On Saturday night I dreamt that I was at home (a very big house—split-level) and we were entertaining a lot of people. Every time I tried to go upstairs I kept seeing snakes in the corners of the stairs, or on the steps. I always retreated and waited for the chance to go upstairs. And when I tried to explain this to a few people at the gathering, they either laughed at me for being scared, or told me to go continue climbing up the stairs. What does that say to you?

–Prindi, Age 34, Single, USA

Prindi has climbed high up the stairs of success. Now that she is a homeowner, and a controller for her company, does she occasionally wonder if she can climb any higher?

The setting of this dream in a large split-level home alerts us that Prindi's recent home purchase is still on her mind. The crowd that is gathered in the home (it is not Prindi's actual new home, but Prindi is the hostess) suggests public recognition, and approval, of her latest accomplishment.

Attempts to climb stairs in dreams are consistent metaphors for attempts to "reach new levels" in our careers and social life. Snakes, on the other hand, are symbols of growth and change. If Prindi's dream is a metaphor for climbing to a new level of success in her life, is it possible that the snakes represent her fears—about her ability to reside at this intoxicating new height?

By finding snakes of change and metamorphosis on the stairs to "the next level," Prindi's dream is a metaphor for fears of success. In the wake of purchasing her first home all by herself, Prindi may be overwhelmed, occasionally, at the heights she has already achieved. If this is true, then her friends in the dream—who dismiss the danger of the snakes and uniformly encourage her to keep climbing—appear to give wise advice. Prindi has climbed far in this world already, and there is no reason for her ascent not to continue. She just needs to take it one step at a time.

"Descending a Stairwell"

Background: I am a childhood sexual abuse survivor, in therapy, and recovering for many years.

My dream: I am in my childhood neighborhood, now grown up to be a young woman. I am lost and ask a man which way to get across a bridge. I did not listen to his advice and went my own way, and found myself inside a school building—a recurring location in my dreams.

I see two women going down a stairwell. I follow, hoping to find a way out. They are far ahead of me. I am descending a stairwell and it is getting narrower and narrower. Then I hear two men. They are behind me, also descending the stairwell.

I can see the light to the street. I keep going down. Now I am squeezing my way through. I cannot go back. I must go forward, but it is difficult, since I am getting stuck. I am down to the street landing and the woman before me gets out onto the street, which is in a very dangerous neighborhood.

I am now wedged in the doorway. My head is stuck so I cannot even turn it. I am trapped. Half my body is on the street in the dangerous town, and the other half is trapped inside the doorway and the men are coming. Either way I am in danger.

I am so troubled by this dream. In my nightmares I am always in the basement of a school building or church. I have many dreams about molestation. I have been working on this in recovery for a long time. I feel this dream is a symbol of something. Is it telling me that I am so fearful that I am stuck in life? And that there is danger in my past and also in the present?

–*Olivia, Age 42, Married, USA*

Olivia's dream is a metaphor for the difficult feelings she is experiencing as she re-explores, in therapy, memories of an early-childhood abuse. As the dream begins, Olivia is searching for a way to cross a bridge. Because bridges in dreams are consistent symbols for transition (they lead us from one location to another), it is logical to assume that Olivia's dream reflects her efforts to leave this painful territory behind.

A man offers directions to the bridge, but Olivia chooses instead to follow the lead of two women, whom she sees descending a stairwell in a school building. Downward movements in dreams (by stairs, elevators, or descents into caves) are common metaphors for the exploration of subconscious feelings and awarenesses. Stairs in dreams also are often associated with sexual activity, due to the motion we make climbing them. Because this stairwell is located in a school building, a recurring symbol in Olivia's dreams, we are alerted that her childhood abuse may have occurred at her school, and also possibly at her church.

As Olivia progresses along this path, the walls of the stairwell begin to close in upon her. Behind her, Olivia can now hear two men following her. (Was she molested by two men in her past?) As the dream draws to a close, Olivia is stuck in a doorway—unable to exit into a street that looks dangerous, and unable to escape from the two men who approach from behind. If Olivia's dream, as she suggests, is a metaphor for her location on the therapeutic path, we can see plainly that currently Olivia is "stuck" in therapy. The past and present both contain men who appear threatening, and Olivia remains frozen in fear between them.

Olivia informs us that she is married when she signs her dream report. If her bond with her husband is strong and supportive, Olivia has already gained a significant foothold on the bridge to transition—where all men are not viewed as potential molesters but, rather, as individuals, with good and bad traits alike identified. As a survivor of childhood abuse, Olivia needs to develop trusting relationships with all members of her social milieu: friends, family, and loved ones. With their continuing support, Olivia will soon be able to climb the stairs from betrayal to trust, and open the door to a future free of fear.

"In the Basement"

I lost a son one year ago, and of course the hurt was so bad I thought I wouldn't make it. About two weeks after his death I had a dream that I was in a castle.

My sister, who has always been there for me, woke me and told me there was someone who wanted to see me. She walked with me down two flights of stairs and when we reached a certain point she said, "This is as far as I can go." I walked further and I came to where her husband was sitting. He is like a father to me, and he said, "Go through that door, because I can't go with you."

Now I was in the basement. All I saw were brick walls and another flight of stairs. I was afraid. I went through the door and saw my son was asleep in his bed in his regular clothes. He got up. I was very afraid and ran upstairs because all I could think was, "Oh, my God, he's dead. What is he doing here?"

When I got to my sister she said, "He is your son. Go to him and tell him it's going to be okay." I turned around and went back down the stairs. I hugged him and told him everything would be okay. I felt so much better, and then I woke up. What could this mean?

—Megan, Age 28, Married, USA

Houses in dreams are common symbols for the self. The upper levels of a house typically reflect higher mental functions, like thinking and spirituality, while basements and cellars function as locations for subconscious feelings and awarenesses. Because Megan's house is a castle, we are immediately alerted to its special symbolic significance. Castles in dreams hold associations with spiritual wealth and the higher self, and to mythic wisdom.

The familiar metaphor employed by Megan's dream is that she is descending down, deep down, into her subconscious. This is a territory where fears and hurts—because they cause so much pain—are often stored. With direction and support from loved ones, Megan steadily overcomes her fears, and is eventually reunited with her son. In this magical space deep within the mythic castle, the separation of death is overcome, and a connection between mother and son is repaired.

When we experience traumatic events in our lives, our minds often bury the feelings associated with the event, to protect us from the shock, and to allow us to carry on with our everyday needs and lives. Our ability to repress our feelings, however, is always only a Band-Aid for wounds that need to be managed consciously, in order to heal properly. Megan's dream, accordingly, is a portrait in courage. A strong woman is beginning the magical journey of healing and renewal.

Teeth

Teeth: Universal symbol reflecting concerns about physical appearance, social presentation, and effectiveness in a competitive environment. Teeth are connected to concerns about appearance because teeth are an integral component of our presentation. "Your smile is the first thing people see when they meet you." Smiles (showing of teeth) are also tools used to indicate sexual attraction and desirability. Teeth are associated with feelings of power and assertiveness because we use them to bite into and to chew food. Animals bare their teeth (show their fangs) to indicate feelings of aggressiveness. Popular expressions—"Sink your teeth into it," "Show some teeth"—indicate feelings of determination and tenacity respectively.

Dreams about repetitive teeth brushing can reflect attempts to "clean" one's appearance—not unlike repetitive hand washing in the wake of guilty feelings. Rotten teeth may reflect concerns about aging and deteriorating health. Loss of teeth in a child's dream may indicate progress and evolution—"getting one's adult teeth." Dental records in dreams are associated with identity. If literal concerns exist, dreams about teeth may indicate thoughts about dental conditions or procedures.

Teeth falling out: Exceptionally common dream associated with concerns about appearance and shrinking feelings of self-confidence and effectiveness. Teeth-falling-out dreams are common in the wake of romantic breakups and divorces, when we are most likely to question our physical desirability and attractiveness. Teeth-falling-out dreams also occur when we are embarrassed or insecure in a social or professional context, or in highly visible professions where appearances are at a premium. During periods of depression or decreasing effectiveness, teeth-falling-out dreams may reflect feelings that we are "losing our bite." The dreams can also be associated with concerns about aging and physical deterioration of the body, as in, "Another year gone by."

The popular superstition "If you dream a tooth falls out someone close to you will die" is false.

Chewing gum: Dreams about chewing gum that fills the mouth of a dreamer, making speech difficult or impossible, reflect feelings of being unable to express oneself clearly, or a reluctance to voice one's opinion. Do you have to "hold your tongue" in your position at work? Is there someone to whom you would like to express your feelings, but cannot?

♦ **Interpretation tip:** Can you identify your appearance or performance anxiety? Was a recent presentation not up to par?

* * *

Who would guess that teeth would be so intimately linked with concerns about appearance? "Teeth in My Hand" shows a dreamer who is concerned about her advancing age. Do her dreams mean she's beginning to "fall apart"? "Shattered Teeth" shows a dreamer who is feeling the heart-sinking emotions of romantic rejection. Now she wonders: Is he worth it? Our next dream, "Losing My Bite," shows a dreamer whose teeth are falling out in rows. Was she a shark in a former life?

Teeth Dreams

"Teeth in My Hand"

I was sitting in a restaurant with my high school boyfriend's sister and cousin (whom I haven't seen in twelve years). We were ordering some food and my teeth began to fall out in my hand. There were lots of teeth (way more than I actually have), and about half fell out.

I looked in the mirror and there were some new rows coming in from the gums, but there were also many holes where it looked like the teeth that were falling out would not be filled. When I looked down at my hand, there was a huge pile of teeth. At the end of the dream, I was trying to get to my dentist.

As for current events in my life, there are a few issues. I recently broke up with a guy that I dated for six years. I was talking about my ex the other day to my best friend (also from high school) and telling her that it would be weird someday when I heard he got married. I don't think of him often, and I don't have any lingering feelings for him, other than that he was a great person and I liked him a lot at the time.

Also, I did just turn thirty a month ago and I have been feeling a little strange about that—wondering if I should get married (I'm single), what am I doing in my career, do I want to live in New York permanently, etc. Probably typical thoughts for a single woman turning thirty, I don't know.

But I have been somewhat obsessive over the fact that my life is passing me by, seemingly more and more quickly. Am I getting anywhere? I work a lot and am very focused—but on the wrong things it seems. I want to get married and have a family, but I spend all my time on my career. I am beginning to date a new guy that I like, but he's twenty-five and I wonder if that's a problem—for numerous, obvious reasons. I have also been thinking that I am looking older (it seems that the day I turned thirty, I started to age—seriously) and that bothers me. So, that's about it.

–Chandra, Age 30, Single, USA

In the wake of breaking up with her boyfriend of six years and celebrating her thirtieth birthday, the hourglass of time appears to have captured Chandra's attention. Is she running out of time to achieve her goals of marriage and family? While her younger boyfriend may temporarily reassure her of her looks and sexual desirability, Chandra is concerned nevertheless. Is this younger man a realistic partner? Specifically, are they on a compatible timeline?

Chandra's recent conversation, in waking life, with a friend from high school about her ex's future marriage plans is a thinly veiled echo of her own anxieties. Accordingly, it is no coincidence that in her dream she is sitting with another friend from high school, who is also associated with one of Chandra's former boyfriends. With this stage carefully orchestrated by her dream, Chandra's teeth now begin falling out by the handful.

In light of her recent anxiety that she has begun to lose her looks, Chandra's loss of her teeth becomes understood as a metaphor not only for advancing age (when teeth really do begin to fall out) but also for fears of losing her beauty and desirability. When Chandra inspects her mouth in a mirror, she is able to identify some areas where she feels her teeth will regrow, but she also notices others where she feels the teeth may be permanently lost. Time, indeed, is passing by.

Chandra's dream is strong encouragement for her to begin taking concrete steps to build the future she wants for herself. Creating this future may require Chandra to leave her younger days (and her younger man) behind, but Chandra has every reason to want—and to be excited about—building a realistic romantic relationship with an available partner.

"Shattered Teeth"

I am in love with a younger man who refuses to enhance our relationship physically. Last night was the first time I dreamed about him. He was with me in an antique shop and questioning me about the use of a silver piece (a small little dish). I felt very uncomfortable. I did not know the answer and realized with pain in my heart his "cold character."

When looking into the mirror later on, I saw that all my teeth were half broken and I was surprised I had not noticed it before.

The dream caused some fear in my heart. Although it may sound cruel, after the dream I told the man not to call me for the next four weeks. I have not dreamed about him since.

–Sigrid, Age 43, Single, Germany

Dreams about teeth falling out almost always reflect concerns about appearance. While the dreams often concentrate on our physical looks, it is important to recognize that they can also signal anxiety about our social, intellectual, or emotional appearance. All of these concerns are reflected in Sigrid's dream.

Based upon her dream report, we know that Sigrid has every reason, currently, to be insecure about her physical beauty. Sigrid has told us that she is in love with a younger man who "refuses to enhance our relationship physically." This scenario, naturally, would drive any person crazy. But it would also cause us to perform an immediate inventory of all our potential shortcomings. "What's wrong with me?" we would ask, perhaps as we stood looking in a mirror, as Sigrid does in her dream. "Why doesn't he want me? Am I too old? Have I lost my attractiveness? Have I lost my sex appeal?"

Not only is Sigrid's physical beauty challenged, but her social and intellectual gifts are also questioned. In the dream, Sigrid feels very uncomfortable when this man asks her the function of a certain small silver dish in an antique shop. At this point in the dream Sigrid realizes his "cold character." The choice of the dream to represent her feelings of inadequacy in the context of an antique shop is poignant. Antiques, generally speaking, are collected and used by the aristocracy. Silver is also frequently a gift at weddings. Does this man come from a "higher" social class than Sigrid, and does he refuse her love (desire for a committed relationship) because of this? If so, is this the "cold character" that Sigrid perceives inside him?

Sigrid's decision to distance herself from this man based upon her dream reflects a high degree of self-esteem and personal confidence. Sigrid appears to have correctly perceived in her partner stumbling blocks to a successful relationship. As Sigrid searches for love in her life, she is wise to look elsewhere for a relationship of equals—partners who love and accept each other with warm and open hearts.

"Losing My Bite"

Last night I dreamt my teeth were falling out—specifically, the top row, and I actually pulled out three "rows" (like sharks' teeth). I tried putting the last "row" back in but my mouth was very sore and bloody and they would not go back in. They ended up sitting in my lap.

While this was going on I was attempting to deal with a mechanic about my car, which was broken-down in his garage. I read that dreaming about teeth often relates to concerns about appearance, but I don't think I'm overly concerned with my appearance at the moment. I have just moved to the West Coast, leaving my family, who I am very close to, back East. I spoke with them on the phone yesterday afternoon and had the dream last night. I cannot seem to reconcile the events myself. Do you have any insights that could help me?

–Lisa, Age 31, Single, USA

These are no ordinary teeth that Lisa pulls from her mouth. The teeth are in rows—as Lisa observes—"like sharks' teeth." Aggression and predation are two qualities that we commonly associate with sharks. Is the true meaning of Lisa's dream, accordingly, that Lisa feels she has lost her "bite" recently—her decisiveness, her aggressiveness, and her killer instinct?

The fact that Lisa's car is being repaired in this dream, as Lisa grapples with her falling-out teeth, is no coincidence. Cars in dreams are consistent metaphors for our selves, for the direction we are headed in our lives, and for our confidence in our ability to get from one location to another. Lisa's dream strongly suggests that she is feeling "run-down" and "without power" in her life.

If Lisa has been feeling overwhelmed—and even a bit depressed—by the challenges of moving to a new and distant location, her feelings are entirely natural. Lisa has left the security of family and friends behind, and now faces the uncertainty of putting down roots in an unfamiliar landscape, without her customary support system. The second message of the dream is that Lisa also is feeling physically run-down. Lisa should consider taking some time off, to allow her body to rest and repair. If Lisa can commit to eat well, sleep well, and include exercise in her daily routine, she will get her sharks' teeth back in no time.

"Chewing Gum"

Last night I dreamt that I was at a school watching a French teacher. I was really impressed how well she kept the children quiet. I decided to wait until the end of the class so I could talk to her. She seemed to be very busy and was running off to her second job. She told me that she only teaches a few hours there, and therefore had to accept a second job. All of a sudden while she was still talking to me I felt a piece of gum stuck on my teeth. I couldn't get rid of it and was unable to talk. It was really bugging me.

Background: I am a French teacher and I have been thinking about my career a lot lately. Like this woman in my dream, I am only teaching a few hours, which does not meet my financial needs. I was even thinking about doing something else this fall, but was worried what to tell the school. Any thoughts? Could this dream teacher be myself?

–Valerie, Age 31, Engaged, USA

Valerie's dream shows that she would like to "spit something out," but that she just can't find the right words.

Dreams about chewing gum and other objects (broken glass, ball bearings, small objects, ice cubes) that fill our mouths and make speech impossible are common. The meaning, as Valerie's dream demonstrates, is that we want to speak up and have our voices heard, but we are experiencing an emotional block that is preventing us from expressing our views.

Through its mirror image of her own professional predicament, Valerie's dream leaves no doubt that the voice that is blocked is her own, and that her dream concerns her dilemma at work. Valerie's teaching job does not provide enough hours to support her financially, and now she fears that she will have to leave in the fall, presumably to pursue full-time work. Her dream shows that Valerie finds the decision emotionally difficult to make, and that she worries about confronting her school with the news. What is the best way to say good-bye?

Given the background Valerie provides, the meaning of her dream is entirely transparent. As soon as Valerie makes a decision about the fall semester—and musters her courage to inform the school of her plans—she will immediately regain her voice.

Tornado

Tornado: Tornadoes are unpredictable, violent storms that destroy homes and separate families. Accordingly, dreams about tornadoes typically reflect memories of family instability, or fears about current family separation. Tornadoes may also represent people who are prone to violent outbursts and unpredictable mood swings, who "destroy everything in their path." Similarly, tornadoes may represent family members or relatives with drug and alcohol problems. (We don't know which personality will show up.)

Dreams that are located back in time—houses we used to live in as children—reflect memories of separation and family instability experienced during childhood. Tornadoes set in the present reflect threats that a dreamer is able to locate "looming on the horizon" in his or her current life. Tornado dreams are common during periods of emotional upheaval—separations and divorces—and during other intense, emotional conflicts involving family.

For people living in tornado areas, the dreams may reflect literal fears of an encounter.

♦ **Interpretation tip:** Can you identify the violent storm that threatens to destroy your home? Are you worried about being separated from your family?

* * *

When a tornado strikes, everyone must run for cover. "Tornadoes Everywhere" reveals tornadoes as symbols of emotional upheaval and destruction. "Twister" shows a powerful storm that threatens to separate a family. "Fist-fighting a Tornado" shows a man with an explosive and violent temper, who wreaks destruction in his path. Our final entry, "Storm on the Horizon," uses a tornado as a symbol of fear and uncertainty for the future. Will our dreamer survive?

Tornado Dreams

"Tornadoes Everywhere"

For years now I have had the same dream over and over. It may vary sometimes but the main thing is that I am in the house that I grew up in and there are storms coming with tornadoes everywhere. The sky gets dark and I see in the distance the tornadoes coming. I run to look for my family and get them in. I search for a safe place but there is no basement and I am running inside and sometimes someone is missing and I hurry to find them.

Some versions are that there is a river, and I see tornadoes popping up everywhere in the river and they are following me. So I keep driving away but they are everywhere. Some repeated dreams are of huge waves crashing and I get caught in them. They knock me down and I can't get up to the surface. I also have some dreams about other catastrophes—like volcanoes or in one case a bomb that was dropped and I lay down for cover on top of my little girl, but we were burning in the fire and I woke up feeling hot as if it had really happened.

I have one daughter and come from a large family with seven younger siblings. I am usually gathering them up in the dreams and they are still toddlers, although in real life they are in their early twenties to late teens. My daughter is usually there, too.

I am the only girl in my family. I divorced my husband, who was a pathological liar who cheated on me a lot. I was also abused by my stepfather growing up, and now I am remarried and have been for four and a half years. I love my husband but have a difficult time trusting him. I had dreams about tornadoes before I found out about my ex-husband's affairs and have recently in the past few years started having them more often. They all seem to be me at my age now but back in time when my brothers were little.

—Barbara, Age 31, Married, USA

Tornadoes, tidal waves, storms, volcanoes, bombs. What a dream life! At any second, the world as Barbara knows it may vanish before her eyes. And in every dream, children figure prominently. The theme that links these dreams is an unstable environment, especially during childhood.

Barbara has told us that she grew up in a difficult family. Her parents got divorced, and instead of her family life improving, things went from bad to worse. Her new stepfather abused her, and then Barbara married a man who was unfaithful and who lied to her. (Can anyone fault Barbara for learning not to trust?)

Given her background, Barbara's chaotic dream symbols create a symphony of sense. Tornadoes in dreams are common symbols for unstable environments; we never know when the next "storm" will strike. Tornadoes are also familiar symbols for forces that threaten to separate our families. We have all heard stories about people being sucked into tornadoes, never to be seen again. Volcanoes and bombs? More instability. (Does someone in her family have an "explosive" temper?) And those suffocating tidal waves? Water in dreams always represents emotions. Does Barbara occasionally feel emotionally overwhelmed?

Next time Barbara has one of these dreams, she needs to take five deep breaths and recognize that her familiar fears—of betrayal in an unstable world—have come to surface. If someone from Barbara's past has proved him- or herself untrustworthy, Barbara should remember it. If an individual hasn't given Barbara cause for suspicion, she should extend the benefit of the doubt—until she is proven otherwise. Otherwise she will prevent herself from living with the kinds of friends and lovers she deserves.

"Twister"

Before I tell you about my dreams, I would like to give a quick background of what's going on. My wife and I have been married for almost five years now. We have had two children together and have an older son from my wife's first marriage. Ever since we have been married, I feel that my wife shows our stepson more affection and attention than she does to me and our other two children. I kind of feel like he has been a wall between the two of us, and that our relationship suffers because of this.

I am a lot closer to the other two children than I am to my wife and my stepson, and recently left her and the kids and then returned again because I could not bear to be without the two little ones. My stepson is hesitant to listen and obey me because his mom has always stepped in every time I have had something to say to him. This doesn't happen too often with the other two. As a matter of fact, they listen and usually obey without question. Everyone says they are "daddy's boy" or "daddy's girl," and I feel a lot closer to them.

The dream I had was that I was outside playing with our three children on their swing set. I heard a loud "rushing" sound and when I looked around to see what it was, I was horrified to see a large tornado heading right for us. I yelled over the noise to the kids, but only the two little ones came right to me. My stepson, as usual, didn't listen to me, yet he was scared to death. He began running toward the tornado. My wife came running outside, asking where he was. When I pointed to him running toward the twister, she accused me of being negligent and went after him. Needless to say, both of them were sucked up into the twister while the three of us made it to safety.

I am disturbed at the possible meaning of this to myself and would like to make a hypothesis of my own. What I think it might have meant is that I would like to permanently separate myself and my own two kids from my wife and our stepson.

—Daniel, Age 25, Married, USA

For better or worse, Daniel's analysis of his dream is accurate and telling. He and his wife married and had children at a young age, and assumed a great deal of responsibility early on. Perhaps more than either partner could manage at the time?

Couples who bring children into new marriages always face challenges of integrating the group into a cohesive unit. Even with the best intentions and efforts, the new family must face the reality of their separate pasts prior to coming together.

Daniel feels that he has not received the support he needs from his wife to allow their new family to develop as a whole. If the scenario is as Daniel portrays it, then certainly his wife's consistent assertion of authority with regard to guiding or disciplining her child (from a previous relationship) has undermined Daniel's ability to assume the role of becoming the emotional, de facto father to the child. In turn, this lack of support has injured Daniel's relationship with his wife. Each time she steps in to challenge his guidance, she is giving her husband a vote of no confidence in this role. At the same time, she is teaching her child not to respect Daniel either in this role.

While it is tempting to point fingers of blame in difficult times, Daniel and his wife both need to concentrate on what the best course of action is, at present, with regard to their children. If they haven't sought counseling already from a professional therapist, they need to do so immediately. Daniel's dream reflects the anger and the blame that each partner holds for the other in this relationship. The tornado foreshadows the emotional storm brewing on the horizon that threatens to separate the family. People get injured in tornadoes, and Daniel and his wife must try not to let the victims be their children.

"Fist-fighting a Tornado"

I had a dream that I was fighting a tornado inside my house, actually fist-fighting it. I was swinging my arms at it and it was just spinning me around and spitting me out. I said the house was my house, but it was not the one I live in now. This house was much bigger because when it spit me out I went up real high before I hit the ceiling and came down. When I got up it was gone. I looked out the window and there were three more tornadoes coming—big and all different. I was startled and then I woke up.

I'm a mother of four, a full-time student, and I work part-time. I am married but my husband and I have been separated for almost four years now. Before that we had a really rocky relationship due to jealousy and physical and mental abuse. Since then he has claimed that he is a changed man. When he gets out of jail next month he would like to show me and the kids that he can be a good father and husband. I am not sure that he has changed, because he has shown me a lot of characteristics of the person I left before he went to jail. He still gets angry at me.

I don't want to bring myself or my kids through that cycle of violence that I've worked so hard to get out of. At the same time I feel like I'll be taking away my kids' father if I don't welcome him back into our lives. But deep down inside I would rather that things stay as they are now because I don't want to take any chances.

–*Linda (Too Tired to Fight), Age 26, Married, USA*

Linda's dream report does a good job of illustrating the symbolic significance of tornadoes in dreams. Tornadoes often represent family members who have "stormy" and unpredictable tempers—from whom we need to take shelter.

Linda's dream about "fist-fighting" a tornado most likely is all too accurate. In her dream Linda is fighting for control of her home. The tornado she fights, however, is much bigger than she is; it soon spins her around and spits her out. When Linda lands on the floor she is done with round one, but when she looks out the window she sees three more storms coming. They're all big.

Linda's dream employs the metaphor of multiple tornadoes to represent the "cycle of violence" that she states she has worked very hard to get rid of. Her dreams also show that she is "wrestling" with the dilemma of whether to reunite with her husband—whether to bring him back into her home—upon his release from jail. Linda clearly fears continued physical and emotional abuse if she does, and she feels that she is no match for him. Accordingly, any person watching from the outside has to wonder: What is the real difficulty in making this decision?

To understand the message of her dream better, it may help if Linda re-explores its metaphor in the light of day. Specifically, if Linda were outside one afternoon with her four children and saw an actual tornado, would she gather the children and run blindly toward the funnel? Certainly not. On the contrary, she would take her children and sprint (not run!) for suitable cover. Regrettably, there is not much difference between Linda's dream and her life when her husband is at home. When her husband raised his arm repeatedly to strike her, he forfeited his privilege to be close to her, and to be close to their children. Linda has worked hard over the past four years to create a safe environment for her children. She should not blow it now—by inviting a tornado in through the front door.

"Storm on the Horizon"

Growing up, I always had a terrible fear of tornadoes. My mother grew up in Oklahoma and also had a very big fear of tornadoes. Whenever the tornado siren would go off in my small hometown, she would round us up and we would race down to the basement until the all-clear siren sounded.

I never actually saw a tornado until I was in my late twenties, and then saw two at the same time, one large and one small. I will never forget the sight, it was so surreal, and at that time I couldn't understand why people had pulled over to the side of the interstate to sit on their cars and watch. I raced out of town to try and get away from them and headed into the mountains to my home. Needless to say, my fear of them at this point in my life was still enormous.

I now have a healthy respect and fear of them and am actually truly fascinated by them. I've even considered trying to become a member of a "storm chaser" team for a summer, just to experience firsthand this incredibly powerful force of nature. But I digress. . . .

I have had tornado dreams for a long time, and have tried to find patterns and meanings for these dreams. Here is what I have discovered. They are always different; sometimes there is just one tornado, sometimes there are many. Rarely are they destructive in my dreams. The one thing that I have always been aware of with these dreams is that they always occur before some big change in my life.

Several years ago, after having an internal ultrasound, my gynecologist discovered that I had a large growth on my left ovary. It was not known whether or not the growth was cancerous. Immediate surgery for the next week was scheduled to remove the growth and to do a biopsy of it. I was absolutely terrified. I had feared for a long time that I might have cancer. My sister made arrangements to come and care for me while I recuperated. I made my doctor promise me that she wouldn't perform a hysterectomy, and she agreed.

A few days before my surgery, I had the following dream: I was riding in the middle of the front seat of a green Pinto station wagon that I had had many years ago when in college. My sister was sitting to the right of me and my mother was driving. My mother in real life had been dead for about five years and I remember thinking in the dream that this, of course, was her spiritual form driving. I was amused and impressed that my mother could drive my little four-speed Pinto. We were driving down a dirt road in the country.

In the distance, directly in front of us, we saw a very large funnel cloud begin to form and then spiral down to the ground. When the tornado was fully formed, it looked just like a uterus . . . and the clouds at the top looked like fallopian tubes and ovaries. In the dream, I thought this was really weird, since I was about to have surgery on these same organs.

We came to a crossroads and my mother turned left. We drove down into a lush, green, beautiful valley where the sun was shining and there was not a cloud in the sky. My mother drove to an inn and they took my things inside. She and my sister told me that they could not stay there with me, but that they would be with me in spirit, and to remember that everything would be fine and not to worry. This is all that I remember.

The surgery went well and the pathologist's report stated that the growths were benign. My diagnosis was severe endometriosis, which I have been treating with natural estrogen ever since.

–Laura, Age 38, Single, USA

Laura's dream uses the symbol of a tornado to represent a period of anxiety (her approaching surgery) that is associated with the fear she felt as a child hiding from tornadoes with her mother. The dream also uses the metaphor of a car (symbol of the self) driving along a highway (the direction we are headed in our lives) to represent her current status. At the time of her dream, Laura's surgery for pain in her uterus was approaching, like a "storm" (tornado) looming on the horizon. In the car Laura sits between her mother, who is driving, and her sister.

The dream reveals the symbolic meaning of the tornado by shaping itself into a uterus, complete with the fallopian tubes represented by smaller, wisplike funnels. At this point in the dream the family trio arrives at a crossroads. Laura's mother turns left, indicating a departure from the main road for a while, and leads her to an inn in a valley that is lush, green, and full of light. Laura's mother and sister tell her they can not stay with her, but reassure her that they will be with her in spirit—an especially poignant remark, since her mother, at the time of the dream, had been deceased for five years. They also tell Laura that all will be well, and not to worry.

Laura's dream effortlessly blends several dimensions and layers of meaning. Laura is vaguely lucid during the dream, and notes her mother's spiritual presence with a lighthearted expression of curiosity and bemusement. (Her mother can drive her Pinto, and drive it well!) The message of Laura's dream is unmistakable. During a period of fear, Laura's mother is visiting in advance of her surgery to tell Laura expressly not to worry—that everything will be all right. What is the symbolic meaning of the valley where Laura, spiritually, will reside during her surgery? The lush, green valley is an unmistakable symbol for fertility—a powerful indication that Laura still will be able to bear children after her surgery.

Train

Train: Trains signify attempts to reach significant destinations in our lives—such as career or romantic goals. Do we arrive successfully? Train wrecks and mechanical failures indicate doubts about our ability to achieve a goal. Watching a loved one or family member depart on a train symbolizes awareness of separation. Missed trains symbolize opportunities lost, or feelings of being unprepared as we attempt to reach a destination (career goal). Trains that move backward suggest that the dreamer feels he or she is moving backward in life—not advancing as hoped for in his or her career or personal life. No train indicates uncertainty about how to reach a goal, and may reflect feelings of abandonment or isolation.

Please see "Airplane."

Train tracks: Trains jumping the track reflect feelings that one is headed in the wrong direction, or that one has deviated from the intended path. Trains that get back on track reflect a realignment of goals and efforts. Elevated train tracks indicate lofty career or romantic goals.

Train station: Symbolizes choice and opportunity for new direction in one's life. Also, a symbol of transition. Are you considering a change in your career? Inability to locate a track, due to too many people or too much luggage, suggests uncertainty about the direction one needs to pursue in order to reach a goal. Inability to board a train (the train is too big, a conductor will not allow passage, insufficient money to buy a ticket) symbolizes feelings of inadequacy in the face of an opportunity, or an obstacle that prevents you from reaching your goal.

Luggage: Inability to board a train due to too much luggage suggests a dreamer is emotionally burdened, preventing him or her from moving on to the next station in life. Forgotten luggage or unpacked suitcases signal emotional unpreparedness and anxiety as one contemplates or prepares for a transition.

◆ **Interpretation tip:** If your train does not reach its destination, consider what goal you are trying to reach in your waking life. Can you identify the obstacles that lie in your path?

✳ ✳ ✳

When trains appear in our dreams, we know our lives are "on the move." Our first dream, "Train Station," reveals a woman who fears she may have gotten on a wrong train. After an initial misstep, will she find her way home? In "Wrong Train," a dreamer learns—with a shock—that she has boarded the wrong train. Our next dream, "Separate Directions," concerns a diverging romantic interest. Is the dream foreshadowing the future, or is it merely wish fulfillment? Our final entry, "Approaching Train," shows that not all romantic rendezvous are the same. Our dreamer wishes this train would pass her by.

Train Dreams

"Train Station"

I had a very vivid dream last night and I'm hoping you might be able to help with it. First of all, a little background on me: I am in a relationship with my boyfriend of seven years that is not going anywhere and has been very rocky. I think I may have feelings for a very good male friend who I met on the Internet and have previously met in real life. We talk every day. He is not happy with the way I am treated at home. He is always telling me I deserve better and that I should get out of my current relationship. I'm quite confused as to his feelings for me. He lives in the USA and I live in the UK, and I will be seeing him again later this year.

The first part is not very clear, but I am lying on a picnic blanket with this friend and he has just cooked me a meal. We're lying on the blanket eating our food and watching the *Jenny Jones* show on a giant TV screen attached to a huge, horrible concrete block of flats. But then I find a strange bug in the food and I'm apologizing for not being able to eat any more.

Then the dream cuts to myself and this friend wandering around a town that I used to live in. All of a sudden I find that I have wandered away from him and onto a train that is pulling out of the station, and I don't have a ticket. The train ride is not particularly smooth and the train is lurching from side to side. I am aware that the train is taking me away from somewhere I desperately want to be. All the time I am on the train I am worried that I'm going to get in serious trouble for not having a ticket. The inspector gets on to check our tickets, but for some reason doesn't ask to see mine and I get away with it.

I'm trying really hard to gather up my belongings and get off the train, but at each station something happens to stop this. For example, I don't have my belongings gathered and I run around the carriage looking for them. The things I have with me are a handbag and an empty laptop computer bag. I don't have my laptop with me, just the case. (By the way, I communicate with my friend in real life using my laptop.)

At one of the stations I think I can get off, but then I realize that the laptop bag I have does not belong to me and it has gotten mixed up with someone else's bag on the train, so I'm trying to find the owner. I then realize that there is some pink writing inside this laptop bag, and I match it up with some pink writing on one of the other passengers' laptops and we swap cases. But the case he has given me doesn't look like mine, and I still don't feel as if I can leave the train.

Eventually I decide to just take what I can find of mine, not worry about the rest, and get off the train. So I get off at a station in the middle of nowhere and I'm asking the ticket clerk which platform I need to get back to the town I started from. I still don't have a ticket. I woke up before I got to the right platform.

–Carol, Age 28, Engaged, United Kingdom

Carol is engaged, but at the beginning of her dream report she informs us that her current relationship of seven years is frustrating, and is "not going anywhere." Is it a coincidence that the new man in her life, with whom she talks daily over the Internet, figures prominently in her dream? At a time when Carol is wondering whether her romantic life is "on the right track," this man appears in her dream as an alternative to her fiancé.

The new man's courtship of Carol is represented by his preparation of a picnic for them to enjoy. Several items included in this dream picnic, however, reflect Carol's doubts about this man as a partner. The picnic is not in a romantic setting—they are surrounded by ugly concrete flats and are watching *Jenny Jones* on a large TV—and there is a problem with the food. Food in dreams is a common metaphor for sensual and emotional nourishment. Carol's discovery of a bug in her food is a clear dream symbol that something about this relationship "bugs" her. After she finds the bug, she kindly refuses to eat any more.

Carol is suddenly wandering through her hometown alone, and steps aboard a train. Trains in dreams are metaphors for significant trips and journeys in our lives—including attempts to achieve committed romantic relationships. As she rides along the lurching train (a metaphor for emotional instability on the journey), Carol grows concerned that she is headed in the wrong direction, away from "somewhere I desperately want to be." She also fears being discovered by an authority, because she does not have "permission to travel" (a ticket).

During a lull in her relationship with her fiancé, the train that Carol boards alone represents her flirtation with "switching trains"—to become involved with another man on the path to a committed relationship. Carol's fear of being caught by the train conductor symbolizes her fear of being discovered by her fiancé. (She does not have permission to look around romantically.) Her search for the laptop case, similarly, indicates concerns about her daily talks. Does her fiancé know how much she speaks to this other man?

Carol's dream reveals that her on-line romance has led her off course, momentarily, and that she fears she may be moving away from her primary relationship with her fiancé—the location where she desperately wants to be. What is the easy solution to this dream? It's time for Carol to log off with her on-line friend, and concentrate on her romance at home.

"Wrong Train"

I had a dream that I was carrying a toilet and running frantically around New York City barefoot, trying to catch a train. I finally caught the train (still carrying the toilet) and, realizing it was the wrong train, jumped off and stepped on the electric rail underneath, electrocuting myself. Then I woke up.

Recent events in my life: I recently broke up with my long-term boyfriend, but I am seeing someone new and exciting. I am also working my butt off in graduate school, and will graduate next spring and start "real life."

—Erica, Age 25, Single, USA

In her waking life Erica has hopped out of one relationship and into another. Is her dream reflecting this recent change in partners by showing her headed in the wrong direction on one train, and then choosing to disembark to get her romantic life back on course?

Two items included in Erica's dream cause it to be exceptional. As she chases the first train (we assume, her first relationship) she is carrying a toilet in her arms. What is the meaning of this seemingly bizarre symbol? Toilets in dreams are highly associated with private emotional issues that we wish we could resolve and "get out of our system." As Erica pursued her first partner, is her dream informing her that she was carrying a lot of "emotional baggage" with her? Does the frantic nature of her search for a train reflect haste in her romantic decision-making, due to her own personal issues, at the expense of a more balanced and realistic selection of a partner?

The second exceptional event is when she dismounts from the train and steps onto an electric rail, and is electrocuted as a result. Dreams about being shocked and electrocuted, when they are unpleasant, are metaphors for emotional trauma in our lives. Was Erica's breakup from her first relationship shocking and emotionally traumatic?

If Erica has jumped from the frying pan into the fire in her relationships, her dream suggests she needs to get the first relationship out of her system (use the dream toilet) before she becomes involved in a new romance.

"Separate Directions"

I am a sixty-five-year-old widow, living with my son and his wife. They have been having some difficulty lately in their relationship.

Recently I had a dream in which I was riding on a train with the both of them. It was supposed to be a local round-trip. I went for a walk with my son and while we were walking, the cars got switched around and we were separated from his wife. She was sent on a one-way trip to another part of the country, while we were still on the round-trip train.

Is this some kind of "wish dreaming"? Or is their marital trouble making its way into my dreams, and causing me to see them separated?

—*Myrna, Age 65, Widowed, Canada*

Trains are metaphors for attempts to reach destinations in our lives. In the context of a romantic relationship, Myrna's dream about her son and daughter-in-law riding on separate trains represents her sentiment that if they don't work out their marital difficulties soon, they may be headed in separate directions. The significance of her daughter-in-law having a "one-way ticket," when her son's is round-trip, also should not be overlooked. One-way means she won't be coming back to rejoin her son.

Myrna asks if her dream is a wish fulfillment, which is an indicator that Myrna is not especially fond of her daughter-in-law. The answer, however, most likely is no. (Sigmund Freud believed that all dreams were the fulfillment of a wish, but most dream researchers do not agree with him.) Instead, Myrna's dream is more simply explained as a reflection of the difficulties she perceives in the relationship.

"Approaching Train"

I am standing on train tracks in an open field. Everything is pitch black and I am walking forward in the center of the tracks. I hear the whistle of a train and I turn around. Through the blackness I see the light of the train screaming toward me. I stand there frozen in place. I see this huge train coming toward me and can do nothing. I keep screaming for someone to make it stop.

Right before it hits me I crouch down. There's a tiny ledge that I press myself against while the train thunders over me. I'm still screaming for someone to make it stop. My hands claw at the dirt, trying to get lower from the train so it doesn't run me over. I can feel the force of it as it roars over the top of me, and its sound is deafening in my ears. All I can think is: "I'm okay right now but when it gets to the end of the train, it's going to go over the ledge, come down, and squash me."

I woke up on the floor of my room with my upper body under the frame of my bed and my fist clutching the carpet. I don't know how I ended up down there, but my throat was hoarse from screaming. I don't normally remember my dreams. The ones I remember are nightmares because I've had people wake me up because I act them out. I also talk in my sleep a lot.

I have never even been on a train, much less walked on tracks. As for my personal life, I am twenty-four years old. I just started going back to school to get a degree. I have been dating a man for seven years and we are supposed to be getting married in a few months. He has medical problems and it looks like I will be the sole provider for our family. Lately I have been having concerns because his attitude has changed toward me and has become bitter. I long to have kids and be a stay-at-home mom but I don't see that in my future right now.

Lately I have found myself growing attracted to another man. I have been staying away from him so I can concentrate on my relationship with my fiancé. But the other man is also a close friend of mine and I feel such a loss because I can't even talk to him now.

–Michelle, Age 24, Engaged, USA

Because Michelle's wedding date is fast approaching in waking life, we know that the train in her dream represents the upcoming arrival of her wedding day. Unfortunately, instead of this dream train carrying her to a romantic destination with her fiancé, Michelle feels she is about to get run over and is worried if she will survive.

Given the background she provides, we know Michelle's approaching wedding day is viewed with apprehension. Her fiancé suffers from a health problem that she fears will dramatically impact her lifestyle, and more significantly, she feels he has recently become bitter toward her. At a time when Michelle is unsure about her commitment and desire, this train ride to an uncertain future (represented by the darkness) appears foreboding, rather than an omen of good times ahead.

When Michelle woke from this nightmare, she realized that she had acted out the dream physically, and was hiding underneath her bed, her throat hoarse from yelling. The stress the dream caused is an indicator of her mounting anxiety.

Michelle's dream suggests doubts that are greater than the usual "cold feet." Has Michelle considered the symbolic meaning of her cries for help in the dream, for someone to "make it stop"? If she hasn't already spoken to a relationship or marriage counselor, her dream is powerful encouragement that she should. Marriage is a commitment that makes all couples nervous, but Michelle needs to be confident she is boarding the right train.

Turtle

Turtle: Feminine symbol associated with fertility, due to the shape of the turtle's shell (womb) that contains life inside. Turtles are common symbols in the dreams of woman who are expecting or actively trying to conceive. Turtles that snap at the dreamer or who otherwise are aggressive reflect fears of emotional injury on the road to motherhood. Smashed or injured turtles reflect feelings of disappointment, or doubts that conception will occur.

Turtles may also be a reference to feelings of slowness or sluggishness, as in the "turtle and the hare," or to feelings of self-defense, as in withdrawing inside one's body armor.

Reptiles: Turtles, lizards, snakes, and other small reptiles often appear in women's dreams during the early stages of pregnancy, an apparent reference to the early stages of fetal development occurring in the womb. The reptiles represent a primitive state of development, and the simplicity of the life force. As fetuses grow, the size and complexity of animals appearing in pregnancy dreams also grows. Dreams about birthing reptiles and other animals (including kittens and puppies) are most common among first-time mothers, who are more nervous than veteran mothers about "what's growing inside them."

◆ **Interpretation tip:** Is fertility on your mind? Dreams about injured or malnourished turtles reflect fears that conception may not occur.

* ❋ *

Who would think that turtles and fertility would be such close bedfellows? "Snapping Turtle" reveals the meaning of aggressive turtles in dreams. Our dreamer wants to get a turtle in a bag, but she keeps on getting bitten. "Turtles in the

Sun" is a happy dream that shows two turtles basking in the sun, with swarms of little ones around them. Our dreamer takes in the view and is ecstatic. Our final entry, "Smashed Turtles," reflects a dreamer's concerns on the road to conception. Will she ever be successful?

Turtle Dreams

"Snapping Turtle"

Hi! My name is Sophia. I live in Florida, and I keep having dreams about turtles.

In my first dream a snapping turtle was attacking my friend so I went to help. Then it started attacking me. It felt so real that when I woke up I ran to the bathroom, put on the light, and started checking my body for blood and missing flesh.

My second dream was last night. I was coming home from work, and a woman had stopped on the road, trying to get a turtle. Well, I stopped to help her. I had a bullion sack in the back of my truck, and I found a stick and pushed the turtle in the sack. When I went to pick up the sack, the turtle busted out and grabbed me on the arm around the wrist area. It bit down until my wrist was bitten in half.

About my background: I am involved in a relationship. My lover is not from Florida; she is from Michigan. She moved here to be with me, so she has been homesick lately. She's been on edge, but we both have been. We are thinking of having a family. She would be the one to carry the baby, not me. Her sister just had a baby. What do you think?

–Sophia, Age 37, Single, USA

Sophia's turtle dreams are recurring, and one was so vivid that Sophia actually ran to the bathroom to see if she was bleeding.

Given the background Sophia provides, the snapping turtle in her dream represents the current relationship she is in, blended with her desires to begin a family. The woman whom Sophia stops on the road to help put a turtle in a bag is her lover. Sophia and her lover have already discussed children—to the extent where her lover has agreed that she will carry the baby. Do we now understand the metaphor of putting a "turtle in the bag"? Sophia is trying to get a baby into her lover's belly.

The baby issue, however, is complicated. Sophia's partner is homesick, which indicates indecisiveness about the relationship. The setting for the second dream, in fact, is a highway, an apparent reference to her partner's expressed desire to move back home. Given the circumstances, is it any wonder Sophia fears becoming hurt in this relationship? Sophia is ready to settle down and watch the young ones grow, but her partner is thinking that she may want to move back home.

Does Sophia remember the pain she felt when she was bitten? These are warning dreams that are functioning to let Sophia know that these are not the best circumstances in which to raise a family. Given the uncertainties, Sophia will be wise to take her dream's advice—and wait to find a more settled home to raise her turtles.

"Turtles in the Sun"

In my dream it feels like this woman and I have just gotten home from work. It feels like we are very much together but I don't know if we are living together. We are kissing and embracing and very happy to see each other. We are in the living room and I know it's where I live, but I don't recognize the house. While we are kissing, she pulls away from me and out of the blue asks, "Will you marry me in four months?"

I'm excited, shocked, and amazed all at the same time. We hold and kiss again and I can see out of the window into the backyard. I see two adult turtles basking in the sun. Then I look further and see that the windows, which are large and low to the ground, have a foot or so of water against them, creating an aquarium appearance. Then I see tons of baby turtles, all around.

I know that I felt good about what I was witnessing—like it was some kind of a good omen. I remember thinking in the dream that the backyard would be too wet to walk in, but I was okay with that.

My background is that I have been seeing this woman for a little over a year now. Unfortunately, she is still in a relationship that she says is unhappy and unfulfilling. I do believe this to be true. It is the most powerful relationship I have ever had and although I'm not real happy or proud of our situation, I somehow feel like this is where I am supposed to be. That I'm supposed to be patient and wait.

What puzzles me is that I have never dreamt about turtles, or someone proposing to me, or time elements such as "four months." I know water deals with emotions and this situation has brought a lot of emotion out of me.

—*Madeline, Age 29, Single, USA*

Madeline's dream is powerful, not only for the positive feelings she experiences, but also because of the extraordinary imagery. Immediately after her lover proposes, the backyard of Madeline's dream home becomes an aquarium—complete with water and turtles.

Turtles in dreams are feminine symbols highly associated with fertility. In its own curious language, Madeline's dream, accordingly, reflects her strong feelings for another woman, and her desire to begin a family with her. The two turtles basking in the sun represent Madeline and her lover. The "tons" of turtles that inhabit the backyard represent a potential future family. Is her dream a foreshadowing of domestic bliss?

Madeline's delight upon hearing her friend's proposal signals Madeline's preparedness for a committed relationship. The date proposed for the wedding, however, is enigmatic. What will happen in four months? Has Madeline correctly estimated the amount of time it will take for her lover to move on from her current arrangement? Will they really begin to live together?

Madeline is advised not to treat her dream as precognitive, but instead to view it as a strong indicator of her preparedness to join her friend in a committed relationship. The danger in believing that her dream is precognitive is that the belief may encourage a passive approach to the future, guided by the hope that her dream will somehow magically come true. Accordingly, Madeline must not allow her spectacular dream to lull her into complacency. On the contrary, if Madeline has seen her future in a dream, now is the time to work hard to create it in the real world.

"Smashed Turtles"

I have been having turtle dreams, and at least twice, smashed-in-the-road turtle dreams. I have been going through fertility treatment for five years, and my husband will take no further action to get pregnant or adopt. Is there a connection here?

It has been a very tough year for our marriage—that almost ended in separation. We have been married five years. I also have a fifteen-year-old son.

–Pamela, Age 34, Married, USA

Like Sophia's dreams about a snapping turtle, Pamela's dreams reflect difficulty on the road to conception. Instead of biting her, however, Pamela's turtles, on at least two occasions, have been smashed in the road.

Pamela informs us that she and her husband have been trying to conceive for five years (the entire length of their marriage). Significantly, she also tells us that her husband "will take no further action to get pregnant or adopt." Is this the clue we need to understand the violence of Pamela's dream metaphor? Pamela, who is already the mother of a fifteen-year-old son, clearly wishes to have another child, even if it means adopting a baby. Her husband's refusal to pursue fertility treatment further, however, or to consider adoption, feels like an attack. Pamela's smashed turtle dreams reflect her concerns that her chances for another child are being deliberately injured, or at least "run over" by another person. Her stress is reflected in her dreams—and in the problems in her marriage.

Vampire

Vampire: Symbol of transition frequently associated with initiation rites. Vampires are common in the dreams of teen girls, who are occupied with questions of losing their virginity. The masculine vampire will draw blood and make the dreamer one of them (a nonvirgin). In the dreams of adults, vampires may represent people who wish to initiate an illicit sexual affair with the dreamer. Vampires can also represent people who are emotionally draining—who suck our vital energy (blood) from us. Vampires hold associations with masculine power. Are you attracted to power, and willing to surrender to it?

◆ **Interpretation tip:** Are you feeling pressured to make a sexual transition in your life? Is someone draining the energy out of you?

* * *

The dreams included in this chapter reflect different aspects of vampires in dreams. "Vampire High School" takes us inside the mind of a teen in transition. Should she allow herself to get bitten? Our second dream, "The Vampire Affair," shows how vampires linger in our adult minds as symbols of sexual initiation. Will our dreamer be tempted to "join the crowd"?

Vampire Dreams

"Vampire High School"

I've been having this whacked-up dream for at least a week now—maybe you can help me decide what it means:

It starts out that I am pregnant (I am a virgin). The father is my best guy friend. Well, he tells me how he feels and all that good stuff, and then the dream switches over and I am at school.

Half the school is vampires but I am normal. Soon these vampire people come in and start biting people and turning them into these things. So I told my best guy friend (the one who was supposed to be the father of my baby) to go ahead and bite me. I knew that I was going to turn into one one way or another. What does this mean?

–Kelly, Age 15, Single, USA

Kelly's dream reflects her feelings about losing her virginity. In the dream she is pregnant (with expectation?) and her best guy friend is the father (what better choice?). He assures her that he cares about her ("all that good stuff") and suddenly the dream switches and Kelly is at school.

Half the school is made up of vampires (nonvirgins), but Kelly is normal (still a virgin). But the vampires who draw blood (like when she loses her virginity) start biting people and turning them into vampires like themselves (nonvirgins). So Kelly tells her best guy friend to go ahead and bite her (take her virginity), because she figures that she is going to become a vampire (nonvirgin) one way or the other.

Losing her virginity is on her mind, and judging from her dream, Kelly might like her best guy friend to be "the one." It is important for Kelly to remember, however, that just because she dreamed about her friend being "the one" doesn't mean it has to happen this way. Kelly's dream simply reflects some of the thoughts she is having. What Kelly decides to do with her virginity, and whom she decides to lose it with, is her decision.

"The Vampire Affair"

I am twenty-six years old, happily married for two years, and my husband and I just had a baby boy (he's eight months old now). He is the light of my life. Before our son, I was an accountant, and now I'm a stay-at-home mommy/housewife. I absolutely love every minute of it. My husband is a hardworking professional and we're still madly in love. He's my best friend as well.

I've had this dream every single night, going on a whole week as of last night. Actually every night is a different version, but they're pretty much the same events. I've been dreaming about a vampire. He visits me every night and we're friends, but I tell him constantly that I don't want to become "one" of his kind.

In the first dream I was hosting a party and all of a sudden I realized my guests were all vampires. I immediately asked everyone to leave. Then the leader (I have a clear image of his face, but no idea who he is—he doesn't even remind me of anyone I know in real life) came up to me and was extremely nice about the whole situation. I was polite, but firm. I ran into my son's room and grabbed him out of the crib. I tried to hide him in numerous places but every time I thought he was safe, he'd squirm out and start smiling at me. The vampire then came into my son's room and asked me who was hiding in here. I ran over and picked up my son and held on tightly while the vampire was trying to take him from me. I awoke to hear my son in his room crying (and he was also crying in my dream).

The next five dreams were pretty much the same, except that most of them took place in my old house that I grew up in (from two weeks old until eighteen years, when I went to college out of state). They all ended with the vampire about to bite my neck.

I've never had consecutive dreams before, and I know there has to be meaning to this. In the dream I had last night I dreamed that Sarah Jessica Parker and I were best friends. (Don't ask me! I adore her, but I've never had a celebrity in my dream.) Anyhow, we were gallivanting around town having a great time when the vampire shows up again. This time he asked me to join him in Hawaii. (That's where my husband and I honeymooned in real life.) I told him no, and Sarah just said, "Oh, of course. You guys can stay at my place." I was shaking my head and mouthing no to her behind his back.

She said, "Well then, let's all just go to a movie." So we're all in the car (I'm driving) and he's in the backseat. He leans up behind Sarah, shoves a spackling tool into her mouth, and it kills her instantly. I just started screaming, "No! Why did you kill her? She was so nice to you!" The dream ended when he just reaches over the seat and is about to bite my neck.

I've never dreamed about vampires before, which is why this dream series is so odd. As for events that have occurred recently: About two weeks ago, an acquaintance confessed to having an affair and yes, I was bothered by it. I couldn't believe what she was telling me. To add to that disturbance, she said she was pregnant by him (he's married as well). I do not want to be associated with people like that, so I haven't really spoken with her since.

–Nina, Age 26, Married, USA

Nina's dreams reflect the disturbing news she learned just before her dreams began. A married acquaintance confessed that she is pregnant by a man who is not her husband. The vampire that has appeared in Nina's dreams, accordingly, functions as a symbol of sexual initiation and temptation. Specifically, could Nina ever commit such an act?

In her first dream, Nina is hosting a party for friends when she suddenly recognizes that they are all vampires. The sexual metaphor expressed by the dream is Nina's awareness that several of her friends and acquaintances are engaged in extramarital affairs. It is clear from her dream that Nina is not interested in joining the ranks of couples who have affairs (Nina politely and firmly tells the vampires to leave), and her commitment to her relationship with her husband is represented by her desire to protect their baby.

In Nina's most recent dream, Sarah Jessica Parker, the star of the television show *Sex in the City*, is her "best friend." Significantly, the character Sarah Jessica Parker plays in the show is associated with sequential romantic partners, and with guilt-free sexual exploration and curiosity. Nina's identification with Sarah Jessica Parker in the latest dream (they are best friends) suggests a curiosity and receptivity to aspects of the lifestyle the actress portrays in the show. Nevertheless, the dream makes it clear that Nina associates that lifestyle with curiosity and frivolity. When the vampire requests Nina's presence in Hawaii (a symbolic allusion to breaking her wedding vows), Nina again firmly declines. This time, however, the vampire kills Sarah Jessica Parker, and is about to bite Nina's neck when she awakens. Is the message of this dream that flirting can have dangerous consequences? Is this the message that Nina also learned—from the experience of her acquaintance? Nina's dreams show that this is one transition she has no intention of making.

Violence

Violence: Common metaphor in dreams used to express feelings of anger, frustration, emotional injury, and pain.

Killing: If a dreamer perpetrates an act of violence in a dream—a killing, shooting, beating, or stabbing—the act does not signify that the dreamer has murderous intent, or desires to physically harm the recipient of the violence. Instead, the act should be considered a representation of anger or frustration, or a desire to make someone, or something, go away. Parents who occasionally dream of injuring a child are encouraged to recognize the dreams as reflections of frustration, rather than of harmful intent. In the aftermath of fights with friends or lovers' quarrels, dreams about murder (anger), accompanied by feelings of regret, are common. Indiscriminate violence—killing lots of people—symbolizes uncontrolled anger and aggression.

Knife: Common weapon in dreams, used to cut and kill. If a male attacker wields a knife, the weapon may symbolize a penis, a general fear of sexual relations, fear of sexual assault, or a memory of a past negative or abusive sexual experience.

Gun: Symbol of power, aggression, and protection. If the dreamer is attacking, he or she should be alerted to hostile or angry feelings toward the persons attacked. If the dreamer protects herself with a gun, it is a positive indicator of self-confidence and self-esteem.

Rape: Dreams about rape reflect fears of violence and feelings of unwanted attention from members of the same or opposite sex. In the wake of an actual rape, recurring dreams about the trauma are common. Rape can also be a strong metaphor to indicate that one's personal boundaries are being "violated."

Stalker: A frequent literal representation of a woman's (especially) fears of being attacked or stalked. May also indicate a disturbing feeling or awareness that needs to be faced and resolved by the dreamer.

Please see "Attacked" and "Chase."

♦ **Interpretation tip:** Try not to think literally about violence portrayed in your dreams. Instead, consider the feelings you experience. Have you been frustrated or angry recently, or have you been wounded emotionally?

✳ ✳ ✳

Violence in dreams is always disturbing. In "Baby Runs Away," a mother is troubled by the casual use of violence in a dream. Could she ever hurt her child? "Beheaded" tells the tale of a woman who feels that someone else is trying to make decisions for her. Finally, "Carrying a Knife" is an unsettling dream that walks a fine line between fantasy and reality. Is our dreamer a steady guy?

Dreams of Violence

"Baby Runs Away"

I am with my son, who is three years old, but in my dream he can speak articulately. We are threatened by some outside force and decide that since we are in danger we should cut off his feet. I take a carving knife and cut through his ankle joints as I would a roasting chicken and amputate his feet.

When I am done and about to bandage the wound he runs away from me crying and others around us express disgust that I would do such a thing. I feel terribly guilty. But I notice that as he runs across a white rug or carpet on the stumps of his legs that the wounds are not bleeding. At this point I awaken with horrible guilt and horror, sickened by the image of myself mutilating my beautiful son, whom I adore. I am naturally troubled by this dream and would appreciate help in understanding these images.

–*Diane, Age 40, Married, USA*

It would be nice if we could speak to our children as adults, and if they would listen and comprehend us. But three-year-olds aren't adults, as Diane's dream quickly reminds us.

Diane has an adult conversation for an instant with her son—in which they both agree that he should not run around as much (amputation) because it is a threat to his safety (the outside force). When Diane is confronted with a literal interpretation of her actions—represented by her friends treating her with disgust—she feels momentarily guilty. As she watches her child run, though, the symbolic intent of her act again becomes apparent. There is no blood, she notes, and her baby boy still can run. Despite his horrific appearance, Diane is aware that she did not intend to injure her son.

The amputation that Diane performs on her son is a symbolic representation of her desire to constrain her three-year-old. Nevertheless, the violence of the metaphor—amputation representing restraint—is disturbing, and begs the question: Does Diane's dream reflect frustration and anger, occasionally, as she works to control her child? The answer, almost certainly, is yes. Similarly, the guilt Diane feels in the dream most likely is an expression of her own troubled feelings when occasionally she is overwhelmed by her duties as mother, and worries that she should do better.

When Diane awakens, she writes that she is "sickened by the image of myself mutilating my beautiful son, whom I adore." The contrast between her emotions in the dream, when she understands that she is protecting her child, versus her emotions when she awakens, when she views her amputation as a literal act of violence, is illuminating. It is important for Diane to be reassured that her dream does not reflect any desire on her part to actually harm her child.

"Beheaded"

I am a twenty-three-year-old student in college, and I will be done at the end of this semester. (Finally! It's taken me five and a half years.) In addition to school, I work two part-time jobs—one in a lab on campus, and the other in a home office. I'm trying to support myself, but now and again I do need to ask the folks for some money. But I never really like to do that.

A couple of days before this dream I was talking to my mom over the phone (my parents have lived overseas since I started college), and we got into a conversation about what I'll be doing in January, when I'm done with school. I was trying to explain to her that I want to stay in my college town for another year—that I plan on getting any job that will pay the bills, saving up some money, and then start looking for a career job. I became very frustrated with her because she didn't understand why I didn't just start looking for a "career" job right away. I hung up extremely annoyed and bitter.

In my dream I remember that my brother and I, along with two sisters (who in waking life are about the same age and are good family friends), are waiting for our heads to be cut off by my parents. My mom has a very strong presence. I can't remember seeing my dad, but I know it is our parents. The four of us getting our heads cut off is some sort of solution (I can't remember the problem), but we're okay with this. It's not something we're very afraid of.

So we're lined up side by side at a guillotine-type contraption (we each have our own). And instead of facing the ground, we're facing straight ahead, so the blade will cut our faces lengthwise. One of my parents (I think my dad) says to us, "Someone pick up the book by your feet." (We each have a book.) I don't want to do it, so I just wait. I can see with my peripheral vision that my brother reaches down (still facing forward) and picks it up and the moment the book lifts off the ground, I hear the *swooosh* of the blade being released. (It was almost as though we were being tricked.)

I just close my eyes and wait . . . and it's not painful in any way. Then I remember Sara and Jane (the two sisters) walking around slowly and then sort of slumping over on top of each other, their head areas just being a red mass. Meanwhile, I'm seeing them headless (as if our heads were cut off at our necks). And I notice that I can still see. So I ask them (sort of in a panic), "Can you still see? Why can I still see?!" And then I don't know what happens to them or my brother; I don't see them again.

So, I'm still able to see, but I see myself and the others as if our heads were cut off at our necks. And then I think (again, in a panic) how can I talk? Will I be able to eat? It's pretty clear that I'll stay alive.

At this point my mom wants to gouge out my eye nerves, to prevent me from seeing, and starts looking through an address book because she thinks she knows some lady (eye doctor, I think) who can tell her which nerves to gouge out. But then she decides that she can possibly do it herself, and I start trying to convince my mom to get instructions first, and it turns into a small argument.

And that's all I remember. So it seems obvious to me that this dream has something to do with my mom and the conversation we had a few days prior, but I have no idea what. It's such a strange dream.

–Karin, Age 23, Single, USA

Karin's dream uses an assortment of violent images to represent the influence of her parents on her career decisions. In the dream, her parents wish to "remove the head" of herself and her brother, and of two friends of theirs who are about the same age. Removing her head is a metaphor for Karin's feelings that her parents do not want her to "think for herself." Karin feels that her mother, especially, wants to control her life, and would be happy if she could. ("Get a good job now; don't take a year off before you start a serious career.") The presence of Karin's brother and her friends indicates Karin's awareness that they all are facing similar pressures.

The physical violence that Karin experiences in her dream is a representation of the emotional pain she felt in the wake of her recent phone conversation with her mother. At a time when Karin most likely would have appreciated some parental congratulations on finishing college—apparently while supporting herself by working two part-time jobs—Karin feels like her mother chopped her head off. It is also clear that Karin feels singled out for torture by her mother. Once her mother realizes she can still see without a head, she consults an address book to locate a friend (doctor?) who can tell her how to remove her optic nerves. As the dream ends, Karin and her mother are having yet another argument. . . .

Karin feels that she is being "attacked" emotionally, but like Diane in "Baby Runs Away," Karin needs to recognize that her dream does not reflect any literal desires, on her parents' part, to actually harm her. On the contrary, her parents' motivations are simple and straightforward. They want Karin to move along in her career path as soon as possible, and to not spend too much time prolonging her college days by working menial jobs. They also want the security of knowing that Karin is settled into her life's work. These are significant transitions, but what parents often forget is how essential it is for their children to arrive at these decisions themselves.

"Carrying a Knife"

It starts out with me behind my friend Joan with a steak knife at her throat. (The knife is a knife I currently own.) I am forcing her to take me to her car. It definitely seems like I want to kill her.

Her car is parked at a friend's house, in a two-car detached garage. While we are in the garage, her friend comes home and her friend's husband comes out of the house. The friend pulls up, rolls down her oversized car window, and asks what's going on.

I explain that I am joking around. The friends both come over close. I have still got a hold on Joan's neck with the knife pressed against her throat. Although the cutting edge is away from the throat, the flat edge is still ready to cut. I strike at one of the friends as I wake up, disturbed.

I am thirty and single, a shy guy, plain-looking, and a little overweight. Joan is twenty-eight and single, a very nice person, and not shy at all. She is good-looking. We work out every morning, and she is having problems with a "Peeping Tom". She is buying a new car, but the old one is in the garage in the dream.

We are very good friends, but nothing sexual has occurred between us and I don't see it happening anytime soon. I don't know of any time we have hurt each other physically or emotionally.

I did not know the friends in the dream.

–*Mason, Age 30, Single, USA*

Joan's "Peeping Tom" problem in real life alludes to Mason's own problem with Joan; Mason is attracted to Joan romantically, but as he himself acknowledges, "nothing sexual has occurred between us and I don't see it happening anytime soon." Mason's daily contact with Joan, at a gym where they exercise together (and where bodies are on display), only serves to heighten his romantic frustration.

The knife that Mason holds against Joan's neck is an unambiguous expression of anger and hostility. Mason's attempt to force Joan into her car suggests that he would like to force himself into a relationship with her, so that they both might be "traveling together" and "headed in the same direction." (Mason tells us that Joan, in real life, is buying a new car. Perhaps he would like to be riding in it?)

Mason would like to force his relationship with Joan, but fortunately he has other people to be concerned about. The neighbor who pulls up in a car with an oversized window symbolizes someone who can see clearly what Mason is doing—what his true motivation is. Mason tells the neighbor he is only joking, but the knife remains on Joan's neck, and his disguise soon fails. Mason awakens, striking out at one of the neighbors, who has spoiled his plans.

Mason's dream reflects frustrated romantic desires for Joan that are transforming into unhealthy feelings of anger, resentment, and aggression. If Mason is not a violent person in real life, and if this dream caught him by surprise, then the dream is a clear sign that it is time to end the relationship. Mason should not frustrate himself unnecessarily with someone who is not available physically or emotionally. He should find another girl who appreciates him, and who wants to be with him.

If the dream represents a fantasy that Mason finds compelling, however, to the point where he thinks he might want to act it out, then Mason again needs to end the relationship, and needs to speak to an anger management specialist immediately. (Has he ever acted out violently before?) In either scenario, Mason's relationship with Joan is turning him into an angry person. It's time to move on.

Water

Water: Universal symbol for emotions. How water behaves in a dream is always significant. Rising water indicates increasing emotions. Turbulent, choppy water, in which a dreamer fears being swamped or drowning, symbolizes feelings of being overwhelmed emotionally. Tidal waves represent specific emotional threats that a dreamer can see looming in the distance. Being caught in a swift-moving current suggests being confused or obscured "swept up" in one's emotions. Cloudy water suggests lack of emotions. Clean, clear water suggests emotional clarity. Swimming or bathing comfortably in water symbolizes a comfortable immersion in one's emotions. The ability to breathe underwater indicates accessibility to unconscious feelings and awarenesses.

Underwater: The ability to breathe underwater reflects easy access to subconscious feelings and awarenesses, and comfort in one's emotional life. Warning! Recurring dreams about being underwater and about feeling short of breath (unable to reach the surface) are important warning signs that you are experiencing difficulty breathing during sleep—a condition known as sleep apnea. If you dream you are out of breath frequently, visit a sleep doctor immediately.

Rain: Release of tension. Water (emotion) that was stored or contained (in a cloud) is now released. Rain can indicate an emotional cleansing and a period of creative fertility. Rain is common in breakthrough dreams, where a dreamer suddenly realizes he or she has entered a period of new direction, purpose, or understanding.

♦ **Interpretation tip:** Are your emotions rising, falling, sweeping you along, clear or confused? Pay attention to water in your dreams for clues to your emotional state.

* ✳ *

Water in dreams is a faithful mirror of our emotional status. In "Waterfall," we see a woman who fears she may be losing her power as she travels upstream on a river. "Pulled Under" reveals a young man swept up in the waters of a romantic dilemma. "Cast Away" shows a dreamer who is struggling to escape a rising emotional tide. In "Walking Underwater," a woman takes a stroll in the garden of her subconscious. If she wants to know the answer to her question, all she has to do is look. Our final entry, "A Swift Current," reveals a dreamer who underestimated the strength of a river. Is she losing the anchor of her faith?

Water Dreams

"Waterfall"

I am in a long-term marriage that has been verbally and emotionally abusive many times. I have been seeing a counselor who seems pretty helpful. My husband started therapy long ago and then quit after a while. He is now reading about abuse. But as you can imagine, after all this time, the effects of the abuse are quite deep in me (low self-esteem, anxiety, doubting my perceptions or even my sanity at times, anger, and depression). My counselor tells me that as long as I am choosing to stay, I can just keep doing my work and focusing on myself, and set my boundaries with him.

I suffer from inertia and lack of motivation in general. Of course, I tackle my "work" (in therapy) with a passion, and seem to focus too many of my thoughts on all of this. I have a fear of water because I cannot swim. Also, usually in my dreams my husband is driving the car.

In my dream, I am driving my car, and I am alone. I am pushing the gas pedal to the floor, and keep pushing it, but I don't seem to be moving. I just can't get going. Then, suddenly, I am somewhere else.

At first I just see huge, tall waterfalls everywhere, and they all pour down together into this vast "waterness." I look and I see that I am in a small raft in this raging river, with rapids, and I am getting close to the edge of this river—where it falls way, way down into this waterness. All the waterfalls around me are dumping into this, too. I get to the edge and I am so scared because I am going to plummet down. I wake up then—scared, sad, and panicky.

–Margaret, Age 45, Married, USA

Margaret's transition from the passenger seat to the driver's seat in her dreams is significant. It shows she is assuming responsibility for the control and direction of her life. No matter how hard she presses on the accelerator, however, her dream car will not budge. The message of her dream is clear: Margaret is still struggling for empowerment in her life.

The dream shifts suddenly and next Margaret is floating on a raft (significantly, another vehicle without an engine) in the middle of a raging river. Turbulent and agitated water in dreams is a familiar metaphor for periods of emotional volatility in our lives. Being carried by water that has a swift current indicates feelings that we are "swept up" and "pulled along" by our emotions. Waterfalls are symbols that combine water with falling to represent feelings of emotional instability, and fears of being emotionally overwhelmed (drowning).

Margaret's dream represents feelings of doubt and fears of "drifting backward" into an emotional "abyss" in her personal life. Because Margaret is alone in this dream, it suggests, as she states, that she has progressed past viewing her husband as an obstacle to her growth, and instead is now concentrating on the steps required for herself to complete her journey of metamorphosis. It's not surprising that Margaret's first turn behind the wheel of empowerment, represented by the car and the raft, is intimidating. Now that she has tasted the thrill of the driver's seat, however, we doubt she will spend much time looking back.

"Pulled Under"

This dream was actually two related dreams that I had on two consecutive days. I will describe as much as I can remember.

In the first dream, I remember having the sensation of sleeping and then suddenly being awakened by something falling on top of me. When I opened my eyes one of my friends, Susan, was on top of me, drunk. Much to my surprise she started cuddling with me and then asked me if I wanted to have sex with her. I declined, reasoning with her that, first of all, she was drunk, and secondly, I didn't have any protection. She said that was just fine with her and then she passed out, still lying on top of me. So I rolled her off me and let her sleep next to me while I went back to sleep.

In the second dream, I was in a wide outdoor area on one side of a stream. Across a bridge on the other side was my friend Susan. She waved at me and smiled, as if asking me to come over with her. Then

I noticed she had a picnic basket. I started jogging across the bridge when I either slipped, or a great gust of wind caused me to fall from the bridge into the shallow creek. I stood up and took a few steps and then slipped on the creek bed into some deeper water. Then the current began to carry me under the bridge. I was able to swim to shore and started to pull myself up from the creek when I noticed that underneath the bridge everything seemed darker and the water seemed murkier. While I was pulling myself up, I looked up and saw Susan laughing at me, but the laugh seemed to be a cruel laugh, not a playful laugh. That is when the current picked up and I was dragged underneath the surface of the water and I was startled awake.

—Bill, Age 21, Single, USA

Bill's first dream is a simple case of incorporation, where an event that occurs in the physical world becomes included in the story line of a dream. Bill was asleep when Susan came in and laid on top of him, which caused him to dream that something heavy had fallen on him. Bill was right. Something heavy did fall on him: Susan!

Bill's second dream represents his mixed emotions in the wake of Susan's romantic proposition the previous night. The picnic basket Susan holds, because it contains food, is a symbol of sensual and emotional nourishment. Bill is excited to join her for the picnic, but as he gets closer he encounters a bewildering series of obstacles. Losing his balance as he crosses the bridge symbolizes losing his emotional balance as he enters into a relationship with her. Next, Bill falls into the creek. The current of the water symbolizes the pull of his emotions—which again causes him to lose his balance. Bill then distinctly notes the condition of the water under the bridge, where it appears he is headed. He describes the water as murky and dark—familiar dream symbols representing unclear and uncertain emotions, and fears of contamination. As the dream ends, Susan laughs at him cruelly, just before he is sucked underwater (fear of drowning emotionally).

One of the great values of dreams is that they allow us to recognize what we already have perceived at a subconscious level of awareness. Bill's dream shows that he was able, literally overnight, to recognize the myriad obstacles involved in entering into a romantic relationship with Susan. Susan has asked Bill to get "swept off his feet," but the absence of support she shows at the end of the dream—Susan's laughing—alerts Bill that a relationship with her would be difficult and one-sided. The message of his dream is plain: Bill should wait for another girl, whose picnic isn't so hard to get to, and who won't laugh at him when he needs help.

"Cast Away"

My life is awful. When I was pregnant with my second child, and my daughter was just one year old, my husband had an affair with another woman. I don't want to divorce him because I still love him so much and I want a family, no matter if it is good or bad.

He has been working in a foreign country since this thing happened three years ago. Although he rarely calls us and rarely comes back, he still pays the bills and gives us money for living. Recently, he told me he wants to divorce me, but I don't agree. I still love him.

My Dream: The ocean submerges everything. Another person and I climb to the top of a building, but the water is still getting higher and higher. I see people say good-bye and hug each other. Some people have already sunk. Some of them cry and some of them smile. I grasp a floating object but I don't have a chance to use it before I wake up.

–Helen, Age 27, Married, USA

Helen's dream reminds us of a sinking boat at sea. As her dream ends, Helen is being forced to abandon ship, with only a floating object to help keep her alive.

The rising ocean in Helen's dream symbolizes a period of rising emotions in her waking life. Helen climbs a tall building to escape the rising tide, but once she reaches the top she encounters a scene of departure and transition. Some people have already sunk in the water. Others are saying good-bye. Just before Helen awakens, she knows that she, too, must jump from the building and try to stay afloat.

Helen's marital woes are the cause of her dream. Despite the lack of communication and contact with her husband, Helen clearly prefers to remain married and keep the remainder of her family together. Her husband's recent request for a divorce, however, has sounded a bell of alarm within her. Helen's dream represents increasing feelings that she is about to be cast into an ocean of uncertainty, including doubts for her survival. The support Helen currently clings to (her marriage—represented by the building in the dream) may be "going under."

If she hasn't done so already, it's time to visit a marriage counselor. Helen should learn what her legal and financial rights are, and begin to prepare for a transition in her life. The sooner she faces these troubling issues, rather than hope they will go away, the quicker this emotional tide will recede.

"Walking Underwater"

My boyfriend and I have been dating for a year. He has never been married and doesn't have any children. I have two children from a previous marriage. About four months ago, we began having issues about my children. He never saw himself with a family and hasn't been certain of his commitment because of them. Even though he tries not to, he resents my ex-husband and sometimes becomes jealous of the attention my children require.

I had a dream that I was walking underwater. I could breathe and speak, but there were bubbles floating up from everyone's mouth. I was looking at elaborate stone sculptures as I walked along the path. As I was walking, I would meet various people I know and each would say to me, "If you want to see the truth, all you have to do is look." That was the message with which I awoke.

I think it means I already know the answer to my questions. I just have to deal with it.

–Melanie, Age 30, Divorced, USA

Breathing underwater is a rare talent. And in Melanie's case, it may spare her a lot of heartache.

Melanie's dream suggests a comfortable immersion in her emotions. Not only can she walk underwater, she also breathes easily. As Melanie strolls along an underwater path, she pauses to read the meaning carved into elaborate stone sculptures. The metaphor implied is that she is looking for a solution or answer to a question. Hearing her unspoken wish, the dream responds directly. "If you want to see the truth," her friends tell her, "all you have to do is look."

Given the background Melanie has provided, we are led to believe that the stone sculptures represent questions she maintains about her current relationship. Melanie's boyfriend's position on children appears to be rigid and inflexible (stony?). As Melanie herself suggests, it appears she has realized in her heart that he is not the right choice to join her family.

The head and heart often view relationships differently. Usually the head talks us into relationships (he will change, she will change) that the heart knows are mismatched. In Melanie's case, the metaphor of "walking underwater"—bringing her head down to meet her emotions—shows that her head, indeed, has caught up with her heart. Melanie is ready to let go, and knows it is the right decision.

"A Swift Current"

In my dream I went to a university to sign up for classes. I parked my red Jeep in a parking lot, and didn't notice that a river was nearby.

Later, when I came out of the building, there was a swollen muddy river in front of me. At first I thought I had come out the wrong door. Then I noticed a dark green minivan float to the top of the water. Next came a new red van, and then my Jeep bobbed up and started floating away.

I went back inside the building for help. I didn't know what to do. The staircase was crowded. It was a tiny spiral thing—like a child's slide. When I tried to get out the door, a Gypsy woman and her children were sleeping just outside it, and it was difficult to get out. I woke up crying over the loss of my car.

I am an American living in Germany. I was married and raising two boys who brought me so much joy when the "Wall" came down in East Germany. At the time, all the horrors of the Romanian orphans were exposed, and I decided that I would adopt a couple of little girls.

I'm sorry to say, that was the biggest mistake of my life. They are not normal children. They are destructive, and they lie and they steal. One of them gorges on food and is not toilet-trained at age eleven. My husband left shortly after the adoption. My oldest son left when he graduated from high school seven years ago, and he has never returned to visit. I go to see him, but he will not come to my house as long as the girls are still here. Therapy and family counseling have not helped.

I have to work to support myself and the children. I feel overwhelmed most of the time. The girls and the family have not bonded, so my chances of having a daughter (a real mother-daughter relationship) have never been realized.

P.S. My eleven-year-old adopted daughter came from a Gypsy family.

–Patricia, Age 51, Separated, Germany

Cars in dreams represent ourselves—the "direction we are headed" in our lives. Dreams about losing a car—Patricia's is swept away by a swollen, swift-moving river—reflect feelings that we do not know how we are going to reach a desired destination in our lives. Given the background Patricia provides, it is easy to see that she feels at a loss as to how to manage her difficult situation.

When Patricia parks in the university lot to sign up for some new classes, she does not notice a river that flows nearby. When she returns from the building, Patricia finds that the river has risen suddenly, carrying her car, among others, away from the lot. The rising water indicates a period of increasing emotions, while the swift current indicates feelings of being emotionally out of control.

Signing up for new classes most likely is a symbolic allusion to the spirit with which Patricia undertook her decision to adopt the Romanian orphans. At the time, she may have intended to "learn something new" and to enrich her life—though her dream does suggest that she underestimated the emotional magnitude of her commitment. (Patricia does not notice the river.)

The interior of the university building also holds allusions to children. The staircase is small and crowded, and reminds Patricia of a child's slide. When Patricia tries to leave the building, a sleeping Gypsy woman, lying with her children, blocks the doorway. Can there be any doubt as to the identity of this sleeping Gypsy? Sleep in dreams is a common metaphor for death, and for unconsciousness. The sleeping woman is one of her absent mother. Patricia feels that this Gypsy mother is now hindering her own progress.

By showing Patricia's car swept away by a fast-rising river, her dream informs us that as a single parent raising a family, Patricia is feeling progressively out of control and overwhelmed emotionally. The primary source of frustration Patricia feels is her limited ability to heal the emotional scars of her adopted children. Because these children were traumatized at such an early age, the truth is that she will always have limited ability to heal their wounds. If Patricia can recognize these limitations honestly, she can begin to relieve herself of the personal blame she feels for not making her children better. Patricia may also wind up appreciating herself, and the altruistic decision she made many years ago, much better. In a world that all too often is full of darkness and need, Patricia is a very bright light, and a genuinely heroic soul.

Wedding

Wedding: Often a literal symbol of our hopes and expectations for "the big day," this includes anxiety that the ceremony and celebration will be successfully accomplished. In the months before an actual wedding, dreams about being unprepared for the ceremony are common (wedding dress doesn't fit, guests arrive late, dreamer is unable to locate the church). These dreams reflect feelings of "cold feet," and should not be interpreted as precognitive, or as bad omens for the marriage. If a bride or groom has no face, then the dreamer is thinking about marriage but does not know who the partner will be.

At a symbolic level, weddings can also represent attraction to, or desires to be close with, qualities that the bride or groom represents. Weddings may represent harmony between feminine and masculine aspects of the self, or a desire to join forces with another person or entity, as in a new business opportunity. Successful weddings suggest confidence in the new relationship. Dreams about a bad wedding indicate concerns that the partners are mismatched, or that a deal will fail to reach closure.

◆ **Interpretation tip:** Dreams about brides and grooms are often transparent reflections of our desire to locate and marry a life partner. Are you ready to meet "the one"?

✳ ✳ ✳

Weddings, indeed, are nerve-racking events. "The Big Day" is a classic representation of wedding jitters. Is our dreamer prepared for her big debut? "Faceless Groom" shows a dreamer pregnant with expectation. Will she ever get to see her husband's face? "Marry My Father" shows a dreamer who is confused by her dream's choice of groom. Isn't her father just supposed to *walk* her down the aisle? Finally, in "A Perfect

Match," our dreamer is searching for that perfect partner, the man of her dreams. Will her next boyfriend be "the one"?

Wedding Dreams

"The Big Day"

I am engaged to be married in October. On the night marking exactly four months to go I had a very real dream about the wedding day— with a similar theme to dreams I used to have when I was fifteen. The main feeling of the dream is frustration.

It was the wedding day and I was all dressed and waiting in a room near the church. I had feelings of joy and excitement. I noticed it was ten minutes before the ceremony, and the makeup was yet to arrive. I saw people arriving and entering the church—all the while getting more and more stressed that I still had a bare face on my big day. I saw my fiancé arrive at the church and got very worried that I was going to be late.

I finally saw an old, old friend of mine (from when I was fifteen) whom I haven't seen or talked to since (and who will not be at the wedding) whom I begged for help. She and I tried to make my face up but the makeup just wouldn't go on. We struggled with brushes and foundation and colors, some of which went on and looked terrible, but others just wouldn't show.

I kept looking over at the church and felt helpless. It was now thirty minutes after the start of the ceremony and I felt frustrated. I can't remember whether I eventually made it to the church, but I woke up feeling so angry and stressed. I had similar dreams about difficulties applying makeup under tight deadlines when I was fifteen.

I don't usually wear a lot of makeup, so I find my dreams confusing. I am happy about getting married, but have some worries about moving overseas before the wedding for my fiancé's job (may or may not happen).

–Amy, Age 22, Engaged, New Zealand

Amy has the wedding jitters, but instead of worrying about cake, flowers, and seating arrangements (literal concerns), the star of her dream, and the focus of her attention, is herself. Amy's inability to apply her makeup reflects concerns about appearance and presentation (it *is* the big day), but the dream's inclusion of a friend from high school, when Amy was first learning to apply makeup, suggests a deeper symbolic meaning. Just as her recurring dreams about makeup as a teen symbolized Amy's anxiety over her initiation into the world of dating (by making herself attractive to potential suitors), her current dreams reflect concerns about her preparedness for the transition from single to married.

Amy's dream is not a sign that she will have difficulties—or be unprepared—on her wedding day. On the contrary, she tells us she is happy with her fiancé, and that she is anxiously awaiting her marriage. What is the message, then, of this curious, recurring dream? It's normal to be nervous about changes and transitions in our lives. When it happens to be our wedding day, it's called "cold feet" and "wedding jitters"!

"Faceless Groom"

I still remember these two dreams that happened a few years ago. In the first I was laughing and running down from a hilltop. It was a beautiful view, so fresh and cool. I felt so free and happy. Suddenly from behind a man lifted me up in his arms and swung me around. I knew instantly that he was my husband. (I don't know how I knew it, but I did.) Then I noticed that I was pregnant!

The annoying part was that I was unable to see how he looked. Suddenly we were at the front door of a restaurant. He opened the door for me and carefully guided me inside. A few people in the restaurant were looking at us, and especially at my husband. When I walked past, I managed to overhear a lady saying to her friend, "He is so handsome." After we sat down, I tried to look straight at my husband's face, to see how handsome he was. I could not. There was no face at all.

In my second dream there were a few females in a room and all of them looked anxious. I had never seen them before but again I knew they were my friends. I was sitting down on a bed. When I looked down, I noticed that I was wearing a strange white gown. Then I looked up again and the mirror in front of me showed that I was wearing a wedding gown. I was quite shocked and could not believe it. My friends got excited when they heard the honk from the groom's car. They took me to another room and then they looked out from the window to see the groom. I was saying to myself, "Today is my wedding day," but my feeling was 100 percent disbelief. I wanted to know what my husband-to-be looked like, so I joined the girls, too. Again I could not see his face. The only visible part of him was from his shoulders to his feet.

For your information, I had the first dream when I was around sixteen years old; the second when I was around twenty-two years old. I am twenty-six years old and do not have any boyfriend or relationship at all. I am very independent. The only thing I aim for now is to achieve my ambitions as a scuba-diving instructor and further up. I also want to go around the world and work in some organizations as a volunteer. So you see, getting married or having a boyfriend is not on my mind at all, as I have so many things I want to do and want to enjoy myself.

–Anika, Age 26, Single, Malaysia

Anika's dreams clearly reflect curiosity about the identity of her future husband. In both dreams, though, just when she thinks she will be able to look into the eyes of that very special man, her mind literally draws a blank. Her dream husband either doesn't have a face, or she is unable to see it.

Anika's faceless groom dreams may be frustrating, but the fact that her dreams do not fill in or create a dream husband for her actually reflects favorably on her sense of reality. Like most dreams, instead of being a precognitive glimpse of the future (she will marry a faceless man?) Anika's dreams are honest portraits of the present. Anika doesn't know who her husband will be. A second, implied meaning of her dream should not be overlooked. Only Anika has the power to "fill in the blanks" in her future, through the careful decisions and choices she makes.

Anika tells us that she does not currently have a boyfriend, and that she is actually so busy with work that she isn't actively looking. That her dreams have come so far apart in time suggests that what she says is true; she is not overly concerned about this question of marriage. Her pregnancy in the first dream, however, suggests she is pregnant with expectation for the relationship, and looking forward to her literal transition to motherhood.

"Marry My Father"

I had a dream in which I was getting married and it turned out that I was marrying my father. Just as we both were about to walk down the aisle, I said that I wasn't ready to get married yet, and called the wedding off.

I will be eighteen years old in about two months, and am engaged to marry my boyfriend in a few years. My father lives in a different state. He is divorced and has been engaged to his girlfriend for over a year. I live with my mother and stepdad.

–Debra, Age 17, Single, USA

Given the background Debra provides, there are several reasons her father may have played such a starring role in her dream. She and her father are both engaged to be married soon, and thoughts of her own wedding plans are most likely associated with thoughts of her father's. Also, because her parents are divorced, Debra is separated from her father, who lives in a different state. Does marrying her father symbolically represent Debra's desire that she and her father could have a closer relationship? Does her dream also reflect wishes that she received more attention from him?

Freud believed that the Oedipal complex was responsible for dreams about marrying a parent, and that it explained why men often choose to marry women who remind them of their mothers, while women choose men who remind them of their fathers. Contemporary observers of family dynamics also point to the influence of familiarity and role-modeling in this decision-making process. Stated simply, if we marry a partner who possesses characteristics similar to one or both of our parents, we usually will feel comfortable and secure with them, because we are experienced with that particular personality type. Indeed, this is the compelling reason people tend to replicate relationships they were familiar with growing up— regardless of whether or not they were healthy.

There's an interesting twist to Debra's dream. Just as she starts to walk down the aisle, Debra decides she is not ready, and calls off the wedding. Debra's dream is sending her two important messages. At age seventeen, Debra is unprepared to make a commitment to marry her boyfriend. Her dream is also encouraging her to recognize that even if her boyfriend reminds her of her father, he won't be able to replace him for her.

"A Perfect Match"

Background information: I've been in and out of several relationships in the last two years, since I broke up with a guy I loved very much (and still do). I got back together with him briefly, but it ended again after just four months when he said he didn't want a serious relationship. Soon after, he began dating someone else. I've been questioning whether I will ever find someone who's right for me, and if so—when.

I keep having these dreams in which I'm dating someone I haven't thought about or seen in years. The catch is the guys I date in my dreams are guys I have never been attracted to.

For example, I keep having these recurring dreams in which I'm dating my ex-boyfriend's best friend, Mike—but I haven't spoken to him or seen him in months, nor have I ever been remotely attracted to him.

Last night I had a dream I was getting married, but I didn't know who I was marrying. As I was putting on my wedding dress, I said to my friend, "I will be wearing this dress two more times after this." Kind of like I was saying that this wasn't going to be my last marriage. I also had a rough time finding perfect panty hose to match my wedding dress.

–Cathy, Age 21, Single, USA

Cathy's recurring dreams about romance show that, even after a disappointment in her past, hope springs eternal for the future. Cathy's dreaming mind is hard at work, thinking about candidates to fill the emotional space left by her ex.

Is it surprising that her "dream dates," so far, have been less than spectacular? Since Cathy's breakup, she has been dating for two years—without success. The dating scene has left her underwhelmed, and now Cathy wonders if she will ever meet an exciting guy again.

The significance of dating her ex's best friend is that Cathy would like to find qualities in another man that are similar to those she admired in her ex. Cathy's wedding dress, significantly worn even when she knows her partner isn't "the one," is dreamspeak for dating men who aren't going to make the grade.

As her dream ends, Cathy is busy searching for panty hose to match her wedding gown. What's the meaning? Cathy is trying to find somebody who "matches" her style and goals in life. Unlike her dream, Cathy wants to walk down the wedding aisle only once; and when she does, she wants it to be a perfect match.

INDEX

ABOUT THE AUTHOR

Charles Lambert McPhee is a graduate of Princeton University and holds a master's degree from the University of Southern California. He is the former coordinator of the sleep research laboratory at the National Institute of Mental Health in Bethesda, MD; the former Clinical Coordinator of the Sleep Disorders Center at Cedars-Sinai Medical Center in Los Angeles, California; and the former Director of the Sleep Apnea Patient Treatment Program at the Sleep Disorders Center of Santa Barbara, California. His first book was *Stop Sleeping Through Your Dreams*. His columns on dream interpretation have been published by Oxygen.com and America On Line. His "Ask the Dream Doctor" columns appear weekly in the United Kingdom on supanet.com. Charles McPhee is the creator of the interactive web site www.askthedreamdoctor.com, and is host of *The Dream Doctor* radio show, heard weeknights from 9 P.M. to midnight on KRUZ FM 103.3 in Santa Barbara. The author encourages readers to share their dreams with *Ask the Dream Doctor* at www.askthedreamdoctor.com.